Feminist Social Work Practice in Clinical Settings

SAGE SOURCEBOOKS FOR THE HUMAN SERVICES SERIES

Series Editors: ARMAND LAUFFER and CHARLES GARVIN

Recent Volumes in this Series

MIDLIFE MYTHS: Issues, Findings, and
Practice Implications
edited by SKI HUNTER & MARTIN SUNDEL

SOCIAL WORK IN PRIMARY CARE
edited by MATTHEW L. HENK

PRACTICAL PROGRAM EVALUATION:
Examples from Child Abuse Prevention
by JEANNE PIETRZAK, MALIA RAMLER, TANYA RENNER,
LUCY FORD, & NEIL GILBERT

DATA ANALYSIS FOR THE HELPING PROFESSIONS:
A Practical Guide
by DONALD M. PILCHER

DESIGNING AND MANAGING PROGRAMS:
An Effectiveness-Based Approach
by PETER M. KETTNER, ROBERT M. MORONEY,
& LAWRENCE L. MARTIN

UNDERSTANDING CHILD SEXUAL MALTREATMENT
by KATHLEEN COULBORN FALLER

GROUP WORK: A Humanistic Approach
by URANIA GLASSMAN & LEN KATES

CLINICAL SOCIAL WORK: Research and Practice
by MARY NOMME RUSSELL

HEALTH PROMOTION AT THE COMMUNITY LEVEL
edited by NEIL BRACHT

TREATING THE CHEMICALLY DEPENDENT
AND THEIR FAMILIES
edited by DENNIS C. DALEY & MIRIAM S. RASKIN

HEALTH, ILLNESS, AND DISABILITY IN LATER LIFE:
Practice Issues and Interventions
edited by ROSALIE F. YOUNG & ELIZABETH A. OLSON

ELDER CARE: Family Training and Support
by AMANDA SMITH BARUSCH

FEMINIST SOCIAL WORK PRACTICE IN CLINICAL SETTINGS
edited by MARY BRICKER-JENKINS, NANCY R. HOOYMAN,
& NAOMI GOTTLIEB

Feminist Social Work Practice in Clinical Settings

edited by

Mary Bricker-Jenkins
Nancy R. Hooyman
Naomi Gottlieb

Sage Sourcebooks for
the Human Services Series
19

SAGE PUBLICATIONS
The International Professional Publishers
Newbury Park   London   New Delhi

For information address:

 SAGE Publications, Inc.
2455 Teller Road
Newbury Park, California 91320

SAGE Publications Ltd.
6 Bonhill Street
London EC2A 4PU
United Kingdom

SAGE Publications India Pvt. Ltd.
M-32 Market
Greater Kailash I
New Delhi 110 048 India

Printed in the United States of America

Library of Congress Cataloging-in-Publication Data

Main entry under title:

Feminist social work practice in clinical settings / Mary Bricker-Jenkins, Nancy R. Hooyman, and Naomi Gottlieb.
      p.   cm.—(Sage sourcebooks for the human services; v.19)
Includes bibliographical references and index.
ISBN 0-8039-3625-7 (c).—ISBN 0-8039-3626-5 (p)
1. Social service—United States. 2. Feminism—United States.
I. Bricker-Jenkins, Mary. II. Hooyman, Nancy R. III. Gottlieb,
Naomi, 1925- . IV. Series: Sage sourcebooks for the human
services series; v. 19.
HV91.F447   1991
361.3'2'.082—dc20   90-27897
                                                         CIP

FIRST PRINTING, 1991

Sage Production Editor: Michelle R. Starika

To Susan Livesay of Western Kentucky University and Kathryn Calderwood, Inge Dolan, Kim Yelsa, and Olivia Zapata of the University of Washington— our sisters and silent collaborators in the production of this book. And for all women who labor as secretaries and office workers everywhere.

CONTENTS

FEMINIST PRACTICE IN RURAL COMMUNITIES

ACKNOWLEDGMENTS

We are grateful to the many people who have contributed significantly to the successful completion of this book. We are especially appreciative of the ongoing support and encouragement of Terry Hendrix, Charles Garvin, and Marquita Flemming of Sage. They believed in the book's importance to social work practice, even in the moments when we questioned whether we would ever finish it. The editorial staff at Sage—Michelle Starika, Tara Mead, and Judy Selhorst—conveyed their support through the speed and accuracy by which they completed their production tasks. The contributors' responsiveness to our many editorial suggestions and their ongoing enthusiasm about the book also kept us going during the more difficult editing periods.

Lee Rathbone-McCuan was particularly helpful in the early stages of formulating the book and in providing editorial assistance to several contributors. Virginia Senechal's thorough and accurate editing of manuscripts made all the authors' tasks easier. Colleagues assisted us by "taking up the slack," particularly Mary's colleagues Joe, MuhBi, Pat, and Will at Western Kentucky University. As our dedication notes, none of this would have been possible without the tireless, behind-the-scenes assistance of our staff at our schools as well as the ongoing support of our families and friends—Peter, Merril, Annie, Gene, Kevin, and Christopher. To all those whose lives were touched by our hectic schedules in completing this book, our thanks.

Mary Bricker-Jenkins
Nancy R. Hooyman
Naomi Gottlieb

INTRODUCTION

MARY BRICKER-JENKINS

Whenever possible, I go to a Saturday morning "women in recovery" group. It is the closest thing in my life today to the consciousness-raising (CR) groups that changed my life (and, I was to learn, the world) in the early 1970s. Although this group lacks the explicit attention to collective social action that was so essential to the feminist CR groups, it does have other similarities that engage and support some extraordinary transformations in the lives of the participants.

First, we attend to the political dimensions of the issues that are reverberating in and often confounding our lives. We are clear, for example, that the "codependency" theme played out in so many of our lives is part of the social script written for women in our culture and, by implication, that our personal dramas of recovery are played on the center stage of a collective cultural arena.

Second, a primary process in our special alchemy is the reaction that occurs when we combine the telling of our stories with the rapt attention we give one another in an environment that assiduously omits advice giving, "probe" questions, empathic reflections, or any of the other interpersonal communication ingredients that typify professional counseling and therapy. Thus, as one friend describes the process, the room becomes an enormous ear, attending to every woman's words as if they are the most important words ever uttered—which, indeed, they are. Moreover, the process accentuates the presence and significance of each of the women, her strengths, her

1

health-seeking and self-healing powers. It is through the elusively simple and utterly equal exchange of personal truths and unconditional listening that each of us gathers the wisdom and strength to rewrite her script in her own words—words of the heart given voice through a community of women who are consciously, deliberately, and proudly being together as women.

Today one of the women, new to the group, spoke of her reemergence into the world of "dating" a year after her divorce. "I was married for 17 years," she said. "During that time something happened. Somebody changed all the 'rules' about dating! It was the women's movement that happened. And though I agree with all that that was about, I realize now that I didn't participate in reframing the rules— and I don't understand them or even know them! Please, maybe some of you who were active in the movement will stick around after the meeting and explain them to me."

A lot of us stayed around after the meeting. What we talked about most was the fact that the "women's revolution" was not over yet. The "new rule" that permits us as women to make more and different choices, for example, left a vacuum in some of the places many women used to reside: over the stove, beside the crib, behind the carpool wheel, at the service clubs, and beside "their" men at the corporate cocktail parties. And who filled the vacuum? Women again— either women paying for their choices by doing two jobs or women being paid minimum wages by other women now "free" to exercise their class privileges in new places.

Many of the women of color and the poor and working-class women in the group wondered aloud what this new "rule of more choices" was all about anyway; somehow it did not have much meaning for women who always had to work outside the home. For many of them, more women making more choices meant more competition for jobs and a suppression of wage scales in those that remained open to them and to the men of their communities. The lesbians among us added another pointed question: To what degree was the increasing virulence and violence of today's homophobia attributable to the sheer panic of those heavily invested in a corrupt patriarchy under siege?

Consensus came quickly: The women's liberation movement is not over yet, reports in the mainstream press notwithstanding. There are more rules to be made—and this time somebody else has to help fill the vacuum and *all* women have to participate in making the rules.

Moreover, we have to get clearer on the nature and extent of systems of domination and exploitation, on who benefits from them and how, and on who is going to be targeted for intensified exploitation if we do not go after *all* those systems. As Blanche Weisen Cook (1979) says, "Revolution is a process, not an event" (p. 10). In this phase, we must not be separated from our natural allies. We must learn new ways to make the rules.

I must confess to feeling an edge of irritation, smugness, and exasperation during this discussion. "If any of these women had participated in CR or read the early socialist feminist works, we wouldn't have to be having this discussion," I thought. Then one of the women referred to me (quite deferentially, to be sure) as a "professional feminist." That phrase urged me back to respectful attentiveness and away from my unfeminist arrogance. I realized that I have had advantages and privileges that many of the others have not: I had experienced firsthand the women's liberation movement and CR processes of the 1960s and 1970s; participated in creating programs of, by, and for women; and received a grant to study, read, and write about feminist social work practice. In addition to all the privileges of the white professional North American, I had in abundance the gifts of riding the great surging waves of several liberation movements. While in a position of relative physical and psychic safety, I have been one of those who had changed the rules.

Now I was being pushed to follow the most fundamental "rule" that we had sought to establish: the rule of empowerment—that each one of us has, as a fundamental right derived from a basic human need, the ability "to speak one's own truth in one's own voice and hav[e] a part in making the decisions that affect one's life" (Pharr, 1988). The rule we insisted upon was that we all get to make the rules. Moreover, we insisted on a consonant rule-making rule, that of praxis—the ever-evolving process of dialogue, reflection, and conscious action to make true our truths again and again and again, as we changed in the process of changing our worlds. Clearly it was time for me to reengage in dialogue and reflection with my sisters who had not participated in the process of "my" rule making. My truth, my theory, was not theirs; if my truth had any viability at all I had to hear others' truths, draw upon my own to make space for them to articulate theirs, and then merge, blend, reframe, and re-create *with* them until we stood on a common ground that had room for each of us in her uniqueness and wholeness—and enough room for others to join us to do it again!

So what does this personal vignette have to do with a book on feminist social work practice in clinical settings? Several things.

FEMINIST PRACTICE
AS A WORK IN PROGRESS

First of all, we are reminded of the ways in which our understanding of the nature of feminist practice and its principles must influence the way we view and work with the content of the book. Each of the editors of this book is to some degree a "professional feminist." We participated in this wave of the women's liberation movement; indeed, we were on the streets and in the endless meetings that churned the ripples into waves. Within the field of social work, we have been working, studying, thinking, talking, and writing about feminist practice for many years. We were cofounders of the Association for Women in Social Work, and we have served on the official women's issues committees of the standing formal organizations of the profession. We have organized and, with hundreds of our colleagues, pushed the feminist dialogue and presence in social work "from margin to center," to use bell hooks's (1984) apt phrase. Now our colleagues ask us to teach them how to "do" feminist social work practice. In this there is danger. We are being asked to stick around and explain the rules. We know we must resist the temptation, lest we become like those we have challenged throughout our professional lives: theorists whose prescriptive pronouncements on practice seemed to exclude or trivialize women's experience, whose practice principles were evidently derived from somebody else's truths and advanced somebody else's interests.

As we understand it, feminist social work practice is as feminist practitioners do; a feminist practitioner is one who defines her- or himself as a feminist. Within that seeming reductionism lies the strength of the approach to practice.[1] Feminist practice is an open and dynamic system that has as its core an open and dynamic world view. Continual self-scrutiny, challenge, and revision are not only ethical imperatives, but the essence of the practice. When the practice (i.e., theory and method) and the experience of the people who do the practice (i.e., workers and clients together) are in any way dissonant, the alarm goes off and the system shuts down. To fail to modify the practice—and its attendant theory—to accommodate newly discovered or emerging realities is to violate the first principle of the practice.

To put it most simply, feminist practice—and any book that purports to document and explain it—must always be considered a "work in progress." Thus we attempt within the limitation imposed by the medium of the printed word to engage the reader in a dialogue and a cocreative process, not to offer a set of instructions on how to fix a broken life. What we can do is to offer another set of truths: some concepts that may help illuminate the practice arena from a different angle; some methodological tools that some of us have found helpful in our attempts to engage and mobilize strengths; some accounts of ways in which some practitioners are attempting to transform their practice by infusing their feminist analyses, commitments, and visions into their work. There are differences and disagreements among the authors—and among the editors—of this book; we offer this as a strength, not a weakness, of the book. We ask of the reader, take what you can and leave the rest. We will not make rules for you; we will only speak our truths in our own voices and invite you to do the same.

PRACTICE THEORY BUILDING AS FEMINIST PROCESS

Second, this book represents in its concept and its content an effort of some members of the feminist practice community to rework practice by engaging in reflective dialogue with people who were left out of the rule making in the first place. We hope this book will engage at least four groups: feminist practitioners, practitioners in conventional settings (i.e., those not in "alternative" programs for women), people of color whose experience and understanding of women's issues and interests are very different from what is articulated (and published) by white feminists, and individuals who have not participated in the women's movement for a variety of reasons but who now identify as feminists, or at least feel drawn to the community of feminists.

The Feminist Practitioner

The principal author of feminist practice theory is the feminist practitioner. We do not know anybody who learned feminist practice in a school of social work (at least not yet); one reason for this is that feminist practice is not the progeny or property of academics. Rather, this new approach evolved from the efforts of feminist social workers to reconcile and integrate their feminist perspectives and commitments with the conventional theories and methods in which they were trained. Those efforts were, and continue to be, a challenge to the legitimacy and relevance of those conventions and their champions. Moreover, in their daily efforts to integrate individual and sociopolitical transformation processes in theory, structure, and method, feminist practitioners challenge the "dual mission" notion of individual versus social change that has bifurcated the profession and the curricula of most schools of social work. Although many of the leaders of our formal organizations and major schools have abandoned the effort in the face of conceptual complexity, feminist practitioners are reclaiming and advancing our common base.

As feminist academics/practitioners with access to publishing resources, the editors of this book take as our responsibility the documentation of the emergence of this practice in a format that is accessible and usable in the practice community. Thus we have departed throughout the book from the conventional mode and form of academic discourse. There are abstractions, concepts, and constructs, to be sure, but the chief currency of practice is made up of case studies and personal reflections. Thus the main body of this book consists of case studies and discussions.

The discussions often reflect the result of dialogues between the editors and the contributors in which the editors explored with the contributors the rationales for practice decisions that were made and the theory embedded in those decisions. In the mode of feminist practice itself, we assume that theory informs every act; we can then set about in dialogue to elucidate, examine, and critique that theory so that our associates can more consciously choose (or revise) the theory and its attendant actions. Essential to good practice in this mode is respect for the language, meanings, and ultimate choices of the speaker; however much any of us might question or even disagree with others' truths, they must be spoken in their own voices. Taken collectively, the case material and interpretations in this book represent the contradictions, confusions, commitments, and creativity of a diverse community of practitioners who are "doing" a new theory of social work practice. We make no apologies for the incompleteness of its articulation; rather, we celebrate the authenticity of its openness to contradiction and change.

Practitioners in Conventional Settings

A second group of individuals who have been underrepresented in the discourse on feminist practice are those who work in conventional agencies, often as the only feminist in the setting. While feminist practice has emerged from a specific analysis of and confrontation with gender-based oppression and its effects, feminist social workers can be found everywhere that social work is practiced, concerned with all systems of belief and behavior that hinder the meeting of human needs. Thus, while much of the early work and writing on feminist practice was conducted by women working with women in "alternative" settings, other feminist social workers were striving in conventional settings to transform their practice as well. Often they had neither the mandate nor the opportunity to work on women's issues, much less the authority to use nonconventional practice approaches. For example, although the feminist literature might suggest a peer support group as the modality of choice, social workers in mental health agencies were restricted in implementing a group approach because those agencies continued to book and bill clients on an individual or family basis. Although the literature might urge a holistic practice that included involvement of physical and spiritual dimensions, prevailing practice and policy in most agencies precluded such "fringe" concerns and methods.

In response, many feminist practitioners established independent or proprietary group practices; these arrangements secured their practice freedom but precluded access to their services by most poor and working-class women. Other feminist practitioners managed to find or establish alternative programs in their communities or experimental programs in their agencies. Their struggles to remain feminist in orientation in the midst of a patriarchal sea are ongoing and complex. As Kravetz and Jones's contribution to this collection demonstrates, the ideological and material forces of professionalization and funding are enormous (see Chapter 11). Although removal of or restrictions on funding pose an obvious and direct threat to practice, the conservatizing consequences of professionalization are more subtle. As such organizations and programs move from a "grass-roots movement" to a "professional service" orientation, the challenges to feminist theory and practice are considerable. This collection attempts to frame that challenge.

The primary focus of this book, however, is on feminist practice in conventional settings, where most social workers who are feminists struggle to integrate their commitments and analyses into their work. In organizing this collection, we wanted to document and nurture the efforts of practitioners who, like nearly all contributors to this book, worry about not being feminist enough, even while they undertake the most compelling work of the feminist movement: securing people's basic needs and safety while urging them to help transform the structures in ways that are essential to their well-being.

What does the feminist practitioner have to say, for example, to the 14-year-old pregnant girl whose relationship with her boyfriend is her only source of pride and protection in her urban community? To the woman whose boyfriend rapes her child but provides the family food and pays the rent? To the social worker whose legal mandate requires that she remove the child if the offender won't go? To the farm wife whose husband's last remaining source of community recognition is his visible hegemony in his family? To the exhausted woman you are asking to provide care at home to her husband because her free labor is far cheaper than your agency's nursing-home beds? And what do you say to your administrator, who expects your complicity in this design to provide care for men by finding new ways to exact a little more, a little longer, from the women whose husbands' wartime service was supposed to guarantee their care and their families' well-being? What do you say to women who, in the absence of choice, affirm their preference for subordination? What do you say to yourself? And what do you *do* that is different from the work of your colleague at the next desk? We put this collection together to address such questions because we see them as urgent for theory building and action at this time.

The historical and material conditions of today increasingly demand that we do our work as if we were in exile. Our "alternative" home, the wellspring of much theory and practice, is increasingly threatened, and the circumstances of our lives force us further away from it. The challenge we face is like that of all people in exile: to build new structures from the material available to us while retaining the forms that reflect and reinforce who we are. Viewing our work from this stance can help us avoid the twin dangers that threaten all people in exile—annihilation and assimilation—while supporting our process of self-definition and redefinition. This is the stance of the book.

People of Color

Those who know best how to live and work in exile were also largely pushed out of the rule-making process in the early days of feminist practice. Although white feminists usually attempted and achieved a liberal politic of "inclusion," we too often failed to see the racist roots and effects of that politic: the imposition of a European-based mode of discourse and interpretation on the experiences of people of color. As women, we know that this "epistemological imperialism" can be much more subtle and insidious than the practice of exclusion; all of our work to affirm the validity of "women's ways of knowing," women's culture, and feminist forms of scholarship signals that awareness. Nevertheless, we have done it to each other too often. We have included women of color—and lesbians, and old women, and women with disabilities—apparently unaware that the very concept of inclusion implies a supremacist belief system.

The emerging politic of diversity holds promise for the theory and practice that is not supremacist. But if the promise is to be fulfilled, we all must practice new ways of listening and learning. We have attempted in this book to contribute to that process not simply by including the work of women of color, but by changing the mode and structure of discourse. We have attempted to present each contributor's work in a framework that supports self-definition and speaking from within that self-definition. We invited the contributors to present their practice within the contexts of their life experiences—to speak their truths in their own voices. In so doing, we affirm the viability of the many definitions of and pathways to feminist practice and the legitimacy of the many ways we learn and create practice theory.

Although many voices are not presented in these pages (nor yet heard in feminist circles), we are slowly learning—primarily from women of color—new lessons in the possibilities, politics, and practice of self-definition. For people of color, they are lessons of survival learned in exile. The chapters by Baczynskyj (Chapter 10), Gutiérrez (Chapter 9), Liddie (Chapter 6), Smith (Chapter 4), and Turner (Chapter 5) provide much of the content from such lessons. We have attempted throughout the book to adopt a form that is consonant with that content—one that permits all of us to listen to ourselves and to each other in new ways.

Newcomers

Finally, this book is for all those who may identify with the woman who pointed out that we were not "following the rules" by asking us to explain them. The newcomers to the feminist community remind us that we have come very far indeed, but we have so far to go. All around us, there is evidence of the distance we have traveled in the last two decades: In the social work community, many more women are directing agencies and organizations; women are deans in many schools; we have a journal—*Affilia*—with an explicitly feminist editorial mission, and there is feminist content in "mainstream" journals; content on women's issues in social work curricula is mandated by the accrediting body. We have day care at our agencies, women's music at our conferences, and even a feminist social worker in the U.S. Senate. But nobody we know has yet claimed that we are a feminist profession or that feminist methods for doing our work—practice, research, and education—are widely adopted, much less the norm. Indeed, despite all the attention to "women's issues" we have managed to claim, feminism is still the "F word," and those who name and challenge sexism continue to risk ridicule and isolation.

Meanwhile, the means by which most of us survived the isolation, learned to do and trust our own analyses, and found the strength to claim a just place in the world—the feminist CR group—is seldom seen as a viable or vital feature of today's political landscape. Many of us seek, in our own versions of the Saturday morning "women in recovery" group, something of that experience and analysis that sustained us in the past, even while we decry such groups' absence of activism and tendency to foster the illusion that private solutions are possible. Our longings and laments do not change the fact that this is the landscape that greets the "newcomer."

The landscape does present some features that we may have overlooked in the heady days of feminist CR-based activism. Women's spirituality and political activism are still tenuously linked in our practice, for example, despite the compelling evidence that our communities seek both. By naming and remembering the terrible violence perpetrated on so many of us by those we trusted to nurture us, we opened wounds that political activism alone will not heal. And in our eagerness to engage in collective action, we often forget that revolution also exacts a lonely, solitary, intimate act of courage from each of its participants. These are some of the features that many of the contributors to this collection now help us integrate into our analysis and practice.

ORGANIZATION OF THIS BOOK

This book contains five types of contributions. Most of the chapters are case studies by feminist practitioners working in clinical settings—health centers, hospitals, and community mental health and counseling centers. Each chapter presents a profile of the practitioner as well as of the practice. This format helps us grasp an essential feature of feminist practice: The relationship between practitioner and client is rooted in the practitioner's consciousness of their common ground. The egalitarianism, collaboration, and strengths orientation of feminist practice derive from and reinforce this solidarity. The format also underscores the diversity of practitioners, approaches, and set tings that constitute the world of feminist practice in today's clinical settings.

Two of the settings represented are not, strictly speaking, clinical. Bernice Liddie describes her practice in a child day-care center (Chapter 6), and Joanne Mermelstein provides an account of her work in rural communities (Chapter 7). Each of them is dealing, however, with issues generally encountered in clinical settings. Their contributions underscore the need to move out of the clinic and into what Bertha Capen Reynolds (1963) calls "the highways and byways of life." Although this need exists in all of social work, it is especially compelling in feminist practice, with its emphasis on depathologizing women's conditions.

Depathologizing—and the concomitant process of politicizing "personal troubles"—is the focus of Marilyn Wedenoja's contribution (Chapter 8). This and the chapter on empowerment practice with women of color by Lorraine Gutiérrez (Chapter 9) represent the second kind of contribution to the book. Each of them illustrates and analyzes in depth some of the central concepts of feminist practice. The concluding chapter also falls into this category. Based on a research study of feminist practice, this summary article synthesizes the core principles underpinning feminist practice, illustrating each by reference to the case studies in this volume.

A third category contains two chapters that focus on organizational and structural issues. Feminist practitioners attempt to create environments that reflect and reinforce their practice. In Chapter 11, Diane Kravetz and Linda Jones discuss their findings on agencies that were explicitly organized as feminist structures. Nancy Hooyman, on the other hand, presents in Chapter 12 her attempts to infuse feminist principles into the structure and processes of a conventional bureaucratic setting.

A fourth category of contribution to this volume is poetry. Some of the poems were written by practitioners. Most of the others were contributed by people writing from their own experience as clients. These were offered as contributions to this volume in response to a call for submissions printed in feminist newsletters. Significantly, nearly all of the contributions we received focused on healing from sexual abuse. The process of women's liberation is, indeed, an intimate political act.

The fifth kind of contribution is external to the text but at the center of its content. In the course of compiling the collection, we learned that most of the physical work of manuscript preparation and production would be performed by women in "home-based employment." We discovered that this is a common practice among publishers in the United States today. The justifications for this arrangement include environmental considerations—decreasing energy consumption and traffic congestion, for example—as well as economic ones. Moreover, the practice is said to enhance the women's economic and life-style choices. Although those presumed benefits are certainly worthy goals, we must examine—in the best social work and feminist traditions—who benefits from this arrangement and what latent consequences it generates for women.

When we pursue these questions, we soon discover that the arrangement renders women highly vulnerable to economic exploitation and psychosocial stress: Most women doing home-based work are hired as independent contractors and thus receive no employment protections or benefits; their social isolation exacerbates the stress of attempting to meet contract deadlines while caring for their families, often working late into the night to do so. Many would choose to work in office-based jobs if their family-related needs could be met through flexible work schedules, employer-sponsored child care, and job-sharing arrangements. For some women, home-based employment is a life-style choice; for many, however, the home is not the workplace of choice, but the workplace of last resort (Joanne Brundage, executive director, FEMALE, personal communication, January 11,

1991; Christensen, 1988; see also Hartmann, 1987; Hartmann, Kraut, & Tilly, 1986). We are left, in the end, with the disconcerting awareness that home-based working women have subsidized the production and consumption of this work, both economically and emotionally. In solidarity with them, and to subsidize the creation of *real* choices for women, the editors and contributors are donating all royalties from the sale of this book to FEMALE—Formerly Employed Women at Loose Ends—a national grass-roots membership organization.[2] Through their support groups, newsletters, and public education efforts, members of this organization attempt to mitigate the deleterious consequences of the choice to remain at home while advocating for the creation of workplace conditions that make viable alternatives for all women.

NOTES

1. We choose not to engage at this time in the important but somewhat distracting discussion of whether "feminist practice" should be called a model, a method, a system, an approach, or a perspective; suffice it to say that, whatever its appropriate classification in the taxonomy of practice theory, the concept "feminist practice" has a referent that is operative enough to inform practice decisions, and indeed to arouse passions!

2. For further information about this organization, contact Joanne Brundage, executive director, FEMALE, P. O. Box 31, Elmhurst, IL 60126; phone (708) 279-8862.

REFERENCES

Christensen, K. (1988). *Women and home-based work: The unspoken contract.* New York: Henry Holt.

Cook, B. W. (1979). *Women and support networks.* New York: Out and Out Books.

Hartmann, H. I. (Ed.). (1987). *Computer chips and paper clips: Technology and women's employment* (Vol. 2). Washington, DC: National Academy Press.

Hartmann, H. I., Kraut, R. E., & Tilly, L. A. (Eds.). (1986). *Computer chips and paper clips: Technology and women's employment* (Vol. 1). Washington, DC: National Academy Press.

hooks, b. (1984). *Feminist theory: From margin to center.* Cambridge, MA: South End.

Pharr, S. (1988, December). [Column]. *Transformation, 3,* 1.

Reynolds, B. C. (1963). *An uncharted journey: Fifty years of growth in social work.* New York: Citadel.

Practitioner's Poem

Nancie Palmer

I honor your act of courage
    inviting me to join your journey to freedom
You—who seek to unchain your bondage
    from a heritage of fear
To banish the ghosts of oppression
To break the silence which surrounds
    your soul.

I am humbled by your presence
    exquisite testimony of a will to survive.

In honoring you I bring with me my work
    —a knowing search of my own soul
That my ears—once full of the raging
    sounds from my own battles—now hear
    the message in your pain
That my eyes—once blinded from lost self
    see your light in the blackness
    of the abyss.

I am strengthened by our humanness
    for are we not—all seeking a way
    to survive.

Come let us walk together—
In gratitude I join your path
For I will never be the same
You have touched me.

Part I

FEMINIST PRACTICE IN CLINICAL SETTINGS

FEMINIST PRACTICE IN HOSPITAL SETTINGS

INTRODUCTION

NAOMI GOTTLIEB

Throughout Part I, the illustrations demonstrate the possibilities for feminist practice in traditional settings. Part I begins with two of the most traditional and bureaucratic contexts: a federal health care system and a large urban hospital. These two case studies have several commonalities.

First, the feminist practitioners were faced with the constraints of the setting. Indeed, Eloise Rathbone-McCuan, Susan Tebb, and Terry Lee Harbert work in the largest single health care system in the country, the Department of Veterans Affairs Medical Centers, with a highly centralized and entrenched structure. Their constraints derived as well from self-perceptions of the veterans' wives themselves, who accepted their traditional roles completely. The woman in Lisa Tieszen Gary's example showed all the evidence of someone beaten down by the battering experience.

Second, in both case studies, the practitioners exhibited great courage in instituting different modes of practice—giving attention to the almost invisible women in the DVA hospital context, and seeing the mother of an abused child as more than the child's caretaker. That courage was enhanced in both instances by collaborative efforts.

In addition, the cases describe important shifts in the practitioners' perceptions of the women they worked with. Those shifts enabled the practitioners to see the women's strengths, to appreciate that, even in light of traditional self-concepts, the women could make modest, but important, changes from their powerless positions toward self-care and self-advocacy. As a consequence, the workers themselves felt less helpless and less frustrated about these women's circumstances and their own work. One has the impression, also, that all of this happened without the word *feminism* being explicitly stated once.

Finally, the case studies show that when organizational innovations can move women away from the role of victim, both women clients and women practitioners can change.

Work in Child Abuse

Marilyn Mesh

ONE DAY
a dead rat
stared
at me
while
flies
buzzed around
feces
on the floor.

Pat yelled
at
Jason
threw Jamie
on the bed
to change his diaper.
The boys' faces,
yellow white
with
malnutrition
and lack of outdoor air,
registered
suspicion
wariness
at a stranger.

We sat
on the couch and talked
while
the boys played
with electrical wires
and garbage.

As Pat spoke around
the soaps on TV
her long history of
neglect
and indifference showing,
I made my way
through the interview
feeling
separate
and
overwhelmed.
When I left
the pain
crept
up my throat
as vomit.

THE NEXT DAY
a long drive
in response to a plea for help
led me
to
Mona Lisa.
She was as her name
serene
and
breathtakingly
beautiful.
Her eyes alive
pleasure
at someone to talk to.
A smile and gentle hands
for each of her five children
as they played
in a house
with
no
indoor
plumbing
or electricity.

She wove
her story
tenderly
around my heart.
In those moments
as Mona Lisa's
history
of
abuse
neglect
rape
beatings
surfaced,
her longings
awareness   responsiveness
sang to me

Chapter 1

FEMINIST PRACTICE
AND FAMILY VIOLENCE

LISA TIESZEN GARY

This chapter addresses the most prevalent form of "family violence": woman battering. *Battering* is defined as "a pattern of coercive control that one person exercises over another" (Schechter, 1987). This coercive control is exhibited in many ways, including physical and sexual violence, threats, emotional mistreatment, and economic deprivation. Although most commonly recognized in married and unmarried heterosexual couples (Bologna, Waterman, & Dawson, 1989; Straus, Gelles, & Steinmetz, 1980; Walker, 1983), battering also occurs among gay and lesbian couples. However, since the majority of victims of partnership violence are women, feminine pronouns will be used throughout this chapter in discussing those victims.

To understand battering fully, one must see it not only as a private, interpersonal problem, but also as a public and political issue. To weave together the individual and societal issues in relation to family violence, I will present the development of the Advocacy for Women and Kids in Emergencies (AWAKE) project at Children's Hospital, Boston. As part of that development, the institution's understanding of family violence, specifically of the interrelationship of violence against women and children, grew. The concerns of a number of clinicians at Children's Hospital caused us to modify our attitudes and practice with abused children; accordingly, we designed a project to make battering of women visible in a pediatric health care setting.

THE PROBLEM

Although no better umbrella term has yet been developed, the term
family violence is a woefully inadequate, gender-neutral term, as are
spouse abuse, conjugal violence, and *family dispute.* The problem
with these terms is the implication that women and men are equally
victimized. Reality is otherwise: In over half of all relationships, men
will in some way hit or otherwise physically harm their partners
(Straus et al., 1980). "Ninety five percent of all assaults on spouses or
ex-spouses are committed by men" (U.S. Department of Justice,
1983, p. 21). In 1987, the FBI reported that every 18 seconds a
woman is beaten by her husband. That agency further reported that
30% of all female homicide victims are murdered by their husbands
or boyfriends. Repeatedly, in the literature and in practice, clinicians,
advocates, judges, and physicians encounter and treat the female victims of this violence, yet they continue to refer to it as "family violence." The inability of society, in which males dominate, to face the
reality that men are responsible for most of the violence within families leaves us with these inadequate terms and responses—interventions that imply mutual responsibility for the violence.

And what about the effect of violence on the children in these relationships? In 40% to 60% of the homes in which a child is abused, the
mother is also battered (McKibben, DeVos, & Newberger, 1989; Stark
& Flitcraft, 1988). Straus (1988), for example, reports that in a home
where a woman is beaten by a man, there is a 129% greater chance of
child abuse. In a survey of 403 battered women, Walker (1983) found
that 53% of the men who abused their partners also reportedly abused
their children, and 33% threatened to abuse their children. She further
found that 28% of the women abused their kids when living with violent partners and 33% threatened to abuse them. Even if they are not
physically or sexually assaulted, children are negatively affected simply by witnessing violence at home. Research and clinical practice
are finding that witnessing violence produces depression, low self-
esteem, generalized fear, separation difficulties, guilt, and aggression
among children (Brown, Pelcovitz, Kaplan, & Kaplan, 1985; Jaffe,
Wilson, & Wolfe, 1986).

Although child abuse has been strongly linked to the battering of
women, child protection, family service, and other child/family-based
agencies have done little to adapt their practices to include helping
battered mothers. For example, in 1984, only 15 states participating

in the American Humane Association's National Study of Child Abuse and Neglect collected data on mothers' abuse. In 1985, this number dropped to 6. In an AWAKE survey of state child protective manuals in 1988, none of the seven reviewed provided information on assessment of or intervention with battered women.

THE SETTING

Since 1972, the Family Development Clinic at Children's Hospital has provided evaluations of families for the courts and the Massachusetts Department of Social Services (DSS, which is the state child welfare agency). With an interdisciplinary team of physicians, psychologists, social workers, and nurses, this clinic also offers consultation to agencies throughout Massachusetts on cases of family violence and on the larger social issues they raise.

Until 1985, the focus of the Family Development Clinic had been on assessing child abuse. As a result, many battered mothers were bringing their children for evaluations and leaving the clinic as unprotected as when they had arrived—much to some clinicians' concern and frustration. Sometimes the clinic even recommended placement of a child because of the mother's victimization. Obviously, a more supportive approach was needed.

RETHINKING PRACTICE:
A CASE ILLUSTRATION

As a social worker who has focused on child protection for more than 10 years, and now on battered women for 4, I can look back and see my own blind spot where woman and child abuse overlapped. My goal was to protect children, and I looked to their mothers as their principal caretakers, their protectors. I, too, was assessing families in the Family Development Clinic and sending unprotected mothers home. The case example below illustrates the work of some of us in 1985 and the gaps in our own practice:

Ms. C is the mother of three daughters who were in foster care when the C family was referred for a Family Development Clinic evaluation by the courts and DSS. Her husband of 10 years had a history of emotionally and physically battering Ms. C, and this had prompted her departure several times. She and her children often found refuge with her parents until they "gave up" on her because she always returned to Mr. C. The children were finally placed in foster care primarily because Ms. C was unable to protect them from her husband's rage. At the time of the evaluation, both Mr. and Ms. C were unemployed and had moved together into a large apartment. Ms. C hoped for the return of the children. However, because of Mr. C's continuing violence against her, we were unable to recommend such reunification. The day of the court hearing we were informed that Ms. C had been brutally beaten by her husband the night before and could no longer advocate for their custody. These children are now being adopted.

During this period, our focus was on the children as victims and parents as protectors and/or perpetrators. Never did I consider the possibility of the mother as unable to care for her children, much less as a victim of violence herself. I looked to both parents "equally" for the care and protection of their daughters. In fact, I even focused more on the mother as "caretaker" (as does society) with an attempt to understand her role (passive or active) in the abuse. I interviewed both parents together, believing the power within the relationship was shared equally and thereby not seeing Mr. C as dominant by virtue of his use of violence. I failed to interview Ms. C individually to try to understand her "passivity" and seeming powerlessness. Although I eventually heard from the DSS social worker about the domestic violence and gave her the telephone number of an area shelter for Ms. C, I had no concept of how to relate to Ms. C or to understand the effects of this chronic abuse. I unrealistically thought that she could "just leave" Mr. C, and never fully considered her level of isolation, dependence upon him (emotional and economic), and sense of despair. My focus was on the children and their safety, without consideration of their mother's situation. This failure began to distress my colleagues and me. We began to question what more could be done for Ms. C. and women like her; how could we more fully and protectively respond?

Advocacy for Women and Kids in Emergencies (AWAKE) was the result. We saw the privatization and secret shame of abuse and the need to validate the woman and her experience. Thus we decided to use a model of peer support—formerly battered women helping currently battered women. By giving women choices about using AWAKE's services, supporting and empowering them as women as well as mothers, and working with them toward the care and protection of their children, we created a new and useful model of practice that bridges services to battered women and their children. Through providing support and advocacy collaboratively with the women and other staff, rather than through creating a dependent relationship or through a distanced (professional/client) relationship, we have joined with women in a new and, we believe, more fully mutual manner.

AWAKE is a unique model of mother-child public health intervention in cases of family violence. Initially funded through a Victims of Crime Act grant in 1986, the project is also now supported by Children's Hospital and private funders, including General Cinema Corporation, Conrad N. Hilton Foundation, Clipper Ship Foundation, and others. It is the first program in the nation in a pediatric setting providing dual advocacy for both battered women and their abused children. Through such dual advocacy, AWAKE is able to institute early detection and intervention, prevent serious violence against children and their mothers, and help children remain out of foster care and at home with the nonviolent parent. AWAKE believes that by bridging two service systems—grass-roots battered women's groups and child abuse professionals—the abused parent and child are far more adequately served.

Since its inception in 1986, AWAKE has worked with more than 430 women and their more than 500 children. In a recent review of 46 advocacy cases, only 2 children had been placed in temporary foster care; the others remained at home with their mothers, safe and free from violence.

At Children's Hospital, an advocate who is herself a survivor of abuse works with a woman to prevent unnecessary foster placement and to refer mothers and children to resources where they can receive help together. Services include court, police, housing, medical, and welfare advocacy, support, and referrals.

A case vignette illustrates the impact that AWAKE can have with a family in which both mother and child are abused:

Ms. Z and Mr. G had been involved in a relationship for more than 2 years and had a 14-month-old son named Paul. Mr. G's violence escalated sharply and classically over time, culminating in a brutal, life-threatening beating of Paul necessitating restorative surgery and 2½ months of recuperation at Children's Hospital. During the first 6 weeks of Paul's hospital stay, despite concern that his mother was also being beaten, no referral was made to AWAKE.

Ms. Z was viewed by staff as uncooperative because she would not say that Mr. G was the batterer. In fact, she vacillated between holding hands with him in the waiting room and asking staff to make him leave the hospital. Some nurses believed that she responded well to her son, whereas others expressed anger that she did not visit often enough. This ambivalence confused, frustrated, and divided the staff.

A month into Paul's hospitalization, Mr. G assaulted Ms. Z on hospital grounds. Ms. Z courageously described this attack to her child protective worker (DSS) and a hospital social worker. Both advised her to try to stay away from Mr. G.

Soon thereafter, the hospital social worker requested the assistance of AWAKE advocacy in this difficult and dangerous situation. With the AWAKE advocate, Ms. Z mustered her courage and revealed again that Mr. G had assaulted her. The advocate, well acquainted with such cases, responded to Ms. Z in a supportive and understanding way, suggesting that they work together to protect Ms. Z and her son. Ms. Z reacted positively to this alliance and went to court with the advocate to secure an order of protection, and arranged with hospital staff to bar Mr. G from visiting the hospital.

Although the child protective and hospital social workers believed that Ms. Z would be unable to protect herself and her son, with the support of the AWAKE advocate she retained an attorney, fought for custody, and moved in with her relatives, pending more permanent housing arrangements. With the advocate's help, Ms. Z finally felt safe enough to say that Mr. G did batter her and her son and decided to be a witness in criminal proceedings against Mr. G for the violent abuse of Paul.

This vignette illustrates many of the issues inherent in a dual case of woman battering and child abuse: initial primary focus on the child's medical and social condition; the mother's seeming ambivalence toward or fear of her partner, thus confusing staff and causing them to blame her; the mother's need for intense, nonjudgmental support, which staff who are directly involved in the care of a severely injured child may not be able to provide; feelings of inadequacy and hopelessness on the part of child protection and hospital social workers, causing them to look beyond the mother to the foster care system for the child's care; constant interdisciplinary collaboration with legal counsel and other staff to protect both the child and the mother and to find them housing, welfare, and child-care resources; and the need for strong advocacy for the mother, without which she may be immobilized and misjudged.

According to many hospital staff, Ms. Z seemed to alter her behavior radically after she began to work with the AWAKE advocate.

AWAKE, however, does not believe that Ms. Z underwent a major transformation; rather, the institution offered her a different response, one that affirmed the conflicts and binds she experienced, and an alternative to enduring those conflicts and binds alone and silently. The advocate's job was to explain Ms. Z's position, so that staff could develop greater empathy for the mother and thus become more supportive.

Further, the advocate, recognizing the alienation and intimidation that women often experience in patriarchal systems such as the court, accompanied Ms. Z to secure an order of protection. Although technically a woman in Massachusetts (and other states) "should" be able to secure such an order on her own, we regularly see women who are blocked in this process by obstinate and daunting clerks and judges, who challenge the women's rights to secure such orders. These women, in crisis and frightened, often leave the court when this happens, unless they have advocates or friends to support and assist them. And, not surprisingly, women are blamed for not "protecting" themselves if they fail to get the orders, rather than the court that refused to provide it.

These are the issues upon which AWAKE focuses, both in service delivery with individual women and children and in discussion and planning for public policy change. The project provides advocacy, consultation, education, crisis intervention, and support to women referred from all areas of the Children's Hospital. Women are referred from both inpatient and outpatient services, from the emergency room to the cardiology service. Referral numbers have soared over the last 4 years of operation: from approximately 50 women in the first year to at least 100 women each subsequent year.

The increasing numbers of referrals demonstrate the need for such a service as well as a shift in service providers' attitudes. Further, these numbers substantiate the findings of McLeer and Anwar's (1989) hospital study: When questions about battering are posed and resources provided, the numbers of referrals of domestic violence cases increase. Also, the woman's "attitude" does not necessarily change with intervention, as the staff presumed in Ms. Z's case. Rather, when the systems/institutions are open, nonjudgmental, and responsive to battered women, those women are able to connect and make use of available supports and resources. This is not only AWAKE's experience; this finding is clearly developed in a study by Gondolf and Fisher (1988). Challenging the idea of learned helplessness in battered women, this study promotes a new understanding of these women as survivors. Further, Gondolf and Fisher posit the notion of the institutions' developing a kind of learned helplessness themselves in their inability to address victims' needs.

PROJECT ASSUMPTIONS

In my own and the project's attempts to understand this problem of violence against women and children in our society, feminist assumptions about woman abuse have guided us. This discussion of AWAKE assumptions will integrate the case material of Ms. Z to illustrate the ideas.

Michelle Bograd (1988), in her introduction to *Feminist Perspectives on Wife Abuse*, presents several important perspectives that undergird this work: (a) The concepts of gender and power are useful in understanding this violence—that is, men as the dominant, powerful forces in this society maintain the oppression of women at both personal and social levels; (b) the family must be analyzed as a historically situated social institution—a separate entity with clearly defined roles (male/female), with women often treated as property; and (c) the importance of understanding and validating the woman's experience must be taken into account.

Mr. G's assault on Ms. Z within the hospital demonstrated his sense of power and entitlement over her. This was reinforced when the hospital initially failed to respond, as is the typical pattern throughout society.

Staff repeatedly failed to grasp the power that Mr. G was exerting over Ms. Z through his severe abuse of their son, his threatening and assaultive behavior toward her, his presence in the hospital, and even his affectionate gestures toward her. Although some of these were obviously coercive, we would be remiss in not considering his more subtly coercive techniques. The staff held Ms. Z accountable for her husband's behavior, from his mistreatment of Paul to his infrequent visits. This corresponds to a commonly held view, that the wife manages the home and is responsible for her husband's behavior. Further, staff were unable to understand, much less validate, Ms. Z's seeming ambivalence toward Mr. G, her "inability" to get him out and to "stay away from him." They did not understand, until they talked with the AWAKE advocate, that Ms. Z felt that she could pacify him by responding positively to such affection. She felt this was preferable to another assault or threat. Further, she was torn over her own desire to get away from Mr. G and her fear that this was impossible. She had

reached out in the past—to her doctor, her priest, and her parents—
and had been told again and again that she should go back home and
try again, like a "good wife."

Further AWAKE project assumptions, articulated well by Susan
Schechter (in staff discussions and presentations, 1988-1990), include
the following:

(a) In up to 60% of child abuse cases where there is also a battered woman
(McKibben et al., 1989), the woman wants help if it is offered in a safe,
confidential, and empowering way. Assisting the mother in these dual
cases of family violence, as in the case of Ms. Z, may be the best means
of protecting her and her children.

(b) Many battered women are not abusive or neglectful of their children.
Whenever possible, these mothers and children should stay together. Ms.
Z believed that the abuse was directed only at her. She had neither
abused nor neglected Paul (and, until the incident of severe injury, Mr. G
had cared for Paul without harm).

(c) The child abuse literature often focuses on the so-called depressed abusive mother while ignoring a large population of child abusers—men
who batter their partners and their children. In fact, at least one study
demonstrates that men are perpetrating the most severe, lethal forms of
child abuse (Bergman, Larsen, & Mueller, 1986). These cases of violence require a different type of intervention: holding those perpetrators
accountable for their violence within the family and empowering the
nonviolent parents.

(d) Many battered women are frightened about contacting child protective
services for fear of having their children removed and placed in foster
care. This fear comes from the batterer's threats and allegations that the
woman is responsible for the harm to the children, even when that is not
true. Further, when clinicians, as in Paul's case, hold the mother equally
responsible for the child's injuries without assessing the violence against
her, or choose to listen only to the batterer, they confirm her fears.

(e) Many battered women are referred to services designed to improve parenting skills. It is inadequate and sometimes inappropriate to offer battered women with abused children these resources, especially if the
women do not lack caretaking knowledge and experience. Rather, they
may be able to provide good child care once they are in a safe and stable
environment. Often, the battered woman is experiencing a situational
crisis of victimization, and her needs for safety must be responded to
first. It is easier for clinicians to refer mothers to parenting classes than
it is for them to make a safety plan, and far less threatening. Again, it is

important to note how this common response can imply to the woman that she is not a "good enough" mother; this is yet more evidence in the power of the patriarchy that holds women as deficient.

(f) Because battered women need multiple services that are difficult and time-consuming to provide—housing, police, and court advocacy, for example—AWAKE assumed that a woman's advocate who was herself a former victim of abuse could best provide help, working collaboratively with the child's clinicians.

PRACTICE IMPLICATIONS

A feminist understanding of domestic violence has dramatic ramifications for our practice, both with individual clients and with the institutions in which we work and with which we collaborate (and which may oppress us). As social workers, we consider not only the individual and how she functions, but also the community/environment in which she lives and what connections she needs to make for a healthy life. As feminist social workers, we add to this view an understanding of women's unique gifts and skills, as well as their lower status in society, where men dominate. It is impossible for us to look at our clients as having individual pathology, as the patriarchal system would suggest we should do. Rather, we must constantly explore the context in which women live and pursue the assumptions under which they, we, and others operate.

In expanding our intervention in child abuse cases to include the children's battered mothers, we confront additional concrete and emotional tasks, but it also gives us the opportunity to understand and respond to family violence in a fuller and more just manner. This evolution began for me when I was a social worker with the child abuse consultation team and the Family Development Clinic at Children's Hospital, Boston. I believe the experiences I have described in this chapter are not so different from those of other clinicians. Rather, I think that my experiences and the assumptions and work of AWAKE can be quite usefully generalized to other clinicians and settings. Let me review again specific issues that are relevant for all practitioners to consider.

Our task often begins in the "assessment" or interview to understand a battered woman. Although AWAKE proposes that a social worker perform an overall assessment and then refer to the battered women's advocate if the woman so chooses, not all settings will permit this division of labor. Therefore it is crucial to know the services beyond your institution that are responsive to women, with which you can connect, since sharing the emotional and concrete load of such a situation is vital.

In beginning to talk with a battered woman, the mother of an abused child, I needed to understand my own thoughts and feelings about her as protector and as victim. As I began to look to a mother for the answers about abuse and for the protection of her children and then found that she could not offer that protection, I began to feel as helpless as she did. This would render me unable to respond to her effectively. I would begin to experience coercive feelings and the desire to take controlling action—demand that she get an order of protection or threaten to have her child removed unless she goes to a shelter—or push her to do what I thought was necessary rather than listen to her needs and plans. I failed to consider how the male-dominated systems—family life, courts, church—kept her trapped at home.

The awareness of my own coercive feelings and actions during times of felt helplessness has been a powerful insight for me. Although I have always considered myself a sensitive and open social worker who works mutually with clients, this deeper self-understanding has shown me where gaps in a sense of "mutuality" have occurred. The clinician can grow accustomed to wielding the power of protection and placement, when necessary, especially when he or she has worked with children for a long time. However, when faced with a battered woman, that same clinician cannot call protective services and have the woman placed in a safe home.

In working with battered women, I have learned to make a conscious transition from looking at them solely as mothers and protectors of children to seeing them as individuals who are victimized themselves. Further, the more I can imagine myself in a battered woman's situation and comprehend the ways in which the man was permitted to continue his coercive behavior, the clearer I become in my empathy and ability to help. Through this transition, I work to understand and validate a woman's experiences by listening to the reality as she perceives it and by believing her. I can then help other staff to understand her response to the violence more fully.

As we have interviewed women, we have recognized more fully the power of isolation. Moving women out of isolation and into contact with others strengthens and empowers them, as it does with us all. Isolation is a key feature of all the women with whom we have worked. This may take many forms: A woman may feel she is the only one in the world experiencing such abuse; she may have no phone, because the batterer ripped it from the wall; she may be prohibited by the batterer from leaving the house to see friends; she may lose touch with her family because the batterer has slowly cut those ties by degrading family members. This isolation can slowly overtake a person, until she is immersed. Once again, this demonstrates the power that a man within our society can exert over a woman.

In meeting with a battered woman, it is vital to do so alone, without the batterer present. This is both for protective reasons and for clarity of the assessment. A woman who is dominated by a partner will probably feel unable to reveal the truth of violence in the home if he is present. Punishment for saying "the wrong thing" and retaliation by the batterer for a perceived injustice may follow a joint interview. Also, seeing each partner individually helps the clinician to keep clear that the partners are not necessarily equally responsible for violence in the home.

In planning with battered women, safety for the woman and her children must come first. Once safety is established, with secure housing, food, and clothing guaranteed, one can better understand whether the woman's and children's behavior is a response to the recent violence and crisis. Some women and children become calm and reassured, and are able to begin their lives anew, once their environment is secure and stabilized. These women and children are able to renew relationships with friends and family and make connections with other supports. Others, however, because of previous emotional difficulties and/or severe or chronic battering, need therapeutic intervention with someone who understands the devastation of such violence. Finally, not to be minimized or dismissed are the realities of a woman's life when she chooses to separate from the batterer: She may or may not locate a shelter that can house her, her economic status will decline, and she may be unable to support herself and her children. Such social problems do not warrant psychotherapeutic intervention, but call for the provision of basic resources. Although shelter staff and others of us working with battered women and their children certainly attempt to assist women in securing these basic provisions, there is a need for a radical systems change that guarantees these goods and services, including medical care for all women and children.

We have grown to respect professional (individual and group psychotherapy) and "nonprofessional" (self-help groups, support groups, 12-Step programs) interventions alike, understanding their unique qualities in the healing process. Too often, clinicians dismiss the benefits of community interventions and buy into the idea that only the "medical model" or patriarchal interventions can be successful. These interventions tend to focus on individual pathology or illness, rather than on the role that familial and societal systems play in a person's functioning.

We have worked hard to help the women and staff to understand the victimization and not to blame the victim. Blaming the victim serves no useful purpose in supporting and empowering women or in furthering society's understanding of this problem. Rather, blaming the victim focuses attention upon her, not upon the male batterer.

CONCLUSION

Finally, it is important to note that institutional and societal change are vital if violence against women and children is to stop. In struggling for institutional change, we must address not only the service deficiencies, but also the underlying assumptions that contribute to the dominance and coercion of women and others who are less powerful in this society. The patriarchal assumptions that must be challenged include that problems are caused by "individual pathology," that the most important form of treatment is the "medical model," and that the continuing "privatization of family life" (Gondolf & Fisher, 1988, p. 24) is desirable. When the institutional response is challenged and begins to change, the battered woman can be identified and understood, she and her children can be protected, and the batterer can be held accountable for his violence. If our society and institutions continue to support and sanction violence, battered women and their families will not be able to maintain any individual change.

Many child protective agencies, courts, and mental health centers maintain preserving the family as their primary goal. But in cases of family violence, that preservation is often at the expense of the least powerful members—women and children—and should not be the goal. For intervention to succeed, courts must evict batterers and mandate treatment for them rather than leaving women and children homeless. These batterers must be held accountable for their behavior, whether they perpetrate violence within or outside of the home. Rape as well as assault and battery are treated much differently if perpetrated by strangers in the street instead of by "loved ones" at home. We, as a society and as service providers, must no longer tolerate violence, whether inside or outside of the home. We must speak out against it and challenge the notion that individuals must solve the problems and stop the battering on their own, for then we only reinforce batterers' power and authority.

REFERENCES

Bergman, A. B., Larsen, R. M., & Mueller, B. A. (1986, February). Changing spectrum of serious child abuse. *Pediatrics, 81*, 113-116.

Bograd, M. (1988). Feminist perspectives on wife abuse: An introduction. In K. Yllo & M. Bograd (Eds.), *Feminist perspectives on wife abuse*. Newbury Park, CA: Sage.

Bologna, M. J., Waterman, C. K., & Dawson, L. J. (1989). *Violence in gay male and lesbian relationships: Implications for practitioners and policy makers*. Presented at the Third Annual Conference on Family Violence, Durham, NC.

Brown, A., Pelcovitz, D., Kaplan, S., & Kaplan, T. (1985, November). *A comparison of child witnesses and child victims of family violence: A controlled study*. Paper presented at the Seventh National Conference on Child Abuse and Neglect, Chicago.

Gondolf, E. W., & Fisher, E. R. (1988). *Battered women as survivors: An alternative to treating learned helplessness*. Lexington, MA: Lexington.

Jaffe, P., Wilson, S., & Wolfe, D. A. (1986). Promoting changes in attitudes and understanding of conflict resolution among child witnesses of family violence. *Canadian Journal of Behavioral Science Review, 18*, 359-366.

McKibben, L., DeVos, E., & Newberger, E. (1989). Victimization of mothers of abused children: A controlled study. *Pediatrics, 84*, 531-535.

McLeer, S., & Anwar, R. (1989, January). A study of battered women presenting in an emergency department. *American Journal of Public Health, 79*(1), 65-66.

Schechter, S. (1987). *Guidelines for mental health practitioners in domestic violence cases*. Washington, DC: National Coalition Against Domestic Violence.

Stark, E., & Flitcraft, A. (1988). Women and children at risk: A feminist perspective on child abuse. *International Journal of Health Services, 18*, 97-118.

Straus, M. A., Gelles, R. J., & Steinmetz, S. K. (1980). *Behind closed doors: Violence in the American family*. Garden City, NY: Anchor.

Straus, M. B. (Ed.). (1988). *Abuse and victimization across the life span*. Baltimore, MD: Johns Hopkins University Press.

Walker, L. (1983). *The battered woman*. New York: Harper & Row.

U.S. Department of Justice, Bureau of Justice Statistics. (1983). *Report to the nation on crime and justice: The data*. Washington, DC: Government Printing Office.

The Trouble Was Meals

Elizabeth Bennett

Dad was the head of the family, for sure.
When he got us all together
it meant either a baby was on the way
or we were moving. So when the question was put,
How would it be if Grandma came to live with us?
I thought, no big deal.
I was glad we weren't moving.

I found a picture of Grandma,
a young dancer in a dress, sequins and feathers.
She had me tape it onto the mirror
over the dresser where she kept Grandpa's remains,
his gold cufflinks, glass eye.

It was all right,
Grandma the dancer in residence,
all right for me, hard for Mother.
Dad would come home, pour a glass of Old Crow Bourbon,
one for Mother, drink them both.

The trouble was meals.
Dad was used to holding forth
and the first night, halfway through Chicken Cacciatore
Grandma turned and said, "Rest your gums, dear."
She called everyone dear, all of us, the mailman,
even the exterminator.
She took to humming in a loud voice
and dropping her knife and fork on the floor.

One night she shouted, "Leftovers, leftovers,
where's the original?" and shoved her plate
on the floor. Baby threw his bottle
on top of the broken china. The plate crash
became a regular occurrence.

Fridays at school our teacher read us poetry,
"Poitry," she called it. One went,
"Old age is a flight of small cheeping birds . . . "*
I didn't like poetry. What I liked was Shop.
I made a wooden bowl, sanded the rim smooth,
carved my initials on the bottom.
I brought it home to Grandma
and we served her dinner in it every night.
She still shoved it on the floor
but nothing broke.

When I was at the orthodontist's one afternoon,
Grandma took a nap and never woke up.
We cleaned out her room. I helped Mother.
She was in a mood to throw everything out,
flannel sheets that smelled of urine, everything.
She only kept the picture. That night after dinner
I found the bowl in the trash.
Dad said, we won't need *that* anymore,
but I washed and dried it
and put it on the shelf next to Old Crow
so I could find it when Mother got old.

*From "To Waken an Old Lady" by William Carlos Williams,
in *Collected Earlier Poems of William Carlos Williams*,
New Directions Publishing Company.

Previously published in Sandra Martz (Ed.),
When I Am an Old Woman I Shall Wear Purple, 1987.
Reprinted by permission of Papier-Mâché Press,
Watsonville, CA, and the author.

Chapter 2

FEMINIST SOCIAL WORK WITH OLDER WOMEN CAREGIVERS IN A DVA MEDICAL SETTING

ELOISE RATHBONE-McCUAN
SUSAN TEBB
TERRY LEE HARBERT

This chapter describes an application of feminist practice with older women who are care-providing spouses to aging veterans. The Caregiver Support Program (CSP) operates under the leadership of the social work department of a midwestern Department of Veterans Affairs (DVA) medical center. Our program, as one of the few designed to meet the psychosocial needs of older women who care for veterans in the community, is receiving significant attention within the large bureaucratic structure of the DVA health care delivery system. To our knowledge, feminist practice is seldom explicitly applied by DVA social workers, the majority of whom utilize conventional psychiatric and medical social work methods. Practice in the CSP incorporates feminist theory, principles, and techniques in a casework model, supporting older women's strengths and minimizing the exploitation they experience in the caregiving role. The increasing number of research and education projects supported within our department are intended to expand interest in applying nontraditional practice approaches to the care of veterans. One reason the Caregiver Support Program has been effective is the innovative administrative climate in this particular DVA social work service,

which helps to reduce some of the bureaucratic constraints that characterize large medical care organizations and that maintain traditional forms of
health and mental health practice.

Before discussing the specific medical setting that sponsors the Caregiver
Support Program and the older women participants in the program, we will
provide a brief overview of the DVA system as it relates to social work
practice.

THE VETERANS MEDICAL CENTER
AS A PRACTICE ENVIRONMENT

The DVA is an immense bureaucracy that is isolated from the mainstream
of most health care facilities. Unlike most mainstream facilities, which tailor
policy and procedures to their organizational needs, the DVA is a highly centralized organization whose policies are formulated at a central office in
Washington, D.C. Although individual DVA medical centers are allowed
some latitude in procedure, they must be in compliance with DVA Central
Office policy. Systemic uniformity is the core of day-to-day DVA operation.
One exception to this is the larger academic teaching hospitals connected to
the DVA through medical school affiliations. These hospitals allow flexibility, which is required to support clinical teaching and research activities.
DVA medical centers without such affiliations are usually uninvolved in the
larger health care systems in their geographic areas. Because of this isolation,
many social work practice innovations that occur outside the DVA are not incorporated unless there is specific sanction from within the system.

DVA hospital settings are filled with tangible and symbolic reminders of
the veterans' experiences in the military. Recreation therapy rooms are filled
with model military airplane kits, and ward holiday parties are an opportunity
to play the patriotic songs popular during World War II. Jungle fatigues from
the Vietnam era are ever present. Aging veteran volunteer drivers and escorts
wear their military insignias very proudly. In these settings, it is sometimes
hard to separate patriotism from patriarchy and to find ways to promote col-
lectivism within the constant influence of hierarchy. Many of the long-term-
stay veterans derive their major source of positive self-identity from their
military service. Their roles—tank gunner, platoon leader, paratrooper, or
military policeman—are anchored in historical experiences that epitomize
military life. Staff tend to dominate over veterans' decision making, despite
the development of patient therapeutic programs in the hospital. These therapeutic efforts are usually small-scale programs that have little impact

on the total institutional milieu of most DVA facilities, especially those authorized to care for veterans with long-term mental illness.

The DVA was established as the Veterans Administration in 1930, the administrative unit to coordinate the services provided to veterans. Almost 60 years later, in 1989, it was elevated to the presidential cabinet level as the U.S. Department of Veteran Affairs. It is the largest independent health care system in the world and the largest employer of social workers, and delivers the greatest concentration of formal long-term care to the U.S. male population (Mather, 1984). The independent facilities include 172 medical centers, 229 outpatient clinics, and 117 nursing-home units (Thompson, 1984). There is great diversity in the sizes and types of facilities that operate within the DVA system. Few programs within medical centers operate without social work staff. Social workers have been especially influential in developing long-term care programs for older veterans.

This health care delivery system is in turmoil over its expectation of increased demands for care from the population of veterans 65 years and older. The vast majority of persons receiving long-term DVA care are men entitled to care by virtue of medical need resulting from prior military service. By the year 2000, the population of veterans 65 and older will grow from 4 million to 9 million. Nearly two thirds of all U.S. males over 65 will be veterans at the end of this century (Veterans Administration, 1988). At first glance, these statistics suggest that aged men with military service background become eligible for DVA care based solely on their chronological age, but this assumption is no longer correct. In the middle of the 1980s eligibility restrictions were introduced that precluded automatic eligibility based on the age of 65. Now older veterans are assured no-cost medical care from the DVA only for those health problems that are determined to be "service connected." For example, if a veteran received an eye injury in World War II and blindness occurred in later life that can be established to be connected to the original injury, the veteran will be assigned category A eligibility for care of the blindness. If another veteran of the same age develops blindness due to some condition not related to a service-connected experience, the DVA is not obligated to treat him at no cost unless he qualifies financially through an eligibility screening process.

Currently, the most common experiences shared by men 65 years and older are that they served in World War II (Rathbone-McCuan & Hashimi, 1982) and that they are married. It is estimated that among male veterans over 65 years of age, 75% are married and 80% live with family. Some 25% of older veterans, or approximately 2.25 million men, currently use DVA services, and the majority of them live with families who will contribute about 80% of the long-term care (Veterans Administration, 1988).

The DVA lacks an adequate data base to project accurately the demands for care from older veterans, because demographic and utilization estimates have not been refined according to information based on new categories of DVA medical eligibility. Furthermore, the general aging population and health and social service providers who are unfamiliar with current eligibility categories may be surprised to learn that age alone is no longer the criterion for a veteran to be eligible for DVA care. Obtaining more precise projections of future long-term care demands and providing better community education about current eligibility policies that control service access are two important challenges now unmet by the system.

In DVA discussions of issues of long-term care, the term *community of care* is a euphemism for family, and the term *family care* is a euphemism for spousal care. Only very recently has the DVA system awakened to the reality that its long-range cost-containment objectives for chronic care are dependent on the labor of older relatives caring for their veteran husbands, sons, and other male family members. Any planning to provide systemwide supports to relatives caring for veterans is made difficult by the lack of data to account for the informal care provided to all the veteran population under DVA medical center care. Individual medical centers may have some information about the amount and type of family care offered within specific programs, but planners cannot tell the full measure of informal care that bolsters the formal care from the DVA.

COSTS OF CAREGIVING TO OLDER WOMEN

Within the DVA, the recognition of family-based contributions does not mean the recognition that women are providing that care. There is much work to be done by social workers to educate DVA policymakers about the human costs of caregiving as it victimizes women and, in turn, the family. The process of education about caregiver burden through the DVA system is a long-term challenge. The well-being of older women as caregivers of the elderly has not been a priority of U.S. health care or social welfare policy (Sommers & Shields, 1987). Because of the immediate demographic patterns of our aging society and the economic and political debates over long-term care and its cost-based rationing, the next few years will be critical for determining the conditions under which older people will live. Women's choices regarding caregiving will either contract or expand. Either they will have more options available to make choices about caregiving or they will be forced through political and economic pressures to devote increasingly more of their adult and later years to meeting the daily survival needs of others who require care (Hooyman & Ryan, 1987).

According to Briar and Ryan (1986), the trend of medical facilities toward advocating home care transfers the necessary services from trained professionals to untrained family members, usually women. Callahan (1988) proposes that the reliance on family caregiving has grown in recent years because of the presumption that care given at home is better, but argues that financial concerns of medical facilities are really the driving force to increase family care. The DVA's recent emphasis on maintaining veterans in the community illustrates this financial trend. Wasow (1986) also questions whether care- givers should be encouraged to remain in the caregiving role for as long as possible, since the result may be two admissions to long-term care facilities instead of one. In the DVA system, the result would be institutionalization for the veteran and his wife.

As Pharr (1988) notes, many feminists consider that economics must be addressed first because it is at the root of sexism. "Free labor" mentality is evident wherever service delivery organizations attempt to save money. Forcing the provision of informal care typifies the victimization of women caregivers. This reflects the pervasive cultural conditions that allow the political definitions of economic crisis to bend and break human bonds of caring through forcing intimate relationships to absorb human costs that society is unwilling to support. This then becomes a process of instrumentalizing human commitments and interpersonal caring (Bricker-Jenkins, 1983).

OLDER WOMEN "ATTENDING" FRAIL VETERANS

Similarly, the motivation of the DVA system to attend to the needs of female care providers to older veterans is driven by economics. The intraorganizational rationale is that if caregivers receive support and services from the DVA, they are more likely to provide care to older veterans for longer periods. If this occurs, the veterans they care for will remain less dependent on the costly DVA long-term care services, perhaps never requiring institutional care from the system.

The feminist perspective that we are trying to evolve in our practice is reflected fully in the words of Balbo (1987):

I would suggest that beyond other more specific goals, the cutting [or minimal provision] of public services . . . and ideological support for the family all have in common: to keep women overburdened with the impossible tasks of satisfying needs, to deny them control over their time, energy, or choices, and to make any different pattern impossible to them. (p. 67)

When this perspective is implemented in practice, it is possible to see the caregivers as caught in pervasive forces that place them in a position of having no choices about caregiving. Feminist practice directs attention to confronting the forces of entrapment and the necessity to create choices.

There are many medical services in the DVA that could develop specific programs for caregivers. For example, the Caregiver Support Program (CSP) in our DVA medical center is part of the extended-care service that coordinates multiple geriatric inpatient and outpatient services. Because of the increasing demand for long-term care, extended care is becoming more diversified and less dominated by 40 years of rigid biomedical structure. Social work plays an important function in both institutional and community extended-care programs. The social work influence helps make extended-care programs more receptive to alternative approaches, such as off-site mobile outreach programs for rural veterans or communitywide resource networking to support adult day care in the local community. Recognition of caregiver burden is much greater in this service compared with outpatient medicine or posttraumatic stress disorder units, because staff become better acquainted and have more communication with caregivers about in-home or community care issues.

Our practice is primarily with spouses of older veterans with dementia. *Dementia* is defined as a loss of intellectual abilities of sufficient severity to interfere with social and occupational functioning. Believed to be the primary mental health problem of older persons, dementia involves progressive intellectual decline and memory loss. Dementing diseases affect more than 7 million people 65 years of age and older in the United States (U.S. Congress, 1987). During the next 25 years, this number is expected to increase by about 50% unless drastic advances are made in treatment and prevention (Jivanjee, 1988).

The most common dementia is Alzheimer's disease; there is no known way to recover mental function lost due to this disease. With Alzheimer's, there are four general stages of progressive decline in cognitive and behavioral abilities. The first stage, during which often no one is quite sure if something is wrong, appears usually as depression or slight confusion. During the second stage, the person becomes increasingly self-absorbed and insensitive to others' feelings, displays an inability to calculate, and has great difficulty making decisions; the individual thus requires supervision. The third stage shows a marked loss of independent functioning, as cognitive capacities decline at varying rates. By the fourth stage, the victim shows no recognition of individuals, is incontinent, and cannot manage any self-care (Tebb, Rathbone-McCuan, & Harbert, 1990). Progression of these stages may be rapid or may proceed over a number of years, but the premorbid outcome of Alzheimer's disease is total dependency. The human toll of the disease is inescapable and tragic for both the ill persons and those who provide their care.

Caregivers participating in our Caregiver Support Program, with an average age of 64, are considerably older than the national average of 46 years for caregivers (Tebb et al., 1990). The average age of their spouses is 67, which is substantially younger than the national average of 77 years for care receivers. These caregivers devote more time to completing care tasks than the reported national daily average of 4 hours (U.S. Congress, 1987). The veterans display various patterns of disability relative to their cognitive impairment. Some have additional medical problems, such as emphysema or the effects of stroke. The combination of medical problems adds to the veteran's vulnerability and places additional care demands on the wife.

For the most part, spousal caregivers have been in long-term marriages. They have devoted their earlier years to children and other traditional home-centered roles that characterize older rural or nonmetropolitan midwestern women of their age cohort. They manifest the take-care-of-your-own persona (Olson, 1988) in their patterns of caregiving and their commitment to caring for their demented spouses. They may continue to emphasize the partnership they entered through their marriage vows, even though their spouses now demand their constant patience and presence. Most have taken on, usually with little or no preparation, the financial management, decision making, and physical labor that were once performed by their spouses. They know what it means to have to be the person who functions to maintain another human being. Many have grown accustomed to performing the most intimate of tasks, such as total supervision of toileting, and many of the wives complain only about their husbands' resistance to their trying to help.

It is indisputable that these caregivers experience major burdens from their care responsibilities. Studies of caregivers of dementia patients have demonstrated that family burden is a major factor in the decision to seek institutional care. However, nursing-home care typically is sought only when the care-giver has become overwhelmed and exhausted, physically ill, or mentally distressed due to the extraordinary care demands (Barusch, 1988; Zarit, Todd, & Zarit, 1986). Older women caregivers frequently experience financial stress. Some face realistic fears of impoverishment, while others either ignore that possibility or lack financial and legal information to assess their true economic situation. These conditions are all present among the women with whom we work.

Our feminist practice base attempts to help the caregivers find their strengths, frame their choices, take steps to empower themselves, and support others to do the same. We did not begin with a well-developed model of feminist practice for caregiver support services, but understood the feminist implications that were not made evident in the earlier research on aging and caregiving. Our clinical contacts with Alzheimer's disease patients and their families in the early 1980s have given us insight into the isolation of those providing many years of home care.

A new meaning of personal powerlessness began to emerge as we came to understand that every aspect of the illness leaves the patient, family, and clinicians feeling powerless. Diagnostic procedures are only now becoming more accurate in early stages of the disease. Once diagnosed, the progression of the illness as irreversible translates to a feeling that life has become uncontrollable and unjust for the patient and family. From this perspective of powerlessness came our impetus to go beyond the framework of traditional gerontology, and to establish a feminist orientation to the program as a direct effort to reduce such powerlessness among caregivers.

FEMINIST GERONTOLOGICAL SOCIAL WORK AS A PRACTICE BASE

The decade of the 1980s was a time for building more connections between feminist and aging concerns and extending these into research, practice, policy formulation, and broader social change initiatives. The 1990s is a time to extend a feminist orientation into all spheres of gerontological social work. Our experience in the DVA suggests that this is a reachable goal.

When the connections were very weak, almost invisible, older radical feminists began to speak out in feminist circles and advocacy groups for older people about their isolating and stigmatizing experiences. MacDonald and Rich (1983) attribute the stereotyping of older feminists by younger feminists to the younger women's tendency to identify older women as part of the "familia" (institution of the family). That identification of women with the prescribed status of caring for others reinforces a basic male institution for controlling others. Projecting older women into mother and grandmother roles perpetuates a definition of older women whose rights to exist are dependent on the love and service they extend to others. Following a similar line of analysis, Copper (1988) expands her critique to confront the lack of age consciousness among feminists; she also critiques the lack of gender consciousness and age consciousness among those professionals who "serve the elderly" and who are directly involved in the social, emotional, economic, and medical needs of older women clients.

In gerontological practice, including the research completed to inform practice, it is helpful to review some of the conceptual linkages between feminism and gerontology. Reinharz (1986) suggests that there are five major categories of such conceptual linkages:

(1) the struggle over the extent to which their group is defined by biology or by social conditions

(2) the strategic use of statistics to demonstrate the existence of inequality and to press for policy changes

(3) the struggle over whether to consider the group as a whole or to be concerned primarily with those subgroups that suffer the greatest inequities

(4) the struggle over the choice of a strategy with which to demonstrate the group's strengths or unfair treatment

(5) the struggle to prevent or challenge a backlash that would arise among powerful groups or other relatively powerless groups

From another perspective, these are the themes that must be factored into the fledging movement to create a feminist gerontological social work practice base.

It is important to explain the meanings we give to and take from feminist thought, based on our operational understanding of sexism, ageism, and ageist sexism. These concepts are relevant to our work with older women, specifically those who participate in the Caregiver Support Program. *Sexism* is the system by which women are kept subordinate to men. *Ageism* is the system by which older women are kept subordinate to younger women and men of all ages. Eliminating the sources and ramifications of ageist sexism is a shared goal in our efforts to practice from a feminist gerontological perspective.

Ageist sexism is a global issue. The global population of women aged 50 and over doubled between 1955 and 1990, from 250 to 500 million. By 2025, the number will reach 1.1 billion. Currently, 17% to 18% of women are 50 and over; by 2050, the proportion will increase to more than 26%. Referring to these international demographic projections, Lois Hamer (1989), an older woman and longtime member of the Women's International League for Peace and Freedom, says this about the worldview of older women:

> The struggle of these numbers [of older women] will greatly influence the future of the thinking about "ageism." The talents of older women may be used to bolster social progress and national economies. Traditional and evolving roles may be reintroduced for the benefit not only of older women, but the entire world. (p. 5)

OPPRESSION OF OLDER WOMEN

The three mechanisms that keep older women oppressed under the powerful influence of ageist sexism are economics, exploitation, and isolation. Each of these specifically affects older women in their caregiver roles; each is discussed in turn below.

Economics

Neither health insurance nor Medicare will provide any real security to older women who face the possibility or likelihood of their spouses' being institutionalized and having to "spend down" their collective estate to the point where long-term care can be covered under Medicaid. Even before the possibility of nursing-home placement, the wife may expend most of the couple's resources on home health care or other programs that are not reimbursed because they are provided in the community rather than in an institution. This leaves the woman with little economic base for her daily living expenses and without any real options to cover her own potential need for long-term care. Recently, federal legislation was passed that limits the financial impoverishment an individual faces if a spouse is institutionalized. However, asset and income protection is limited. If still of an age to be employed, the wife may need to leave the work force to care for her spouse, thereby reducing her ability to accumulate full retirement benefits from pensions and other entitlements. Pharr (1988) instructs us to look at economics not only as the root cause of sexism but also as the underlying driving force that keeps all oppressions in place. These conditions are most vivid in the lives of older women, but adult women of every age face economic inequity because of differential earning power, low access to and preparation for jobs, and financial discrimination.

Exploitation

Traditional role socialization is a very effective means of keeping older women engaged in their "attending activities" as unpaid attendants (Mac-Donald & Rich, 1983). Socialized to accept this role, women frequently receive strong reinforcement from within their family and community environments to provide what is expected of them as wives to disabled men. Of all the discussion and writing on the risks of caregiving arising from its oppressive conditions, one of the least mentioned is the psychic and physical violence to which many of them are exposed (Rathbone-McCuan, 1984). Only recently, as the elder abuse movement has gained some political position and found some collective grass-roots connections with the battered women's movement, have we come to understand that older women caregivers can be battered verbally and physically by their bedridden spouses, who inflict punishing resentment on them and keep them isolated.

Isolation

Interdependent with economics and exploitation, isolation is a psychosocial-physical malaise that can easily evolve from the objective and subjective burdens of caregiving. In situations where the spouse's problem is Alzheimer's disease, in itself the most isolating illness among the old, the ill person withdraws into his own world, the social connections to the couple fade away, and the woman is cut off from supports while still burdened with the daily, hourly, and momentary demands of her spouse's regime. These burdens are not easily escaped. Respite care lasts only so long, support groups do not follow the caregiver home at night, and spiritual life may be greatly weakened by soulful distress (Rathbone-McCuan & Hashimi, 1982).

If feminist practice emerges from a worldview (Bricker-Jenkins, in press), then practice designed to support work with older women caregivers assumes that there is a commonality among all caregivers as a woman's experience. Such commonality can be understood while still maintaining respect for diversity; hardship can become a source of strength, and political and cultural change must be present for growth and transformation of individuals and groups.

Few of us really understand these assumptions until we experience them in our daily lives and see the meanings behind the assumptions as they play out in the life struggles we share with others. Economic resources do not necessarily protect against the demands of caregiving. When any woman is left to be the sole provider of care, her fate mirrors the same psychosocial experiences of other women, irrespective of age, race, and socioeconomic status. Each woman assuming the responsibility of a caregiver travels her own journey, but her interconnection with other women struggling with the hardships of that journey eventually makes them traveling companions and potential comrades. As human beings come to believe that there are alternatives through the experiences of others, new ways are introduced to turn illness into health, pain into joy, and isolation into companionship.

As collaborating authors, we have traveled very different routes to reach our feminist perspective. We know the power of collective change because we were young adults in the 1960s and saw individuals in our profession of social work join and sometimes direct the flow of social change. We have confidence that our political diversity, as reflected in our individual feminist perspectives, shares a common value base that we bring to this work. We practice with a sense of community that we try to share with our clients and work to change our shared powerlessness.

DESCRIPTION OF THE CAREGIVER SUPPORT PROGRAM

The CSP program is staffed by M.S.W. students, placed through their field practicum as caseworkers for small numbers of caregivers. Students have an average of five to eight cases, and assume responsibility for facilitating participant caregiver group sessions. Their supervision is provided by the social worker who originally adapted the program from a health/strengths model and a staff social worker who has a feminist practice orientation. Both social workers are trained in the health/strengths model as presented by Weick and Freeman (1983) and subsequently developed by Weick (1983, 1984, 1986). The health/strengths model emerges from the values embedded in conventional working definitions of social work practice (Bartlett, 1958). However, these values had lost importance in practice as social work shifted its care of the mentally and physically impaired to a biomedical model. This shift increased social control by the clinician and reduced the voice of the client.

The key assumptions of the health/strengths model are based on self-actualization as a process (Weick & Pope, 1988) that we know to be threatened and sometimes extinguished by the burdens of caregiving relationships. The ideology of the health/strengths model prescribes attention to clients' knowledge as a basis for finding their strengths and applying them as the major focus of practice. When combined with and extended by feminist theory, principles, and methods, this orientation directs attention to clients' self-actualization experiences based on applications of personal and environmental strengths that encourage social change through collective work.

Creating opportunities for self-actualization is fundamental to the quality of life for most caregivers. The values about self-actualization incorporated into our program are as follows:

(1) Caregiving can be a self-actualizing experience (for some women), as it offers purpose and meaning to life.

(2) Caregiving can increase as a self-actualizing experience if women are empowered to make choices about the conditions of and their commitments to caretaking.

(3) Caregivers can attain self-actualization by connecting to their inherent strengths and the strengths derived from the collective experiences of caregivers.

These assumptions seem to be valid, but must be understood in the larger context of ageist sexism that traps older women in the isolation of caregiving. Our caregiver participants do not yet benefit, to any major extent, from material and ideological conditions introduced into our society through the *collective social change work for and by caregivers*. Rather, patriarchy produces specific and profound injuries to older women directly related to the cultural, economic, and social circumstances of their caregiving.

The stresses experienced by older women caregivers are not inherent by virtue of their gender roles, but rather due to their lack of socially valued resources, a lack that, in turn, creates and intensifies life stresses for them. In the program, these factors are recognized as realities. In other words, caregiver burdens are seen as an outcome of older women's interaction with an environment that does not reduce/eliminate stress or provide them access to resources. In practice, this means that the social work staff do not approach the caregiver with any preconceived notion that there is something wrong with her. Rather, they explore the quality of her environment and the patterns of her interaction with it. From this position, the social worker's purpose is to interact with the client to reduce her burden and to increase her well-being. The health/strengths model gives foremost attention to the regenerative and resilient capacity of women who are participating in the program; the feminist framework then extends this into clinical and programmatic work. The social worker supports this capacity for health and strength that is a link between the health/strengths model and feminist practice.

Another essential aspect of the program is the work conducted to support an older woman's desire to have positive life experiences with caregiving. If one accepts that a woman has the right to make the choice to continue to give care, irrespective of her reasons, and wants to derive satisfaction from that decision, the social worker joins her to find ways to make such satisfaction possible. The social worker encourages the caregiver to examine her inner knowledge of the best ways to care for herself. Opportunities for self-actualization come from drawing on her knowledge and applying it to choices and actions. The worker believes that each caregiver has the ability to affect positive change for herself in the ways that she copes with caregiving stresses. The caregiver-social worker relationship is an opportunity for learning and extending knowledge into transforming interactions with the environment.

As a first step, an open-ended assessment form and the Well-Being Scale are completed by the caregiver and the social worker as a shared learning experience. The assessment form covers areas relevant to the caregiver, particularly to her situation and her ability and desire to give care. It does not address the veteran's situation and health. Separate sections are designed to address burden and self-actualization: onset of the care provision, personal history of the care provider, information available about the veteran's illness and needs, knowledge about procedures for the caregiving tasks, use of informal and formal support services, and the caregiver's patterns of self-advocacy. In the process of completing the Well-Being Scale, the social worker looks for the areas of well-being affected and the caregiver's understanding of these in her life. The scale is used only as a tool, and does not force choices on the caregiver (Tebb, 1989).

COMPONENTS OF THE HEALTH/STRENGTHS MODEL AND FEMINIST PRACTICE

The program has outlined three steps to develop the relationship needed to implement the health/strengths model. Listening is a key skill. Listening is a skillful intellectual and emotional process integrating the physical, mental, social, and spiritual environments of the social worker and client in a search for understanding. The social worker hears what is said without words, by noting body language and what the caregiver is feeling and thinking but not expressing through her words. Expressing one's own emotions is also part of listening and communicating with the caregiver. The social worker needs to be aware of and to express her own feelings in a way that supports and assists the exciting work of change shared between social worker and client. If the social worker is to participate in the change process, she must be able to self-disclose as part of listening. Self-disclosure is the ability to talk openly and honestly about oneself. The atmosphere supporting the client's comfort for self-disclosure is established only if the social worker consciously engages in a reciprocal process.

The second step in the health/strengths model is that of exploration. The social worker credits the giving of care, patience, and loyalty, and supports the caregiver when she wants to share feelings of fear, depression, courage, or joy. At this point knowledge and education are also needed. As mentioned previously, Alzheimer's disease has a complex progression that is unfamiliar to those living with its patterns of deterioration for the first time. Caregivers also benefit from knowledge about services in the DVA medical center and in the general community. Also part of exploration is the process of learning together how self-advocacy can become a utilized strength of the caregiver for meeting her own needs as well as those of the veteran.

The third step involves the social worker's caring for the client. The social worker, in caring about the older woman, encourages her to seek self-knowledge and to make decisions and plans that are important to her. When she knows another person cares for her, the caregiver finds an open door for greater self-caring anchored in self-value. One of the most meaningful experiences reported by the staff occurs when a caregiver transforms from a position of self-neglect to one of self-care. This, by our definition, is personal empowerment and is the basis for self-actualization to meet physical, social, emotional, and spiritual needs.

CAREGIVERS' EXPERIENCE OF SELF-ACTUALIZATION

Before discussing the actual case application of feminist practice as we have incorporated it in the program, it is important to identify how conventional social work approaches reinforce ignoring the social system surrounding the aged veteran. Most social workers in the DVA have knowledge about family systems as drawn from general social systems theory (Rodway, 1986), but they have little experience applying a family systems perspective to the geriatric client (Rathbone-McCuan & Hedlund, 1989). Conventional theories must be rethought in view of the family systems dynamics that emerge around caregiving. Experienced practitioners may not conceive of the caregiving spouse as a legitimate client separate from the veteran's client status. One general consequence of the presence of the CSP at our medical center is that some of the other social work staff have become educated about and sensitive to the importance of referring spouses of older veterans to the program. Because our program is independent and available to any caregiver thought to be caring in a home-care situation for a veteran with a dementia, it is dependent upon referrals.

Caregivers often come into the program through a referral from the Geriatric Evaluation Unit (GEU), which is a special inpatient interdisciplinary program designed for integrated assessment of aged veterans thought to have dementia. The GEU has developed a strong psychosocial care orientation. It differs from GEU programs at other DVA settings because of the extensive emphasis placed on the involvement with the family, specifically the caregiver, who is referred to the CSP. Feminist practice is not applied, however, in every component of the GEU service, and it will take considerable time to extend a feminist orientation into other areas such as respite care and DVA-sponsored home health care. The GEU coordinating social worker has been a major source of referral to the CSP. She reports that many older women do not see themselves as entitled to the special attention that CSP offers them. Active outreach is therefore necessary as part of the CSP social work role. It is at the point of outreach, which immediately follows a referral, where we have started the most comprehensive application of feminist practice. As mentioned before, even in cases where other staff have made direct referrals, many of the caregivers will decline services that attend to their needs if those services are not directly connected to medical care for their spouses.

There are two interrelated reasons caregivers may not feel deserving of specialized support. The first is connected to the lack of self-actualizing experiences, including the personal recognition of one's own needs, associated with caregiving as a basis for peer support and professional service. The second is the conditioning they may have received from the DVA setting that reinforces their feeling that they are invisible and have no important role in their spouses' medical care experience. One caregiver who was angry that she had not been referred to the program sooner described her feelings of invisibility: "My husband's medical care needs are taken care of by me every time I take him home from the clinic, but there was never an opportunity for me to talk to the doctor directly. I was there every visit and never did the doctor ask to speak to me without my husband present."

One strategy derived from the feminist principle of collective action has been to emphasize support groups. In planning the structure of group support, we applied some of our experiences with grief management and depression in all women's groups. Through the group component, caregivers have an opportunity to meet and interact with each other for the purpose of building networks that can exist outside of the formal program. Several caregiver participants have become spokeswomen for the CSP and make themselves available to talk to other caregivers. The limits of their time and energy, however, make it impossible for them to spend extended periods in clinics where they might meet other caregivers and tell them about the program. Some caregivers have participated as presenters at community forums to describe the DVA program. Others have found it valuable to participate in non-DVA community Alzheimer's disease support groups and bring back current information to others who do not attend non-DVA programs.

Another example of a DVA caregiver program, using older women's natural capacity to build support networks in group situations, is now operating in an eastern DVA medical center. This program is based on an action-oriented practice model (Toseland, Rossiter, & Labrecque, 1989), which is complementary to the self-empowering processes derived from feminist work with groups. The program became associated with the New York State Office for the Aging, which had funds to produce videotapes about caregiving issues. The real "stars" in the video *Coping with Caregiving* (New York State Office for the Aging, 1986) are DVA caregivers. This film and a social work training manual developed at our medical center have been distributed to all DVA medical centers. When the video was first previewed in Washington before senior DVA administrators, it was very evident that these caregivers had been heard. Having observed the follow-up activities of several key DVA policymakers, we are convinced that caregivers' experiences can be a force for social change. Participation in activities such as making the video gives caregivers an opportunity to influence policy change as well as to experience personal empowerment.

At both individual and group meetings with caregivers, there is discussion, sometimes very direct, about their choices: to walk away from the situation, to demand more support from other family members, or to initiate earlier institutionalization of the spouse when his cognitive functions start deteriorating rapidly. Caregivers often approach discussions of such options with pain and a sense of guilt, thinking "maybe I've not done enough." This is where the feminist model becomes a framework for drawing out the strengths of caregivers to make their own choices. It is sometimes very difficult for us as practitioners to realize that caregivers believe there is more they could or should do for their spouses when the "objective evidence" points to increasing burnout. Many times, however, this process of considering options reinforces their awareness of personal control. Caregiver participants have explored their own definition of *obligation* as prescribed by traditional gender-role values and norms and have observed that other women in similar situations have found alternatives affording them more self-actualizing experiences.

In our program, many new alliances are formed for caregivers of veterans to fill needs that otherwise might be ignored. One of our nation's greatest underutilized sources of volunteer service can be found in the network of veterans' organizations and the volunteer service offices maintained at each medical center. We have been successful in recruiting veteran volunteers to provide a range of important services to caregivers, including home repairs and farm maintenance tasks. A repair such as a floor replacement may represent a financial expense that the couple cannot afford, or locating someone to do the task may take more energy than the caregiver has. Program staff try to find ways to expand the resources that caregivers can call upon with the certainty that assistance is available and will be provided in a manner that does not reduce dignity or reinforce feelings of obligation.

We have encouraged the development of self-help for these caregivers and have observed what they can accomplish to reduce their own sense of isolation. It has seemed inappropriate, however, to follow a path toward consciousness-raising per se, because these clients are unprepared to be assertive when they first enter the group. The norms of the group seem to minimize any expectations among members that self-disclosure is necessary in order to reduce personal pain or isolation. In this respect, the approach does seem to be that of more conventional social group work. Collective action is encouraged for those who have the emotional and physical energy to become engaged in group supports. On the other hand, we have had to temper our enthusiasm for such participation when it becomes just another energy drain on caregivers. Some of our clients will never become comfortable with egalitarian or collegial relationships with program staff, but they do respond to our consistent respect for their knowledge about what is best for them and their spouses on an individual basis. Group members have consistently displayed a natural understanding of how important it is to support each member in her role while also helping her to identify the risks of giving care. We have found that using the Well-Being Scale to have each client set her own goals based on her strengths is compatible with the reinforcement of strengths that members receive in the group.

We have evidence that our program has provided a voice for the caregivers of veterans, a voice that was not heard two or three years ago at either the local or national level of the DVA. Our work has been selected as the programmatic example for how to serve caregivers through the resources of DVA medical centers. As a team, we speak about the principles of feminist practice to colleagues who normally shrink from any professional activity associated with a feminist perspective. However, we also choose to use language that is not always feminist. Although this becomes frustrating, it is a necessary condition of our communication within an interdisciplinary environment where negative stereotyping is frequently associated with feminism.

CASE EXAMPLE

In the case we have selected to present in this chapter, the work of CSP social work graduate students who perform much of the clinical casework with caregivers is highlighted. The feminist orientation presented as part of their practicum instruction for this specific field placement is often a new and uncharted perspective for students. From their academic course work, most students enter the practicum with some reading in the health/strengths model, but only a small percentage have had any exposure to feminist practice or literature. Even those in that minority with a feminist orientation have never attempted to apply it to social service practice in a bureaucratic medical setting comparable to a DVA medical center or with older women clients.

Caren was a first-level M.S.W. student who was placed in the CSP unit because of her interest in extending her feminist practice background from working with battered women in a mental health setting. At 35 years of age, she had a rich history of feminist organizing and ample experience with support groups for abused women. On the other hand, she had never experienced her feminist perspective as applicable to older women.

Mabel, her client, was a caregiver who had been referred to the program earlier and had declined to participate based on her own health problems. Her congestive heart failure was hard to regulate through medication and she complained of constant exhaustion from providing care to her husband Fred. Fred was in the middle stages of Alzheimer's disease.

The first visit Caren made to Mabel's home was part of the ongoing effort made by the CSP to recontact caregivers who initially decline the service. The first meeting provided Caren with an opportunity to understand the frustrations caregivers experience in completing their daily routines. To celebrate her 62nd birthday, Mabel had wanted to prepare a special dinner and birthday cake to enjoy with Fred. By mid-afternoon, two cakes had been burned in the oven because she had been distracted by Fred's constant demands for attention. A second visit by Caren was necessary in order to complete the Well-Being Scale, to be used as a basis for identifying Mabel's strengths and desires. From the scale Caren learned that Mabel missed her interactions with old friends at church and in a quilting group. She also wanted to have some time for herself to be outside in the fresh air.

The student's case log provides some important insights about her feminist perspective with this client:

> I could feel my identification with Mabel grow as she talked about her guilt at leaving her spouse to participate in her own life activities and desires. This feeling of guilt was no less powerful for her than what was experienced by women in the shelter who felt guilt about seeking their own physical and psychological safety. These women facing very different crises all need to experience their sense of self as a priority and learn to give themselves permission to feel the anger of their exploitation and then move beyond it into a process of transformation.

The arrangement of formal respite care at the DVA medical center enabled Mabel to begin participating in the CSP support group. It took her only a short time to relate to the experiences of other women whom she recognized from sitting in the clinic lobby at the medical center. She gained encouragement and confidence that respite care was appropriate for her spouse and came to believe that her friends from church were sincere in being willing to attend to Fred in an empty classroom while she participated in the choir on Sunday mornings. With support from Caren, Mabel contacted the local Red Cross and made arrangements for weekly free respite to match the time when her quilting group met.

Caren's time with the client was spent working with Mabel to transcend the cultural and ideological reinforcement that had left her, like the majority of adult women, unprepared to forgo meeting the needs of another person in order to consider her own. Strong conditioning that had demanded her lifelong duty to care for her dependents, now symbolized in the full care of her spouse, was her form of entrapment in late life. Her own goals were implemented, and this brought about a change in what she considered necessary to improve her quality of life and increase her self-actualization.

CONCLUSION

It is easy to grow weary at the thought of attempting to apply a feminist social work vision to the caregivers of veterans and at the same time provide a bridge to link the DVA to the national feminist caregiver movement. It is there, in that growing social change movement, that confrontation of the broader economic and political issues is accomplished. We know that the

DVA needs to hear the messages of that movement, which is independent of DVA professional staff. We agree with the position stated by MacDonald (1988): "If we do not take our analysis further [beyond the immediate objective of relieving some of the crises of caregivers of veterans] we are likely to come up with only bandaid solutions, or in fact, find ourselves contributing to the very problems we are here to solve" (p. 32). Extending the labor of women to care for their veteran spouses seems to be facilitating exploitation of a vulnerable group. At the same time, if women are committed to providing such care based on informed choice and with adequate supports, then we have actualized what we consider a fundamental principle of feminist practice.

There is no way for the DVA to escape from the issues of long-term care for "old" veterans. In fact, there is already strong pressure on Congress to increase funding to a level where it can assure quality geriatric health to several million older veterans. The national veterans' political advocacy and lobby network can be a "rumbling giant" on almost any issue that implies inadequate attention to veterans' welfare. These organizations have yet to realize, on a large scale, that the medical centers serving the veterans could also be sources of assistance to their wives and daughters who are likely to care for them and benefit from DVA assistance because local non-DVA services are often very meager or too expensive to be accessible. Our feminist vision of social change includes a future of collective action that can draw together ever broader and more diverse sectors of our society to reframe new responses to human rights for all caregivers in our country.

REFERENCES

Balbo, L. (1987). Crazy quilts: Rethinking the welfare state debate from a woman's point of view. In A. S. Sassoon (Ed.), *Women and the state* (pp. 45-71). London: Hutchinson.

Bartlett, H. H. (1958). Toward clarification: An improvement of social work practice. *Social Work, 3*, 3-9.

Barusch, A. S. (1988). Problems and coping strategies of elderly spouse caregivers. *Gerontologist, 28*, 677-685.

Briar, K. H., & Ryan, R. (1986). The anti-institution movement and women caregivers. *Affilia: Journal of Women and Social Work, 1*(1), 20-31.

Bricker-Jenkins, M. (1983). Nothing from nothing leaves nothing/rostando nada de nada queda nada. *WREE: View of Women for Racial Economic Equality and Economic Equality, 8*(6), 7-10.

Bricker-Jenkins, M. (in press). *The changer and the changed are one: An introduction to feminist social workers and their practice.* New York: Columbia University Press.

Callahan, D. (1988). Families as caregivers: The limits of morality. *Archives of Physical Rehabilitation, 69*, 322-328.

Copper, B. (1988). *Over the hill: Reflections on ageism between women.* Freedom, CA: Crossing.

Hamer, L. (1989). Ageism: A global issue. *Peace and Freedom, 49*(1), 5.

Hooyman, N. R., & Ryan, R. (1987). Women as caregivers of the elderly: Catch-22 dilemmas. In J. Figueira-McDonough & R. Sarri (Eds.), *The trapped woman.* Newbury Park, CA: Sage.

Jivanjee, P. (1988). *Family caregiving to elderly people suffering from Alzheimer's disease and related disorders: A review of the literature.* Unpublished manuscript, University of Kansas, School of Social Welfare.

MacDonald, B. (1988). Health and economic needs of old women: Major issues. In N. Gottlieb (Ed.), *A working conference on older women: The state of knowledge and the need for action* (pp. 32-37). Salt Lake City: University of Utah, Graduate School of Social Work.

MacDonald, B., & Rich, C. (1983). *Look me in the eye: Old women, aging, and ageism.* San Francisco: Spinters.

Mather, J. H. (1984). An overview of the Veterans Administration and its services for older veterans. In J. W. Rowe & T. Wetle (Eds.), *Older veterans: Linking V.A. and community resources.* Cambridge, MA: Harvard University Press.

New York State Office for the Aging. (Producer). (1986). *Time to care: Title 1. Coping with care* [Videotape]. Albany, NY: Producer.

Olson, C. S. (1988). Blueridge blues: The problems and strengths of rural women. *Affilia: Journal of Women and Social Work, 3*(1), 5-8.

Pharr, S. (1988). *Homophobia: A weapon of sexism.* Inverness, CA: Chardon.

Rathbone-McCuan, E. (1984). The abused older woman: A discussion of abuses and rape. In G. Lesnoff-Caravaglia (Ed.), *The older woman.* New York: Human Science Press.

Rathbone-McCuan, E., & Hashimi, J. (1982). *Isolated elders.* Rockville, MD: Aspen.

Rathbone-McCuan, E., & Hedlund, J. (1989). Older families and issues of alcohol misuse: A neglected problem in psychotherapy. *Journal of Psychotherapy and the Family, 5*(1/2), 173-184.

Reinharz, S. (1986). Friends or foes: Gerontological and feminist theory. *Women's Studies Institutional Forum, 9*, 503-514.

Rodway, M. R. (1986). Systems theory. In F. J. Turner (Ed.), *Social work treatment* (3rd ed., pp. 514-540). New York: Free Press.

Sommers, T., & Shields, L. (1987). *Women take care: The consequences of caregiving in today's society.* Gainesville, FL: Tread.

Tebb, S. (1989). *An aid to empowering: Well-Being Scale.* Unpublished manuscript, University of Kansas, School of Social Welfare.

Tebb, S., Rathbone-McCuan, E., & Harbert, T. (1990). *Caregiver manual.* Topeka, KS: DVA Medical Center.

Thompson, F. G. (1984). *Health policy and the bureaucracy: Politics and implementation.* Cambridge: MIT Press.

Toseland, R. W., Rossiter, C. M., & Labrecque, M. S. (1989). The effectiveness of peer-led and professionally led groups to support family caregivers. *Gerontologist, 29*, 465-471.

U.S. Congress, House of Representatives, Select Committee on Aging. (1987, January). *Exploring the myths: Caregiving in America.* Washington, DC: Government Printing Office.

Veterans Administration. (1988, February). *Trend data 1963-1987.* Washington, DC: Government Printing Office.

Wasow, M. (1986). Support groups for family caregivers of patients with Alzheimer's disease. *Social Work, 31*, 93-94.

Weick, A. N. (1983). Issues on overturning a medical model of social work. *Social Work, 28*, 467-471.

Weick, A. N. (1984). The concept of responsibility in a health model of social work. *Social Work in Health Care, 10*(2), 13-25.

Weick, A. N. (1986). The philosophical context of a health model of social work. *Social Casework: The Journal of Contemporary Social Work, 57*, 551-559.

Weick, A. N., & Freeman, E. (1983). *Developing a health model for social work.* Unpublished manuscript, University of Kansas, School of Social Welfare.

Weick, A. N., & Pope, L. (1988). Knowing what's best: A new look at self-determination. *Social Casework: The Journal of Contemporary Social Work, 69*, 10-16.

Zarit, S. H., Todd, P. A., & Zarit, J. M. (1986). Subjective burden of husbands and wives as caregivers: A longitudinal study. *Gerontologist, 26*, 260-266.

Come to Me

Sue Saniel Elkind

Come to me looking
as you did 50 years ago
arms outstretched
and I will be waiting
virgin again
in white that changes
to splashes of roses
as we lie together
Come to me smiling again
with your mortar and pestle
and vitamin pills
because I am given to colds
and coughs that wrack us both
Oh come to me again
and I will be there
waiting with withered hands
gnarled fingers
that will leave their marks
of passion on your back.

Previously published in Sandra Martz
(Ed.), *When I Am an Old Woman I Shall
Wear Purple,* 1987. Reprinted by
permission of Papier-Mâché Press
and the author.

FEMINIST PRACTICE
IN MENTAL HEALTH SETTINGS

INTRODUCTION

NAOMI GOTTLIEB

At the outset of this book, Mary Bricker-Jenkins said that the members of each generation of feminist social workers need to speak their "own truths" about themselves and their work. Part of those truths encompass each worker's continuing and changing journey to a feminist practice that helps his or her clients to change their lives. Making one's self-discovery explicit and public is an additional way in which feminist social work practice differs from mainstream practice. In the latter, case studies or reports of research are ordinarily offered in the third person, as if a neutral person were describing a piece of "objective" professional work. When feminist social workers disclose their own developments as they have influenced their practice, they are illustrating another facet of the fact that "the personal is political." Not only are our personal lives influenced by the gender politics of our society, but, in turn, our own development influences our political work. Part of that political work is our professional practice with clients, and one of the contributions of feminist social work is to make that connection explicit.

In most of the chapters of this book, the authors describe the personal aspects of their feminist development. The three chapters in this section are particularly vivid examples of the value of doing so. Here especially the reader is invited to see the contrast between this kind of self-disclosure as related to practice and the distance created in other accounts by a neutral stance. And if we were to ask these three authors, as well as the other contributors, to write about the continuation of their journey at a point 3 or 5 or 10 years from now, their stories might be considerably different—which would show again that this is a continually evolving process.

In the chapters by Armando Smith and Clevonne Turner, the authors' self-disclosures illustrate the complex interaction of gender and ethnicity. From her own experiences, Turner demonstrates how her personal development is interwoven with her intellectual development. She argues for an enlargement of the self-in-relation theory to encompass women of color, particularly African-American women, and then describes how both personal and theoretical understandings inform her work with African-American women.

Smith's personal evolution and its relation to practice is made complex by virtue of his masculine gender, African-American and Hispanic ethnicity, and feminist stance. He is honest and forthright in acknowledging the influence of his gender on his practice and, particularly, that his work with the young father in a teenage parent couple might be very different from that of a feminist woman social worker. Part of the "truths" that both Turner and Smith help us to see are the complexities that emerge from the mixture of gender and race.

Nancie Palmer tells of the connection she sees between her own feminist development and her work with incest survivors. She is particularly concerned with the issue of power and the importance of trusting relationships. She writes eloquently of the betrayal of trust experienced by the incest victim and the necessity to restore that sense of trust. She makes the contrast between traditional modes of therapy and a feminist approach in the handling of power and in restoring trust, advocating the latter approach in order to aid the client in moving from "victim to survivor to the potential of thriving." A somewhat similar case might be reported in another kind of anthology of case studies, but in a nonfeminist context it is likely that connections would not be made among the professional's personal evolution, political stance on gender issues, and the work with the client.

We believe that this development in feminist social work practice is a more vital definition than the earlier, gender-neutral social work concept of the "use of self." These case studies show a more dynamic connection between personal evolution and social work practice.

Voices of Many Women
24 Women, Survivors Group, Little Rock, Arkansas

Compiled by Auralie Tortorici, L.C.S.W.

This reading is part of the collected writings of 24 Arkansas women who over the years have participated in therapy groups for adults healing from child sexual abuse. The women are 18 to 57 years old. Their poem is in 4 parts: I Remember Now; Things I Heard; I Want to Say; Now I/We Know.

I REMEMBER NOW

I remember now
—Sitting on the swing set
    afterwards in the backyard
    wearing old clothes and
    feeling bad . . . pitiful
I remember
—Fear of shadows in my doorway
—When I found out it was abuse
    I asked mom about me having
    a baby
—I rolled my own hair for my
    7th grade school picture
    because mom had to work that
    evening and couldn't fix it
    for me. That night, among
    other abuse my dad busted my
    lip and it was swollen.
I remember now
—Being in the back seat of a
    red and white car . . . my oldest
    brother fondling me . . .
—having me straddle him to
    have intercourse
—I was only a child . . . a
    teenager . . . a young woman.

I remember
—being hand tied to the rail
    of the bed, then some kind of
    material was stuck in my
    mouth. Frozen fear all over
    my body. I felt a tremendous
    amount of fear.
I remember now
—My father's stomach coming
    down on me.
I remember now
—We were playing hide-and-seek
    by the house on Elm Street.
    The teenage boy from the next
    block found me in a bush. He
    put his hands in my
    underwear. I must have been
    four years old.
I remember now
—the laughter that was
    pretend.
—I was molested by my
    grandfather. I remember his
    hands; his large, terrible
    hands.

I remember

—The old road by the airport
where my uncle raped me every
Sunday afternoon—after I
spent the weekend at my
grandmother's house, playing
with my cousins.
—He paid me $5.00 to keep
quiet. I was 11. He
threatened to do the same to
my cousin Pam, she was 7
then.
—I remember as a child lots of
times. I would hide to get
out of doing things. Two
places I would hide were the
closet and behind the couch.
I remember now
—My stepfather's nude
body . . . and his saying "kiss
it."
—I remember my mother's
laughter. She called me a
liar.
—As a child I rebelled against
all that was happening by not
eating.
—My memories come in
flashes—like my dad taking a lot
of nude polaroids with me
crying and posing in different
positions as he instructed.
This started when I was 6.
I remember now
—Feeling so scared,
so crazy,
so alone.

THINGS I HEARD

—Don't let any little boys do
this to you.
—You'll make someone a good
wife someday.
—Dad, how can you keep doing
this to me? (having sex)—I
asked.
—He said he could do whatever
he wanted as long as he asked
God's forgiveness just before
he died.
—I love you kid, you know I
would never hurt you!
—Keep quiet.
—Don't tell.
—Don't tell or you'll get in
trouble.
—"You and I are just alike"
whispered my father to me
during the sweet talking time
to encourage me to
participate.
—He kept telling me how my
body wanted it.

I WANT TO SAY	**NOW I/WE KNOW**

—You are the sorriest creep I
   have ever known.

—How dare you sexually abuse
   me and then say maybe
   something is wrong with me!!

—You are the one that is
   mentally off!

—I hate your guts.

—How could you do this to me?

—What you did to me was the
   worst thing that has ever
   happened to me.

—Do you have any idea how much
   you have screwed up my life?

—Leave me alone.

—I don't want you to care
   about me or even play like
   you care—its disgusting to
   me.

—If you ever touch another
   child, I'll get into the
   computer bank and slash your
   credit ratings.

—I just wanted you to love me.

—I am not alone.

—I have courage to stretch and
   grow.

—We are not awful people.

—We are here and now together,
   glad that we are starting to
   LIVE!!! We deserve it—
   healing, struggling, toward
   healthier lives.

—You are not to blame.

—The abuse was not my fault.

—The abuser was wrong.

—You deserve someone to love
   you the way that love is
   supposed to be given . . . with
   trust and respect, with care
   and honesty.

—You never forget it but life
   can get better.

—Healing is possible.

We say all these things because our lives matter.

We say these things so it will never happen again.

Used by permission of A. Tortorici.

Chapter 3

FEMINIST PRACTICE
WITH SURVIVORS OF
SEXUAL TRAUMA AND INCEST

NANCIE PALMER

> Every injury to the health of the individual is . . . a public injury. It is an
> impediment to the general freedom, so much deduction from our power,
> as members of society, to make the best of ourselves. (Thomas Hill
> Green, quoted in Foley & Sharfstein, 1983, p. vii)

Sexual exploitation of the vulnerable by the powerful is a haunting
legacy of human beings. What is changing is the way such exploitation is viewed by society. It was not until the momentum of the civil
rights and women's movements reached sufficient magnitude in the
1970s that issues of sexual abuse first appeared on the agenda of mental health professionals (Finkelhor, 1983).

Legal definitions of incest and rape vary from state to state and in
such criteria as degree of consanguinity, age of victim, degree of force or
threat of force, and the nature of the overt or covert sexual activity.[1] By
any of these general criteria, sexual assault is defined in legal terms.
Such terms reflect the dominant value and belief system of a patriarchal society. The prevailing medical model that predominates in mental health practice likewise mirrors such beliefs.

To the victims of incest and assault, the experience of trauma goes
far beyond these limited prescriptions. What is crucial in incest is that the

"relationship, not the biology, is betrayed" (Gelinas, 1983, p. 313). Rape and incest are violations of power from positions of strength, authority, or trust. This violation of trust has significant consequences for survivors.

The basic tenet here is that all human survival depends to some extent on other human beings. "When security and trust are present, we begin to develop an interpersonal bond which forms a bridge of mutuality. Such a bridge is crucial for the development of self worth" and one's sense of value as being wholly human (Bradshaw, 1988, p. 5). Mutuality extends from a person's first one-to-one survival with a caretaker to the society at large, which creates certain influences and attitudes that affect the well-being of all populations. From this perspective, individual mental health is indeed reflective of the larger human condition. Betrayal of trust and violent power have a profound personal impact. Yet such betrayal may be subtly reinforced by traditional practices that inadvertently violate the tenets of trust and authority.

This chapter presents a feminist view of mental health practice with survivors of incest and sexual assault. Limitations of traditional practice models and settings, particularly in community mental health, are contrasted with a feminist practice perspective. This perspective considers the needs of survivors both on a profoundly personal level and within the context of their larger social experience.

It is not possible within the context of one chapter to present a comprehensive practice response for survivors of sexual assault. Rather, presented for consideration are those issues and needs most often overlooked, minimized, or distorted through prevailing mental health practices. Such practices may also reflect the larger social context, which, through its values, beliefs, and attitudes, further alienates and disenfranchises certain vulnerable populations. Of great concern is the recognition that these populations are conspicuously absent from or underserved by the community mental health system.

A case example of collaborative work with an incest survivor is used to illustrate the responsiveness and power of the healing alternative of feminist practice. In conclusion, implications for further research and practice approaches are discussed.

Throughout this chapter, it may appear that the words *victim* and *survivor* are used interchangeably. However, the two are distinguished in that a victim is conceptualized as a person who experiences injury, destruction, and sacrifice, and a survivor as one who lives through and attempts to restore him- or herself beyond the moments of assault. A victim of incest can be viewed as a survivor when moving toward healing yet may be revictimized or reassaulted by an insensitive sociopolitical system.

A DEFINITION OF FEMINIST PRACTICE

My social work practice begins with myself. In essence I have been a feminist, to some degree, all of my life. My foremothers and forefathers struggled in the wilderness to farm, minister, and teach. As the only descendent in two generations to wear the olive skin of my French-European ancestors, I was claimed by, or relegated to, various cultures throughout my life. I felt a kinship with the world and felt special to have been claimed by so many others, yet I also experienced rejection by those who believed I was nonwhite. The name-calling inflicted upon me still resounds in my memory. Perhaps the pain was eased somewhat by the knowledge that secretly I possessed a certain status because I wasn't "one of them." I feel embarrassment that I too was influenced by those in power. I find common solidarity in my own experiences of oppression. I work from that place toward a greater humility, knowing that my existence is temporal and any status an illusion.

My feminist roots also spring from and are nurtured by loving parents who, through their own courage to grow, followed paths that were nontraditional. My father, a professor of life sciences, was also a painter and potter, a craftsman, a nurturer of children, and an athlete. He took the time to share his vast knowledge and love of natural history with us, thus forming my respect for life and the connectedness of all living things. My mother, speaker of many languages and particularly enthralled with Hispanic art, widened my appreciation for other cultures. Her courage to earn a doctorate when schools considered her too old gave me a role model for womanhood. Always an advocate for those without power, she had the audacity to paint her room and door a bright yellow among the sea of gray walls in a state institution. The many rooms so decorated along the way illustrate the legacy of her need to humanize mental health care. And I draw upon my sisters' courage to seek for themselves their own paths. I was and am all of this.

Believing that being and practice are one and the same, I work to achieve congruence among what I carry in heritage, my beliefs and values, and how I live. This authenticity sounds wonderful but is difficult to achieve. Suffering is inevitable, and to be authentic is to risk rejection. I have found strength from others who have touched my life. Feminist practice is part of my commitment to be there for others in their quest for authenticity.

Practice within a feminist perspective is a process of fluid thought and living without a hierarchy of power and status. By its nature, it is a casting off of delusions of who and what we are as defined by dominant others, and a recognition of the social and political effects of oppression, subordination, and definition. It is the experience of our interconnectedness, the mutual relationship, the oneness with all living things that is crucial to our fragile existence. When we desecrate, subordinate, alienate, and oppress, we are doing the same to ourselves. However, to view feminism only as a women's issue is to overlook the implications of how a patriarchal society oppresses and diminishes males, preventing them from being all they can be.

Drawing upon Far Eastern traditions for a definition of mental health, I believe that it is the ability to live in harmony with oneself and nature, to show compassion to one's fellow human beings, to "endure hardship and suffering without mental disintegration," yet find meaning in it, to "prize nonviolence," and to "care for the welfare of all sentient beings" (Fontana, 1986, p. 35). This then requires that we each take ultimate responsibility for our lives in both personal and practice arenas.

Feminist practice supports the mutuality of persons in work together. It allows and encourages a personal connecting with others. This connection provides the opportunity for survivors to experience a personal bonding while at the same time ameliorating some of the effects of personal and social oppression. In addition, mental health practice becomes an evolving process; that is, there is no specific outcome that finishes work. This means that there is no grand "cure," no final "fix." Persons will work to grow, to take on their sufferings when they are ready. Readiness may require periods for processing, rest, incubation, and even reexperiencing life themes. Utilizing these concepts creates an atmosphere that can free the practitioner from knowing all the answers and the client from performing all the outcomes. Both are free to be, which is what counteracting oppression is really all about.

What matters in this collaborative effort is the choreography taking place and the meaning each ascribes to the dance. Ascribing one's own meaning to experience is empowering and thus healing.

SURVIVORS OF SEXUAL TRAUMA: SPECIAL CONSIDERATIONS

When an intensely significant social problem such as incest is "discovered," the next step frequently is to determine the true scope of the phenomenon. Estimates of prevalence of incest vary widely, ranging from 25% to 50% for females and 16% and up for males (Finkelhor, 1983; Sgroi, 1988). The incidence of rape shows similar variations. Since there are methodological limitations with all such findings, consensus does not exist among social scientists about the prevalence of sexual exploitation and assault (Finkelhor, 1983). Such lack of clarity, however, does not diminish the significance of even a single episode or the salience of trauma evidenced through the voices of thousands of survivors.

Given our passion for scientific inquiry, it is tempting to quantify and categorize various types of assault experiences by frequency, progression of sexual contact, or presence of violence, and then to equate such factors with specific treatment regimens or interventions. With few exceptions, such an approach creates a misleading linear perspective that diminishes the capacity of mental health and other social systems to respond adequately to individuals with critical needs.

COMMON NEEDS OF SURVIVORS

The common needs of sexual assault survivors may be magnified by social attitudes and responses. Whether through violent attack or a subtle means of coercion, victims experience an underlying distortion of trust and a seriously damaged belief in the benevolence of others. These combine with an overwhelming sense of helplessness to leave victims feeling totally violated. Victims quickly learn that in order to survive, one must give oneself over to the power of another. In a close relationship or family, the primary resource for ameliorating the effects of trauma is destroyed. The effect is giving up oneself in hopes of survival. Lerner (1975) calls this process "de-selfing," which means "too much of one's self (including one's thoughts, wants, beliefs and needs) is negotiable under pressures of the relationships" (p. 20). De-selfing can result in deep despair and rage at ceasing to exist without the power of another.

Unsupportive and judgmental system responses may exacerbate the impact of trauma and prolong its duration. For children and for dependent disabled or elderly people, sexual assault takes on another terrifying dimension when their very survival depends upon those who betray them. The young may experience significant cognitive confusion because their "appropriate dependency, love and trust" in their caretakers is turned against them (Gelinas, 1988, p. 25). Friendships, marriages, and living arrangements, whether heterosexual or homosexual, also involve issues of loyalty that are distorted through the assault.

SPECIAL POPULATIONS

From a therapeutic perspective, the unique meanings survivors ascribe to events are most important. It is also relevant to consider that survivors' beliefs, expectations, and internally generated meanings are influenced by their relationships with their environments. Looking at the conditions of special groups of populations illustrates this point. Some of these groups are briefly identified here. In addition to their general emotional needs as survivors, people in these groups experience further victimization and alienation through lack of a sensitive and viable mental health response reflective of a supportive social system.

Older Women

"Physical aging, social role changes and ageism are the major conditions in industrial societies which contribute to the older woman's vulnerability and victimization" (Davis & Brady, 1979, p. 7). Rape and other sexual offenses are typically portrayed as the victimization of a "seductively dressed young woman attracting the attention of a man who is seeking to satisfy a sexual need" (Davis & Brady, 1979, p. 7), rather than the brutal assaults they are. In fact, rape and incest are not primarily sexual crimes, but rather acts of violence and power for which older women are particularly easy targets.

In working with older victims of sexual assault, it is important to understand that they grew up in a time of differing attitudes toward matters of a sexual nature. Likewise, when they were young, the mental health profession was not viewed as a scientific remedy for human suffering. Seeking outside help was an alien concept to a generation that saw rugged individualism as a way to overcome hardships. The lack of significant laws protecting children during their maturing years has created a population of wounded women who have never known relief from incestuous assault or rape or from feeling that they were responsible for their own suffering. This need was vividly illuminated by an 80-year-old grandmother who brought her granddaughters to our mental health clinic upon court referral. During the process of education about incest, the grandmother's eyes reflected a new awareness as she softly murmured through her tears, "Honey, I'm so glad you are here for my granddaughters." Pausing and grasping my arm, she looked at me with deep sorrow and said, "There was no one there for me."

Male Victims

Male victims also face particular pressures exerted by a patriarchal system. "Our culture provides no room for man as a victim. Men are simply not supposed to be victimized" (Lew, 1988, p. 62). Real men, according to the script, are to be strong, silent, and in control of their emotions (Bruckner & Johnson, 1987). Males are expected to deal with adversity through aggressive means. Consequently, male victims of assault may lose total identity with their masculinity and perceive themselves as feminine, gay, less than human, or as "irreparably damaged freak[s]" (Lew, 1988, p. 62). Male survivors live in excruciating fear that their vulnerability as victims will be exposed. The existing social system, and mental health philosophy that fosters the belief in "mastering and controlling" one's life, may fail to provide a sensitive and supportive response to such deeply felt human needs. As one male rape survivor put it, "You learn to cry on the back of your eyeballs."

Disabled Victims

Another special population, whose conditions cross all age, economic, ethnic, and sexual-orientation barriers, is made up of persons with physical or mental impairments. Similar to the elderly, this group is typically viewed as asexual. Since rape and incest are often considered sexual crimes, victimization of the disabled is often overlooked, or their trauma is construed as a manifestation of their disabling illnesses or conditions. Assault of the disabled may be even more problematic, because their physical, mental, visual, or auditory impairments may impede their ability to report evidence. In addition, social response systems, including mental health agencies, may lack skilled and sensitive persons to elicit such information.

The disabled, similar to the physically impaired elderly or children, may depend upon the offender for life support and care. The victim of incest or rape often experiences both the reality and the threat of physical violence, which can include being expelled from the household or withdrawal of major life supports (Rowe & Savage, 1988).

Gay Victims

Both heterosexual and homosexual persons experience similar stress reactions. However, homosexual persons have the added burden of being ostracized and even hated by society. Additionally there is a significant lack of practitioners and programs specifically focused on the needs and issues of lesbians and gay men. Current mental health practices still value the dominant cultural norm of heterosexual marriage and relationships. For these reasons, alternative resources, women's groups, and groups or coalitions particularly supportive of alternative life-styles are needed to provide necessary emotional support, to normalize the choices of living, and to break through the silent isolation. Practitioners' negative feelings and attitudes regarding homosexuality may preclude a safe environment and validation for the gay survivor.

THE CONCEPT OF CHRONIC SHOCK

Several frameworks can be used to view the needs of most survivors. I have found the concept of chronic shock (sometimes known as posttraumatic stress disorder, or PTSD) helpful in clarifying these needs and suggesting pathways to survival. Chronic shock is of such magnitude to the survivor that failure of the practitioner to recognize the full meaning of these trauma conditions may significantly diminish or render ineffective any treatment approach. Further, when the mental health response is to view such trauma as pathological (a response more likely to be used for persons who are "deviant," elderly, or physically/mentally impaired), the end result may be a continuation of victimization.

Some indicators of chronic shock in victims are (a) periods of unexplained grief or rage; (b) experiencing only a limited range of emotions, particularly extremes; (c) "numbness," or an inability to feel or have any sense of being connected with any feelings within themselves; (d) reporting events as though they happened to someone else; (e) confused thinking—disjointed thought patterns when recalling events; (f) significant memory lapses, usually spanning years; and (g) denial that the traumatic events had any effect on them (Kritzberg, 1986). Shock may also result in hypervigilance to one's surroundings and others' behaviors.

Shame or distortion of reality, due to real or threatened force accompanying prolonged internalization of worthlessness, may evolve into a chronic shock state that, unresolved, can last many years if not a lifetime. Shock may manifest itself through physiological changes, such as vacant staring or rapid shallow breathing. Practitioners should be alert to the recurrence of physical shock symptoms when exploring trauma with survivors and should take immediate steps to assist the survivor—for instance, in slowing the breathing to a deep, slow pace—and, if necessary, seek medical assistance. Most often, by the time a survivor comes into contact with a mental health resource, the manifestation of shock has been integrated on a deep emotional level. Emotionally, the person shuts down, or becomes "numb." The numbness is often accompanied by an overwhelming fear of injury, abandonment, or death, all of which can be very real. For many survivors, the choice is between living and dying. For rape victims, the experience may be further compounded if they are survivors of childhood assault or incest (Burgers & Holmstrom, 1983).

Chronic shock is a manifestation of a survivor's attempt to reconcile trauma. As further explored in the discussion of the medical model, perceiving these behaviors as pathological fails to appreciate them for the strong, creative, and courageous acts they are. This perspective leads to the use of intrusive therapy, such as hospitalization, medication, or electroshock, and creates a process of continued invalidation of feelings and experiences for the survivor.

In the phases of recovery, the person experiencing the trauma begins to be flooded with the feelings associated with the event. Healing involves the experiencing, sharing, and validation of these feelings. In my practice experience, children who must survive abusive and rigidly restrictive homes, where explicit rules forbid talking about what is really going on or expressing negative feelings, are unable to negotiate this phase of reclaiming themselves. The child is left to interpret what the trauma means, and the interpretation often takes the form of self-blaming. The social and legal responses to adult females also foster self-blaming. In its extreme forms, chronic shock may be expressed through perceptual disturbances or dissociative experiences ranging from a feeling of fading into a wall to the development of multiple personalities to handle the trauma.

Perceptual disturbances are frequent among adult survivors (Ellenson, 1986). The terror invoked with abuse is so powerful that, even though perpetrators are long absent or deceased, survivors experience their presence. Ellenson (1986) has shown that such perceptions are remarkably similar across ages, cultures, and socioeconomic statuses. These hallucinations generally consist of singular visions or auditory hallucinations and are significantly different from disturbances of functional psychosis. For example, a survivor may see a shadowy figure, usually static and usually positioned at the foot of the bed. Mobile figures may be seen moving rapidly and furtively, darting past doors or reflected in mirrors. Auditory hallucinations may include the sound of footsteps, a knob turning or door opening, or a single name being called, such as "slut" or "whore." More elaborate visions are usually associated with particularly prolonged or vicious sexual assault or with sexual assault of a very young child. Such experiences are not accompanied by delusional thinking or associational disturbances consistent with actual psychosis (Ellenson, 1986).

Working through chronic shock requires a very safe environment and safe persons. This is of crucial importance because chronic shock occurs when there is no safe place to work out powerful and frightening emotions. A practitioner must be able to be with the survivor, to cradle the rage, confusion, anger, and terror. In this regard, practitioners must have a good sense of themselves and be well centered internally. Practitioners also need to be clear about any of their own experiences that would interfere with their providing adequate service to survivors.

Other common results of sexual abuse and rape include damage to the survivor's organizing framework for conceptualizing the power of others and self, damage to sense of worth and self-esteem and regard from others, and reduced capacity for intimacy with self—that is, the ability to comfort oneself and be empathic toward and trusting of others. Recovery is a reclaiming of oneself. The significance of this concern is further expanded upon in the following exploration of the medical model.

LIMITATIONS OF TRADITIONAL
PRACTICE MODELS AND SETTINGS

In spite of many practitioners' efforts to move away from traditional practice, core concepts of the medical model remain the driving force in many mental health settings. In this model, the professional expert is the agent of change, empowered to diagnose and treat the patient from a position of authority and domination. Patients are viewed as the sites of pathology and seen as unable to cope. They are rewarded for giving over themselves and being "good clients." The practitioner ascribes meanings to the patient's experiences and assesses his or her capacity for growth and change. In essence, control is once again given over. Feeling out of control is a significant issue for survivors. Regaining control, by assigning one's own meaning to events, is crucial to the survivor's experience of competence as a human being.

Some practices may be subtle yet powerful; the issue of pacing is one example. We must respect survivors' readiness to move on their agendas. Imposition by the practitioner of "what is best" for the survivor may exacerbate the shock or produce such flooding that retreat is the only recourse for emotional survival. If survivors are encouraged to equate survival with giving over to authority, they may, in order to please a practitioner, punish themselves if they receive the message that where they are is not okay. The needs of survivors are paramount in all therapy situations, whether individual, self-help, or other groups. The imposition of the medical model, which equates outcome (client recovery) with "doing something" to the client, inadvertently may encourage or pressure practitioners to push their clients along in order for the practitioners to feel professionally competent. For this reason, it is important that practitioners pay attention to the dialogue they carry on with themselves about a person's response. It is also crucial to remember that survivors adopt behaviors in order to gain a perception of control. These behaviors must be respected and gently worked with in order not to strip survivors of their only means of coping.

As influenced by psychoanalytic theory, incest and rape trauma are still interpreted by some practitioners as sexual fantasy, a wish for the father or a wish to be raped. These concepts, framed in a patriarchal value and belief system, continue to create further distortions of the survivor's reality. Survival behaviors are interpreted in pathological terms rather than seen as courageous acts carried out for the preservation of the individual's life and humanity. The social order continues to subordinate and minimize survivors' abilities to describe their experiences accurately. Persons disenfranchised or held in contempt by society experience a lack of empathic connectedness and validation by others. To be "cured" through practices that negate one's own experiences exerts incredible pressure to produce a false self. The giving-over process is maintained.

In the medical model, belief in the superiority of professionals limits the endorsement of self-help groups. Members of these groups foster an equality and kinship through shared experiences. These groups may be helpful by offering the survivor tangible evidence that persons can and do move through what feels like an abyss of never-ending confusion and pain.

The traditional belief in a separate and "objective" stance toward a patient or client may create further estrangement for devalued persons and their social environment. Alternative models, including self-help and feminist practice, allow interpersonal bonding based on mutual respect and the realistic acknowledgment that one is really never separate from another.

The prevailing medical model reinforces traditional socialization of women. Passive giving over is expected in the process of change. The result is a continued inability to intervene on one's own behalf and on behalf of others in powerless positions. Many treatment programs continue to blame the female for an incestuous condition and foster only one recovery perspective—that espoused by a dominant patriarchal society and heterosexual marriage.

In addition, traditional therapy (individual or group) continues to rely almost exclusively on auditory communication as a treatment modality. Yet the socialization of females and children fosters a passive silence. The power of voice in expanding conceptions of the self and of experience has been evidenced in the growing field of sociolinguistics (Belenky, Clinchy, Goldberger, & Tarule, 1986). Suppression of voice is often used to describe survivors' condition of silence. For example, in writing of life in the death camps of the Holocaust, Terrence Des Pres (1986) says that "terror dissolves the self into silence, but in its aftermath . . . men and women are seized by an involuntary outburst of feeling which is very much like a scream—and in this crude cry the will to bear witness is born" (p. 34). The sense of voice may be construed as an internal and external dialogue. These dialogues are critical to our ways of knowing about ourselves and each other.

The power of suppression is easily understood in working with victims of abuse. Intuitive and instinctual knowing or awareness of danger, discomfort, or incongruity between experience and what authority says happened is suppressed in order to survive. In the process of surviving by meeting the needs of someone else, the victim's internal communication to the self and communication to others becomes silent. In the process the sense of true self is lost. Socialization of children and women fosters the belief that acceptable conduct precludes the expression of their pain or discontent. The medical model provides few if any alternatives for healing these issues.

Since the individual is considered the site of pathology, little attention is given to the effects of the mental health environment. The medical model creates a sterile, middle-class environment, neither inviting to persons of various ages, life-styles, and cultures nor safe in the messages conveyed to survivors. Given that survivors develop a hypervigilance to their surroundings and to persons in order to sustain a sense of control, the setting and the covert messages emanating from that setting are crucial.

FEMINIST SOCIAL WORK PRACTICE WITH SURVIVORS

Feminist practice, through its perspective of interconnectedness, operates from a collaborative base, valuing the competence of all human beings. This practice recognizes that victims do what they have to do to survive the brutal assault to body and spirit. Such behaviors are viewed as acts of tremendous courage and strength in the face of annihilation. Feminist practice seeks to restore the shattered trust of survivors and does not require victims to give themselves over once again. Appreciating the oppression, feminist practice provides alternative avenues for breaking the silence, such as the therapeutic use of art, poetry, and clay, which serves as both a personal and social outlet.

Emotional work and healing take place when and where there is a sense of safety. Physical needs include accessibility, climate, appropriate furniture for sitting and doing work (children's needs must be considered), freedom from interruptions, and privacy. Artifacts or objects in the environment are important as well. For example, in my work environment, the Navaho rug, the picture of a sleeping Hispanic child, a ceramic lamp thrown by my father's hand, a weaving from my mother's loom, books, and clay, paper, and toys all serve as a beacon to those young and old of many heritages. For children who must stay in the waiting room while a parent works, there is first a trip together to see where the parent will be. This practice gives parent and child a point of anchoring. Clarification of what names are to be used is also a point of respectful contact.

Other environmental messages to the participant are conveyed through the preparation for work together. This preparation includes the necessity of informed consent. Informed consent includes a determination of the participant's primary language, and of his or her ability to use written material such as completing the required intake forms or signing consents. I make it a practice to read, review, and discuss with participants all written consent forms, noting any concerns in writing. Informed consent includes awareness of any visual, auditory, or other impairment participants may have that would affect their ability to appreciate fully the nature of the transaction. Consent is the right to services under conditions that are most supportive of personal liberty. This includes the right to refuse services and the awareness of the legal obligations that a practitioner must follow in reporting suspected child abuse or imminence of danger. Informed consent should include a review of alternative resources, such as use of clergy, self-help groups, native or folk healers, and a determination of choice. The medical model excludes the value of these alternatives and discourages discussion of them as well. Informed consent includes my review of how I work with people and my assumptions about change.

It is also important to review with survivors some of the risks involved in the attempt to change. One such risk is a familial response of resistance to change. Familial response can include both the family of origin and the immediate family, in whatever form family takes. This point is critical because "relational distortions" precede incest; that is, "for one or more members of a family to be exploited by another family member requires pre-existing long-standing relational patterns of unfairness, which progressively converge and focus on the child who becomes the primary victim" (Gelinas, 1988, p. 25). Participants are told that I will be with them to walk through the pain and that others can be sought to walk and be there with them even if the family chooses not to participate or reacts to their efforts to grow. Survivors are told that they are not responsible for what happened to them as victims. And finally, survivors are told that I believe in them. All of these factors can begin to create a sense of safety and validation for the participant.

FEMINIST PRACTICE: AN EXAMPLE

Other safe messages and behaviors, as well as the contrast between traditional and feminist practice, are illustrated in the following example. The person and situation have been modified to protect confidentiality.

This example involves a 40-year-old woman whose teenage daughter was referred to the community mental health clinic as a victim of date rape. In the process of initial interview, I learned that the mother was an adult survivor of incest. Through the initial process, which covered the establishing of a safe environment and informed consent, the mother was able to request additional services for herself.

In the process of ascertaining what services would be most useful, Jane (the mother) expressed the need for individual rather than group therapy. Even though the power of collective personal resources in the form of self-help or clinical groups could be very useful in providing emotional support, validation, and normalization of the survival experience, it was important that Jane be able to make a choice. Given her need to please other people, her ability to voice any opinion was a significant sign of strength and courage. Groups, for all of their benefits, may present a terrifying collective to persons who are experiencing particularly deep shame and inability to trust (Black, 1989). Were this survivor to be put into such a situation, the likely result would have been an intense flooding of emotions and exacerbation of loss of control. Adult children who have experienced especially severe and sadistic abuse at an early age in an environment that rigidifies goodness and badness are particularly vulnerable to experiencing deep shame. Those experiencing deep shame may most benefit from individual therapy as a beginning point (Naitove, 1988). In voicing her needs, Jane was beginning to reclaim herself at her own pace.

Jane, a single parent, learned to make pottery after her divorce. I made clay readily available for her use, and she found it comforting to mold and shape the clay while we talked. The molding and shaping served as a voice medium through which feelings could be safely accentuated. Moreover, playing with the clay may have assisted Jane in integrating compensatory developmental stages arrested through trauma (Belenky et al., 1986). Jane's own references to persons being only good or evil were evidence of this developmental arrest. Additionally, play is considered a precursor to symbolization and meaning-making by offering experiences and opportunities to create metaphors, which facilitate dialogue (Ackerman, 1989). Through this process Jane began to break her silence and the authority bound to it. Periodically Jane would also write a poem and share it. I participated in these processes and also shared with her educational material to take and read at her own pace. Through these collaborative experiences, Jane began her dialogue.

Although Jane gave some initial indications that she was a survivor of incest, she was not ready to talk about it. So we worked together on forming a trust and a process of beginning to see herself as a valuable and worthwhile person. We also worked on identifying the strengths she possessed that enabled her to survive, and explored the issue of her fear that her feelings would consume or destroy herself or others. Through the various media we developed a language for identifying and then expressing feelings. It was important to reinforce and validate each small step that Jane took. This is particularly important for women, since as a result of their socialization they tend to focus on one flaw and internally generalize it to encompass the core of what they are. We talked about how women are socialized and the impact of social, economic, and legal forces.

Work was not smooth, by any means. There were periods when Jane would resort to the use of alcohol, seek sexual activity with multiple partners, and occasionally return to one boyfriend who would physically abuse her. Yet through these periods of crisis she continued contact and remained resourceful in securing food and shelter for herself and her daughter. I referred her to other community resources—a Catholic agency that offered a GED program, the victim witness program, and state social services.

It took months of being with Jane before she felt sufficient trust and strength in herself to share her secret agony. She began slowly, first by sharing that she was an only child born to parents late in their lives. Having been abandoned by Jane's natural father, her mother remarried. Her stepfather (now deceased) was a mechanic who developed a ministry that was to become an integral part of their lives. Her mother was a silent woman given to periods of deep depression that confined her to bed. Sexual abuse of Jane by her stepfather began when she was 4 years old. The abuse progressed to full intercourse by the age of 6. The sexual abuse was mixed with violent battering of both Jane and her mother. During these raging episodes, her stepfather would berate them for not being good, or for not being silent and respectful. He verbally and publicly humiliated his wife for not being sexually responsive. At times the stepfather would shout scriptures as a means of augmenting his authority. Physical punishment of Jane also took another form of sexual violence—being stripped and battered on her buttocks with belt or hand. The trauma was so severe Jane recalled being unable to walk to school or sit at her desk without extreme pain. The remembering brought forth flashback nightmares and perceptual disturbances.

Because of the extremely vicious trauma experienced at an early age, Jane experienced one particularly strong perceptual disturbance in my office. In sharing her nightmares, Jane suddenly became tense, her body went rigid, and she stared wide-eyed at an empty chair near her. Her terror and horror were clearly evident. In a panic-stricken voice she reported seeing her stepfather in the chair. I immediately reassured her she was not crazy, and that I believed her. In response to her need for the protection that she never got as a child, I moved the chair in which she saw her stepfather behind me. I told Jane what she was experiencing was a natural response to the terror she felt as a little girl. The ongoing education about sexual abuse enabled Jane to grasp this information. We talked about the reclaiming of herself and in this process the breaking of silence. We talked of this process as one of beginning to break the power of her stepfather. Throughout this episode Jane was very frightened, so I told her our work was stronger than her stepfather. Survivors need a sense of safety and protection. The physical removal of her stepfather to a position of powerlessness and verbal reassurances of protection validated Jane's experience of her reality and afforded her safety.

This was clearly not a time to observe the 50-minute hour. In this instance it was critical that I stay with Jane through this process of discovery to a position of recovery. The processing took several hours until she was able to regain some equilibrium. What was crucial was that Jane's most vulnerable needs be met until the adult within her could regain her strength. At the end of the process Jane asked that the chair with her stepfather be placed forever outside of the room in a corner of the hall. With accompanying reassurances that this request was not "silly," as she feared, the need was met. Before each session thereafter I made sure the chair was where Jane wanted it. I told Jane that these decisions were from her position of growing strength. She now could command where her stepfather was to be, and in time the terror associated with the chair disappeared. We had been together through a major episode of recovery.

Jane's experiences as a survivor presented a dramatic situation that could have led to significantly different outcomes, given a choice of a medical or feminist perspective. Using the latter approach, Jane was supported and validated. By letting work happen in a collaborative fashion, Jane began to reclaim herself as a whole and valuable human being. This reclaiming was not achieved by a giving-over process, so that what she accomplished for herself was genuine and enduring. She moved from victim to survivor to the potential of thriving.

FUTURE PRACTICE MODEL DEVELOPMENT

Although sexual assault is experienced on a profoundly personal level, its effects are magnified in the social context. Thus the shattering of one's relationship to another extends far beyond the encounter. For healing to occur it is necessary to consider the need for a mutually satisfying relationship on both intimate and social levels. Given the fact that through assault a person or family has destroyed trust and failed to nurture an individual's humanness, it becomes even more crucial that social resources not do the same. Examination of the existing social conditions and medical models that reflect such conditions makes it clear that survivors are not getting what they need in order to recover from grievous wounds. It appears that the beliefs and practices fostered through the existing paradigm may exacerbate the effects of trauma. Clearly, alternatives are needed.

We must be open and willing to listen to what survivors have to say, for they alone know the depth and reality of what they have experienced at the hands of others. *Openness* in this sense means valuing all others and their competence as human beings. This means that continued work is needed to advocate and work for change where there is oppression, and educate where there is ignorance. It means a willingness to work collaboratively with each other, using the best of our natural resources to ameliorate personal and social suffering.

Traditional diagnosis and treatment pervade community mental health and other health-related systems. Changing this system is difficult; therefore an orchestrated effort with other professionals, advocates, citizens, and disenfranchised persons is needed if we are to begin to demonstrate the validity of alternative services. It is also clear that community mental health has failed to be responsive or inviting to persons of age, color, disabling condition, or alternative lifestyles. Change must come from within by the very professionals who serve. It means taking risks to advocate and educate from within. Outreach and collaborative efforts with natural resources such as clergy, native healers, and self-help groups are also needed to create meaningful and viable programs. We must be honest with ourselves, and we must be willing to look at our own bigotry and biases.

If one believes that person and practice cannot be separated, the conduct of oneself is crucial to relationships with others. Compassion for and belief in the competence of others must be lived out before real change can occur. To this extent it is hoped that both practitioners and their clients will begin, as best they can, the process of change within themselves.

NOTE

1. For an excellent resource reviewing legal issues in mental health care, see Herr, Arons, and Wallace (1984).

REFERENCES

Ackerman, R. (1989, May). *ACOA's: Does gender make a difference?* Wichita, KS: Governor's Conference on Adult Children of Alcoholics.

Belenky, M. E., Clinchy, B., Goldberger, N., & Tarule, J. (1986). *Women's ways of knowing: The development of self, voice and mind.* New York: Basic Books.

Black, C. (1989, May). *The child within.* Wichita, KS: Governor's Conference on Adult Children of Alcoholics.

Bradshaw, J. (1988). *Healing the shame that binds you.* Deerfield Beach, FL: Health Communications.

Bruckner, D., & Johnson, P. (1987, February). Treatment of adult male victims of childhood sexual assault. *Social Casework*, pp. 81-87.

Burgers, A. W., & Holmstrom, L. L. (1983). Rape trauma syndrome. In F. Turner (Ed.), *Differential diagnosis and treatment in social work.* New York: Free Press.

Davis, L. J., & Brady, E. (1979). *Rape and older women: A guide to prevention and protection.* Rockville, MD: National Institute of Mental Health.

Des Pres, T. (Ed.). (1986). *The survivor: An anatomy of life in the death camps.* New York: Pocket Books.

Ellenson, G. S. (1986, March). Disturbances of perception in adult female incest survivors. *Social Casework*, pp. 149-159.

Finkelhor, D. (1983). *A sourcebook on child sexual abuse.* Beverly Hills, CA: Sage.

Foley, H. A., & Sharfstein, S. (1983). *Madness and government.* Washington, DC: American Psychiatric Press.

Fontana, D. (1986). Mind, senses, and self. In G. Claxton (Ed.), *Beyond therapy: The impact of Eastern religions on psychological theory and practice.* London: Wisdom.

Gelinas, D. J. (1983). The persisting negative effects of incest. *Psychiatry, 46*, 313-323.

Gelinas, D. J. (1988). Family therapy: Characteristic family constellation and basic therapeutic stance. In S. M. Sgroi (Ed.), *Vulnerable populations: Vol. 1. Evaluation and treatment of sexually abused children and adult survivors.* Lexington, MA: Lexington.

Herr, S., Arons, S., & Wallace, R., Jr. (1984). *Legal rights and mental health care.* Lexington, MA: Lexington.

Kritzberg, W. (1986). *The adult children of alcoholics syndrome.* Pompano Beach, FL: Health Communications.

Lerner, H. G. (1975). *The dance of anger.* New York: Harper & Row.

Lew, M. (1988). *Victims no longer: Men recovering from incest and other child sexual abuse.* New York: Nevraumont.

Naitove, C. E. (1988). Using the arts therapies in treatment of sexual offenders against children. In S. Sgroi (Ed.), *Vulnerable populations: Vol. 1. Evaluation and treatment of sexually abused children and adult survivors.* Lexington, MA: Lexington.

Rowe, W., & Savage, S. (1988, May). Sex therapy with female incest survivors. *Social Casework*, pp. 265-271.

Sgroi, S. (Ed.). (1988). *Vulnerable populations: Vol. 1. Evaluation and treatment of sexually abused children and adult survivors.* Lexington, MA: Lexington.

Mary Jane's Story

Mary Jane Hall

Untitled #1

Rage of feeling
  Response to
    Knowing facts

    Mind's eye blinks
      Not understanding
        Heart's response

Untitled #2

There are wounds
    Flesh and Blood
    Heart and Soul
    Essence of Being

There is hope
    Mantle soft
      Gentle steel
        Deeply penetrating

There are wounds of hope
    Hope for wounds
      Wounds cradled not yet
          touched by hope.

AUTHOR'S NOTE: Untitled poems #3 and #4 were written during the months of October and November of 1987. At that time I chose to confront the person responsible for the incest in my life. After I sent the first letter I had feelings of uncertainty about it. Untitled #3 was written at that time. The response that came from this individual was not perfect but it did break "the secret." It was a very important part of my process of healing. At the time #3 was written it was difficult to own it. There was something that remained unsaid. Thus Untitled #4 was written and it freed something in me to own #3.

Untitled #3

Faint fear,
    anxious sense
Tremulous Words present
Brother dear, omnipresent
Captive memory of intent

        Equal, empowered
        Inspired words writ
        Uncertain confidence
        Words hopefully sent

Response unfolds
Elation tears descend
Hope fulfilled
Mute feelings ascend

        Relationship melds
        Harm and hope
        Barrier's burden
        Eased, maybe revoked

Untitled #4

Inward spiral
Spectrum a swirl
Feeling ignited
Unfocused whirl

        Past to closure
        Present released
        Forgiveness waiting
        Openness the need

Wells

Wells of Silence
Dug of whispered rage
Filled by tears
Withheld, unclaimed

Wells of Silence
Transformed by sadness
Now wells of pain
Sealed, retained

Wells of pain
Forged, mute the rage
Flaming tears, erupt
Dry, contained

Wells of pain
Fractured infinity
Wells of silence
Finite remain

Wells of Me
Open, emptying
Fluid being
Dignity reclaimed

Wells of Me
Unfolding image
Converge, emerge
Kaleidoscope rebirth

Victims

There is something in us
  Walled for protection
There is something in us
  Hidden from abuser's plan

In the passing of time
  Walls built to stand
In the passing of time
  Hiding becomes life plan

Someone's touch awakened us
  To wall's abusing confines
Someone's touch awakened, beauty
  Hidden in our inner lives.

Changes

Changes
    Unfolding new realities
    Re-entering old ones

Changes
    Fear escorting loss
    Hope courting gain

Changes
    Mixed blessing
    Pleasure among the Pain

Changes
    Leading edge
    New, yet revisited

Untitled #5

At moments
  life flows
    memories diverge

      At times
        links come undone
          inside in disarray

Over long moments
  events freeze
    memories submerge

      Sometimes
        things fray
          outside wears away

In a moment
  past thaws
    memories emerge

In time
being reunites
Self, connected array

Untitled #6

Looking long
Seeing part
Pausing a long
Sensing the rest

Grown quietly
In places deep
Stored gently
For a time to weep

With fearful ache
Portal opened
In painful longing
Acceptance unfolds

Dancing

I'm dancing
So near the edge
I'm a flutter
So not to fall

I'm dancing
So to test the distance
I'm a whirl
So afraid to settle

I'm dancing
So removed the harmony
I'm a blur
So lost the focus

I'm dancing
   So off the pace
I'm motion
   So out of phase

I'm dancing
   So near my center
I'm silence
   So loud, unheard

I'm dancing
   So near the edge
I'm hope
   So gently led

Untitled #7

   Broken trust
Foundation of Relationship
   Secrecy
Jailer of inner hallways built

   Incest
Empty aching need
   Therapist
Companion of inner labyrinth

   Victim
Wounded, hated Self
Survivor
Cautious, hopeful Self

   Me
Core of inner being
   I
Inner self of full expectancy

"Changes" was previously published in 1988 in *Bread and Roses: A Poetry Anthology for Adult Children*, by Health Communications, Inc., 1721 Blount Road, Suite 1, Pompano Beach, FL 33069. Reprinted by permission. Other poems all copyright 1991 by Mary Jane Hall.

Curry in the Morning

Nikky Finney

a jump rope hangs in the closet
behind an apron
worn and unfitting

            they do not make aprons
            for women of fourteen

a skate key
bound in cloth
lies next to the discolored gold band
she wears on occasion only

            they no longer stock dreams
            for women of fourteen
            out of season
            out of style
            out of reach

she was against tying the knot
in the first place
but the eyes of her mother were constant
so she married him
for consistency's sake

sometimes she would ask about going out
anyplace
the answer was always no
so she'd return
to the back room the scent of the soap
and the security of the ironing board

            fourteen
            with no business
            being a wife
            but there are rules
            for women
            who are mothers at fourteen

in the morning
she reach past the apron
fondle the jump rope of her youth
and drape it around her neck

                              girl-scouting taught her
                              the proper way
and from its innocence
her life will dangle
a tribute to her creativity
the girl scouts of america
on display for once
without his approval

From Nikky Finney, *On Wings Made of Gauze*,
William Morrow, 1985. Reprinted by permission.

Chapter 4

FEMINIST PRACTICE
WITH TEENAGE PARENTS

ARMANDO SMITH

This chapter describes my practice with pregnant adolescents and their families in an adolescent health program. During the 5 years I have worked in the agency with this population, I have struggled to integrate my feminist beliefs and ideology into this traditional, sometimes hostile, setting. A brief description of my practice setting is presented, and then I describe my own process of development as a feminist and the gradual, yet unfinished, process of integrating my feminist thoughts into my clinical practice. The practice example selected from my caseload illustrates what this integrating process involves and how it guides my work with clients. The chapter concludes with my assessment of what future developments are needed in terms of psychosocial work with teenagers and what revisions are necessary in the way we conceive of and manage adolescent health in the United States.

THE METRO ADOLESCENT
HEALTH PROGRAM

The adolescent health program is a separate program within a comprehensive community health center. The center was started approximately 20 years ago, when the federal government actively supported the concept of community-based health treatment for low-income and indigent populations. It is located in what is euphemistically called an "inner-city" Midwest urban setting. The population that we serve lives with and deals with the many problems that afflict poor urban communities. The neighborhood boasts three major housing projects that are ill suited for most of the residents who, because of their financial situation, are forced to live there. In addition to poverty, we have many of the social ills that often accompany poverty—namely, street violence, gang involvement, and drug use and sale. Medically and socially, our adolescent population and the community in which they live have the highest rate of infant mortality and morbidity, and a high incidence of sexually transmitted diseases and teenage pregnancy.

My position as coordinator of the program requires that I supervise a multidisciplinary team of nurses, social workers, case managers, and vocational counselors. As a team we are responsible for providing medical and social services to about 500 pregnant and parenting teens per year. Although most of my duties are administrative, I provide individual and couples counseling to young women and men in their late teens who are often not married but are trying to raise their children jointly. I also conduct small group discussions on health issues for teens and a similar group for their parents.

DEFINITION OF FEMINIST PRACTICE

My definition of feminist practice stems necessarily from my own view of what feminism means. Feminism for me is an ideology that supports the belief that women's experience, perspective, and knowledge are essential and necessary ingredients in every consideration of social, political, and historical issues. The poet and scholar Adrienne Rich (1976) taught me that history has been written largely by and for male scholars,

> many of whom suffer from an intellectual defect called patrivincialism or patriochialism: the assumption that women are a sub-group, that a "man's world" is the "real" world, that patriarchy is equivalent to culture and culture to patriarchy, that the "great" or "liberating" periods of history have been the same for women and men. (p. 16)

Rich (1976) states that when she was writing the book *Of Woman Born*, she kept this question in her mind: "What was it like for women?" (p. 16). That question, or a mutation of it, is a guiding principle in my work with clients. I accept that as a man I am limited in my ability to understand the question fully, or the answers that women may give to it. In some ways, my response is an extension of the old social work tenet of accepting the client where she is. Yet, in other ways, it is altogether a different proposition because it requires that, as best as I can, I put aside both my formal training and socialization as a man and assume the realities of a woman.

The first lesson I learned as a feminist therapist, which is now a central part of my work, is that clients are teachers, and if I allow myself to listen, there is a lot I can learn from my clients. The best client-teacher I had was Diane.

Diane was a young white single mother who met the standard criteria of *DSM III* (*Diagnostic and Statistical Manual of the American Psychiatric Association*) for clinical depression or dysthmic disorder. She had frequent crying spells, irregular eating and sleeping patterns, low self-esteem, and vague thoughts of suicide (American Psychiatric Association, 1980, pp. 213-214). At the start of treatment I thought that we were mismatched. I am a Black male therapist, and I soon discovered that the above "symptoms" of this young white single mother were related to two main issues: She felt unattractive or, more correctly, that only African-American males found her attractive. In fact, the father of her only son was an African American. The other issue was that she felt unappreciated and exploited in her job as a legal secretary to a man she described as an "old tyrant." So I was faced with a young woman who in one way or another felt exploited by men, yet she seemed to seek validation from them.

Fresh out of a clinical social work program, I was ready to deal with issues of transference and countertransference. But Diane soon set her own agenda; she demonstrated by her resilience and motivation that she was primarily interested in gaining understanding of herself, especially as it related to her role as a mother to her young son. I felt drawn to her sources of strength (or was I forced to look at them?), yet I also felt that my combined approach of humanistic psychology and client-centered therapy was providing her, at best, symptomatic and temporary relief.

The breakthrough for us came when, crossing what I considered to be therapist-client barriers, I asked her to type my thesis at her usual free-lance rate. For her, this development had the effect of validating her skills and expertise, something I had attempted to do verbally.

She also became interested in and amazed at some of the revelations in my thesis. Due to the nature of the project, my thesis contained personal information about my own struggles. This information, as well as the fact that our relationship was now on a different level, probably contributed to the demystifying of both therapy and me as the therapist. I lost my status as the all-knowing, ever-correct therapist and assumed the status of a human being, much like her, who was in a process of becoming. The two added benefits of this were that our sessions now focused on discussions about our growth and struggles. The second benefit was that she became aware of the struggles of men and women as documented in my bibliography. She realized that some of her issues were applicable to other women and that most of them had their roots in society. Now more than ever she took responsibility for her own "work." During therapy, she began to read feminist books. Eventually she and other women were instrumental in getting the agency to start a support/therapy group for women.

I still remember how I mourned the loss of her as a client. In retrospect, I think that although all my actions and processes were not thought out as feminist, Diane helped with my development as a feminist therapist. I realize that having her type my thesis was not what most practitioners would have done. However, I did not consider that her reading my paper gave her the only view of me as a person. Rather, I assumed that I was doing this as a therapist. She also demonstrated to me that for clients who are able and inclined, the use of bibliotherapy is an effective technique. Perhaps my most important lesson was that power and control are strong issues in therapy, even when the therapist sees him- or herself as benign. It was in my own therapy that I realized that my mourning the loss of Diane had to do with giving up control (she did not need me) as much as it had to do with any other loss. It was her newfound ability to make changes in the system (e.g., the agency starting a group) that eventually led Diane to find a new employer.

I took from Diane the ability to trust the client, a better understanding of control (especially as it related to gender roles), and a whole range of techniques and interventions that have now become an integral part of my work. I believe that Diane took from our work together a better sense of herself and an ability to trust that self, and, most important, the courage and the wisdom to look outside herself for explanations of problems or tensions she may be experiencing. Thanks to the women's community, she also learned to look outside of herself and beyond men for sources of support.

DEVELOPMENT AS A FEMINIST

My own development as a feminist began in the late 1970s, when I became involved with a group of men who were part of a small but growing number of men looking at the changing male roles vis-à-vis the emerging women's movement. Like most of the men in my small support group, my initial interest in the group was for personal growth. I was looking for ways to develop close male friendships that were not based on competition. I also was interested in developing friendships with men that allowed us to share ourselves and seek support in ways that I had not experienced as an adult male, but knew to be possible from reports of my women friends.

I soon realized that this was no easy task for us men. It took many hours of consciousness-raising for us to give up learned competition and begin to trust and support each other. As we struggled with our own personal issues, we realized that many of them are related to society's expectations of how men and women should behave. I recognized, for example, that one of the barriers that kept me from developing close male friendships was the fear that one or both of us would be defined as gay. Then, as now, homophobia was a strong deterrent.

During this time, I began my own bibliotherapy and began reading both popular and scholarly work by women and men who were identified with the feminist movement. Popular authors like Betty Friedan (1963) pointed out historical oppression of women. Scholarly authors like Adrienne Rich (1976) provided new and sometimes disturbing analyses of traditional female roles. Later, I began to read books by men who attempted to examine the implications of women's changing roles, both for men and for their relationships with each other and with women (Nichols, 1975). Warren Farrell (1974) not only delineated some of the issues about traditional male roles, but also offered a new vision of what males become. But it was Joseph Pleck's (1976) scholarly analysis of the traditional male roles and all their dangers that led me to select the subject of my master's thesis, the socialization process of males. The process of writing my thesis led to three personal growth areas: my working definition of feminism, the incorporation of that definition into my practice, and my further involvement in the men's movement.

The feminist men's movement is a national movement that helps men to examine the damaging effect of traditional male roles, such as competitiveness, isolation, and poor health. It also helps support men in finding new ways of being and relating to each other and to women. Politically, it supports the feminist agenda of equality in all areas of our lives. It supports the notion that the oppression of any one segment of the population is morally wrong and damaging to all of us. Ironically, it was my involvement in the national men's movement that provided me with an avenue for developing close male friendships, a better sense of my masculinity, and the courage to call myself a feminist.

INTEGRATION OF FEMINISM INTO MY PRACTICE

Integration of feminism into my practice has been a struggle, not only in terms of individual client issues, but also in terms of institutional racism and sexism. Although the individual struggle is often challenging, I find that I frequently have to challenge systems and agencies that have certain preconceived notions about our clients due to their race, their gender, and the fact that they are pregnant or young parents. This type of advocacy often allows me to assist the client in attaining basic needs, but on another level I believe that it gives the client a sense of security and the knowledge that I am on her side.

Although my racial/ethnic background is Black and Hispanic, my feminist development occurred almost exclusively in the white middle-class arena. So when I started my work in the field of teenage pregnancy, I found from experience what I had already known intellectually from reading authors such as Toni Cade-Bombara. Although feminism and feminist viewpoints have a place in Black culture, the application has to be different. As Cade (1970) states: "I don't know that our priorities are the same, that our concerns and methods are the same, or even similar enough so that we can afford to depend on this new field of experts [white females]" (p. 9).

In a setting such as the one where I work, the concept of feminism becomes expanded, and its application takes on a new face. It becomes important to ask myself hard questions about my practice.

For example, how do I convince a young woman age 19 with two children that dreams are worth having, when all around her nobody has dreams? How do I respond to a young man who gets a girl pregnant because if he doesn't perform sexually with a girl, people will know that he is gay? How do I convince a 33-year-old grandmother to help her young daughter take care of her newborn baby when the grandmother says to me, "Who is going to take care of me?"

One of the great benefits of feminist theory is that it allows me to think about the causes and solutions to problems in a variety of ways. I acknowledge that some issues have a personal component to them. That is to say, each individual responds to issues based on his or her own idiosyncratic personality. But I also see a direct connection between these personal idiosyncrasies and the larger societal system, especially in my agency setting and its environment.

According to Bricker-Jenkins (1988), one of the foundations of feminist practice is the acknowledgment and incorporation of cultural and social differences in the assessment of individual strengths. Before her, writers such as Angela Davis (1983) and Toni Cade (1970) taught me that Black women, like their white sisters, have been brainwashed by "Hollywood and other dream factories" into hoping for certain tangible benefits (Cade, 1970, pp. 7-8). Some of these anticipated benefits, such as motherhood and marriage, were seen as desirable because they might elevate a woman to a "cherished and protected" status. Other benefits such as having material possessions were supposed to free the woman from the burden of housework and parenting so "that she can realize herself and nourish her sense of identity" (Cade, 1970, p. 8).

White women saw these benefits as attainable. Later, however, they came to realize that the achieved dreams were in many ways oppressive and destructive. Many Black women were far removed from these "benefits." Yet, however unattainable they might be for women burdened by poverty and racism, the dream was slow to fade, sometimes living on forever.

Given this common hope among some African-American women, part of my treatment goal with the grandmother who wanted some protection for herself was to help her find ways she could feel "taken care of." Sometimes this meant pushing her to use her own sources of strength and other times it meant taking care of herself. This differs from a conventional or even woman-centered approach, which requires that the client eventually give up her wish to be taken care of and learn to rely on herself. I believed that this client would eventually reach the point where she did not need to be taken care of, would grow to rely on herself, and could then feel personal strength and power. My short-term goal, out of necessity, was to get her to the point where she could help her young daughter in ways that were manageable for the grandmother.

Perhaps my major difficulty as a Black male working with pregnant teenage women is that the medical center is committed to a maternal-child health model, with all of the social service and case management supports going to the needs of the mother and child. This model assumes that the male counterpart is either absent or harmful, or both. These perspectives lead staff to "help" these women accept the status of teenage single parenthood, with its concomitant problems.

This sometimes means that I have to help others see that the young man who engages in premature, unprotected sex for fear of being labeled or discovered to be gay is responding to pressure in much the same manner as young women often respond to pressure. Anecdotal reports from many of our clients suggest that many young women do not plan to become sexually involved. They do so out of fear that their mates may leave them or in response to family problems. Or they feel left out of a circle of friends, all of whom have children.

For young men, pressure may take the form of ostracism, harassment, and, in not a few cases, physical abuse. My support of young fathers may be defined by some as abandoning the young women clients and advocating for their perpetrators or oppressors. From both my client-centered background and my feminist background, I know that validation is an important part of change (Bricker-Jenkins, 1988) and believe that young men have the right to experience empowering growth and change free of racism and sexism.

I trust the process that tells me to acknowledge their fears and threats as real and to share some of my own struggles regarding masculine identity in order to help these young men. Relying on some of the techniques identified by Bricker-Jenkins (1988), I explore options with them, such as joining groups for young people who are struggling with their identity, reading books on coming out, and seeking competence and skill-building opportunities. These are a few ways that I can help young fathers realize that the power of domination over the women in their lives is not real power. It is my hope that they can find new and better avenues for expressing masculinity as they explore these options.

My feminist perspective encourages me to think of hopelessness as a sense of frustration due to lack of control, especially over one's own life. It is often useful for me to spend several sessions with some teenage women clients encouraging them to fantasize about what they would like to do. We look at their dreams from the standpoint of the strengths they have that can be further developed in order for them to experience control. In this context, possibilities become real options, and we begin to strategize; we examine their interests and skills, and choose small, attainable goals that are designed to provide a sense of personal competence. I have seen the growth of young women from writing poems that get published, preparing résumés, or challenging issues that reflect racism and sexism in their lives. Although these clients have an uphill battle against an environment designed to keep them down, I now see former clients who are realizing some of their potential. Armed with this insight, they become more confident to tackle new situations.

My professional goal still remains the client-centered mandate of being "where the client is at." However, having fully embraced Bricker-Jenkins's (1988) propositions and assumptions of feminist practice, I know that pain and problems have cultural dimensions, and that we grow within supporting and validating environments. Therefore, the goal is to support the client by creating an environment that is safe and then encouraging and watching the client grow in new and promising ways.

CASE SUMMARY
FROM MY FEMINIST PRACTICE

Debbie was a 20-year-old single African-American female who lived with her boyfriend Joe and their two children, Tamara, age 3, and Sean, age 1. She lived in a two-bedroom apartment in one of the Chicago Housing Authority's projects. She had known her boyfriend for 4 years and had lived with him for the previous year because he "just up and moved in one day." She was supported by a grant from public assistance that was now in jeopardy, as she refused to give them any information about Joe. Joe was unemployed and Debbie stated that he "comes and goes as he wants." Debbie described her major daily activities as watching TV and taking care of the children. Her social history showed that she was the fourth child of six children. She stated that she moved out of her mother's apartment "as soon as I was able to get an apartment in my name." She denied any major problem with her mother, saying, "I moved because there were too many people in that small apartment." She stated that several of her siblings were also living at home and that some of them also had small children. Debbie reported that when she was in her teens, her father died from complications of his drinking. She dropped out of high school at the age of 16, even though she was a B student. There is no history of mental health treatment or counseling.

Debbie was in her second trimester of pregnancy and had received little prenatal care. She stated that Joe did not like it when she came to the clinic because he had to stay with the kids. She had a history of repeated gonorrhea infection. Her two previous deliveries were by C-section. Both the medical staff and the social work staff had observed multiple lacerations and bruises all over her body that she was reluctant to explain. She eventually said that sometimes she and Joe fought and that he became physically abusive. Debbie voiced no clear goals for herself, but stated, "I don't know what to do with my life. I want Joe to move. I can't sleep at night. Most of the time I feel like crying or I feel angry."

Regardless of one's school of thought, this case required clear assessment of evident needs. Almost any observer would have identified behavior consistent with low self-esteem, acceptance of abuse, and suppression of the individual's own interest on behalf of others. There were also some clear signs of depression.

My relationship with Debbie was guided by some assumptions about her relationship with her boyfriend. I knew that Debbie was ambivalent about that relationship, partly because her emotional dependency prevented her from totally letting go of the relationship. Consistent with Bolton's (1983) proposition that one of the motivations of the prematurely pregnant adolescent is to form attachment with others when she has failed to do so with her parents, Debbie's ambivalence can also be explained by her fear of failing to form attachments again in the relationship with Joe.

Given this assumption, I thought it would be productive to engage Joe in the therapeutic relationship. I persuaded Joe to come to a session with Debbie, and we began to look at some issues that affected him. Specifically, I convinced him to get medical treatment for gonorrhea without putting the blame on either himself or Debbie. Since he saw himself as a good father, I pointed out that his children were about to lose their monthly income because Debbie had not cooperated with the public assistance office with information about him. We explored his options: He could voluntarily provide the information to the public assistance office, he could find a job and support the children, or he could move out, thereby allowing Debbie to say truthfully that she did not know his whereabouts. I also told him that many of his and Debbie's problems would eventually affect the children, so coming to therapy with Debbie would be a good idea.

Treatment with Debbie focused, at least in part, on examining her dependence needs. Without challenging her relationship with Joe, we looked at some possible ways of managing her concerns. Through many sessions, we were able to break down what "I don't know what to do with my life" really meant for Debbie. We began to focus on such manageable areas as career, parenting, budgeting, and relationships, which were not limited to Joe, including those with her family members.

Reflecting on the feminist beliefs and knowledge that guided my course of treatment with this young couple, I believe any hesitancy came from the unfinished process of integrating the feminist perspective with other more traditional social work practice approaches that I have found to be effective. Although some of my decisions may not be feminist in origin, I know that my practice has been supported and nourished by feminist ideology.

One of my decisions with Debbie and Joe is not congruent with the practice framework of many feminists: I engaged Joe in treatment and shifted some of the counseling to issues that were affecting them as a couple in their efforts to accomplish joint parenting functions. As mentioned earlier in this chapter, I have many serious questions about whether the maternal-child model of practice is exclusionary. It frequently fails to help the practitioner recognize the many nontraditional strengths and meanings woven into the interpersonal relationships of young African-American women and men. By the nature of the assumptions made in the maternal-child model, the mother and her children can be isolated from relationships that the white middle-class agency and its professional staff define to be destructive, or at least counterproductive, to the young woman's attainment of goals that support her children and herself.

As a male feminist practitioner, I also take issue with traditional models of casework that see "the putative father" only as a source of support for the teenage mother and her children. Even with the advent of male involvement in teenage pregnancy prevention programs, the emphasis is primarily on the male finding a job, not a career, with the more advanced programs involving the male only in sports and recreation.

Many feminist practitioners will take issue with my decision to validate Debbie and Joe as a couple by engaging them as such in therapy. Some practitioners might question whether or not I was aware of the cycle of domestic violence or why I did not give priority to the greater risk of abuse of Debbie and perhaps her children from Joe. Joe and Debbie's relationship illustrates Lichtenberg's (1986) "relationship of equals" (p. 106). It became apparent that although Joe was seen by everyone, including himself, as the oppressor, Debbie also had a role in that dynamic. In order to make any changes, it was essential for them to understand their oppressor-oppressed relationship. My decision was to engage them as a couple in treatment, with no preconceived idea that they would remain together. Given the closed community of the housing project, even if they lived apart they would invariably interact within the community as well as with each other as parents. Joint therapy at best would allow them to do so in a manner that would be healthy.

The realization that this couple would probably decrease their involvement with the center after the baby's birth, as well as my assumption that this couple needed to feel competent, led me to keep treatment short term and focused. It was also evident that both individually and as a couple, Debbie and Joe needed to feel that they had options that they had not previously experienced. The decision to see them as a couple validated their tenuous relationship and gave them a sense of belonging. For Debbie, her need for attachment represented a complex and painful dynamic that had little likelihood of being changed unless she could begin to realize that "attachment" could control her rather than free her to select other options in relationships. Joe's involvement in the counseling process offered an opportunity for him to redefine the relationship as something not to be neglected, abused, or destroyed. Redefining, validating, creating options, and feeling competent are some of the "feminist assumptions" that are identified as foundations of feminist practice (Bricker-Jenkins & Hooyman, 1986).

I harbor no illusions about Debbie or Joe as individuals or as a couple. Neither had attained a viable sense of autonomous empowerment or even formulated many goals toward that end. As a couple they lacked insight that is often necessary for permanent, systematic change. Yet they did have some guided and supported experiences related to forming a new kind of relationship and were exposed to sources to help them deal with the stresses of relationships. This was important, regardless of whether or how long they remained together.

FUTURE DEVELOPMENT OF THE FEMINIST PERSPECTIVE FOR PRACTICE

One of the problems that has plagued the issue of teenage pregnancy is that it is often defined according to the professional bias of the experts. Consequently, social work has participated, along with other health professions, in supporting the medical definition of teen pregnancy as a health problem, which emphasizes treating pregnancies and delivering healthy babies. Teenage pregnancy is also often defined as a social problem that is merely a symptom of the disintegration of the family and society at large, or as a political/economic issue of the Black community. Now the medical and social perspectives are gaining an even stronger hold as more young women and men, such as those I have described, become involved in rampant drug use and suffer AIDS and other HIV-related infections that may kill them and their children.

It was not so long ago that radical members of the African-American community were resisting the notion of birth control because it was seen as institutional genocide. Of necessity, that leadership must now be drawn into a different dialogue about ways to empower this generation of young inner-city Blacks to survive. We have yet to consider how feminist principles and collective movements toward health and survival might help to inform that dialogue in order to reverse the patterns of human destruction in communities similar to that described in this chapter.

Teenagers in the United States have a much higher rate of childbearing, abortion, and pregnancy than their counterparts in other developed countries (Rosoff, 1988). Future practice and research must concentrate on ways to foster minority youths' personal esteem and self-worth that can then be actualized into alternative ways of living and being.

The intolerant attitude of our culture toward sex differs from the attitudes of other developed countries. More cross-national research might help to inform U.S. policies and programs related to pregnancy prevention. In my own program, the great majority of pregnant teenagers were high school dropouts, and most of them did not plan to get pregnant, but had very little knowledge about their bodies. Feminist research could lead to some much-needed answers about how to build self-esteem and self-knowledge into pregnancy prevention programs for both young women and young men. If feminist social work principles can be directly incorporated into program design, such programs may encourage skill and competence building. These are important programmatic aspects that should help provide teenagers with the wherewithal to delay sexual involvement or, at a minimum, to take precautions that would diminish the probability of an unwanted pregnancy. In turn, this may prevent many other social and health risks interconnected with high-risk sexual behaviors among teenagers across the country.

REFERENCES

American Psychiatric Association. (1980). *Diagnostic and statistical manual of mental disorders* (3rd ed.). Washington, DC: Author.

Bolton, F., Jr. (1983). *When bonding fails: Clinical assessment of high-risk families.* Beverly Hills, CA: Sage.

Bricker-Jenkins, M. (1988). *Foundations of feminist social work practice: The changer and the changed are one.* Unpublished doctoral dissertation, Fordham University.

Bricker-Jenkins, M., & Hooyman, N. (Eds.). (1986). *Not for women only: Social work practice for a feminist future.* Silver Spring, MD: National Association of Social Workers.

Cade, T. (Ed.). (1970). *The black woman: An anthology.* New York: New American Library.

Davis, A. Y. (1983). *Women, race and class.* New York: Random House.

Farrell, W. (1974). *The liberated man.* New York: Random House.

Friedan, B. (1963). *The feminine mystique.* New York: Norton.

Lichtenberg, P. (1986). Men and feminist practice. In M. Bricker-Jenkins & N. Hooyman (Eds.), *Not for women only: Social work practice for a feminist future* (pp. 106-111). Silver Spring, MD: National Association of Social Workers.

Nichols, J. (1975). *Men's liberation: A new definition of masculinity.* New York: Penguin.

Pleck, J. (1976). The male sex role: Definitions, problems and sources of change. *Journal of Social Issues, 32*(3), 155-164.

Rich, A. (1976). *Of woman born: Motherhood as experience and institution.* New York: Norton.

Rosoff, J. I. (1988). Not just for teenagers. *Family Planning Perspectives, 20*(2), 52.

Hattie on the Block

Dolores Kendrick

Remember me?
    I'm the woman you nailed to a tree
      after the twilight died.

Carrie, you be still, now,
    don't make no noise.
Mama will protect you
    from all the shoutin' an' screamin'
    an' biddin' that's goin' on
      right now. Hold on. Hold onto Mama.
    Won't be long now,
    they done had they lunch,
    an' somethin' will happen to take
    the fear outta your bones
      an' the sweat off of your eyelids
    an' drain them to the sweet winds
    for the birds to eat. Somethin' will happen:

Happens that I be a slave woman,
maybe that makes me property,
not a human bein' like all
you who come to buy me,
see if I'm sturdy, can hold ground,
can withstand the elements, bear fruit
when the seed is in me, like the Lord's land,
sing for my supper when the seasons come,
give death the mortgage on my bones.

Don't come near me! Stay away!
I'm not buyable yet,
I'm a bit unleavened.

Still, Carrie, be still, child. Don't cry,
      don't let them see you cry, honey,
there's a victory in that. Keep the tears
      inward, outta they sight.
Hold onto my apron, tear it, if you want,
      hold hard while we crush the evil
pushin' its way through that crowd of shoppers
      yellin' before us an' standin' there
mockin' us with money an' all the changers
      in the temple, but they all look good,
      don't they? Nice coats an' trousers,
      bright shoes, sturdy hats. Ever seen
      a finer lookin' peoples than that?

Evil be pretty sometimes, don't it?

Money look good, even if it be for your soul.

Souls cain't be bought.
I won't be of much use to anybody
who buys me without my Carrie here
I be crippled, needin' crutches: who gonna
pay for them? Or will I have to work
the fields limpin' about with my mind
catchin' butterflies, when I should be
pickin' cotton, 'cause my soul be amputated
when you bought me without my Carrie
for a few dollars cheaper?

No, don't, I beg, you, don't touch me!
Stay back. I cain't leave this block
in holo-cust!

That's it, Carrie, hang tight;
    My, your forehead be hot,
fever comin' on I 'spect, an' your
    mother's fever gone cold
makin' it more dangerous when
    it be exposed to the elements
that gather up 'round her now,
    this early, bright mornin'
spoiled an' festerin' in the mouths
    of all these happy buyers who need
the disease of your Mama's wrath
    so they can recover from their own
dyin'.

Dyin' today if I be sold without my Carrie.
I promise you that.

Look on us before you lay
your money down. What we cost? $2500?

Good price. Buy what you breed.

Masters, Owners, Buyers, Fathers, Sons,
Take vengeance on your dollar!
God help me, I be His maidservant,
I be His witness to this sale of womanflesh
in the twenty-eighth year of my delivery!

Carrie, look! Wipe your eyes, child.
See. They finished the biddin'. Money
be paid. We's together, God heard my
haltin' words through the ears of these
deafened people; you an' me from this strange
pulpit. Look lively, child. We be sold,
but we ain't bought.

Chapter 5

FEMINIST PRACTICE WITH WOMEN OF COLOR
A Developmental Perspective

CLEVONNE TURNER

Just what do my race and sex have to do with my social work practice? In short, everything. I am an African-American, female, self-employed clinical social work practitioner and consultant. In every way, my practice reflects all that I am, all that I have been exposed to, and all that I continue to work at in order to change the paradoxical world in which we live. For this reason, this chapter starts with a description of my personal and professional development and leads to illustrations of how I use my personal and professional self in my work with Black women clients. That practice is informed by the "self-in-relation" theory developed at the Stone Center for Developmental Services and Studies (Surrey, 1984), but it is also informed by who I am.

PERSONAL DEVELOPMENT

Being born and raised in the South and educated in parochial, public, and private coeducational as well as single-sex integrated and segregated schools has given me a rich, multidimensional view of myself and others. I have lived and worked in the South, the Midwest, and the East, with occasional yearnings about one day working out West. My initial mentors and role models were my parents, who are still together after 48 years of marriage, being dual-career earners, and raising my brother, sister, and myself. I am married, and I have two adult daughters and one teenage daughter.

My "play aunt," Donnelda Ryan, was my first African-American female social work model, in Nashville, Tennessee. She was one of my mother's best friends, and she was like a second mother to me. She was the ideal social worker in every way, true to her race and sex, as she was perfectly suited for the community-based services and advocacy work she so untiringly performed. My mother, Isabelle Watkins, was an excellent, highly respected elementary school teacher before and during her marriage, who took time away from her career to stay home with her children until we had started school. I grew up knowing that I would be successful and that I would be engaged in some type of meaningful work while providing a service to other people. I inherited a "learned talent" to survive that was passed on to me chiefly by my mother and her network of women friends, relatives, and neighbors in the Black community. They modeled the difficult yet successful integration of working inside and outside the home, preserving relationships, providing community service, and maintaining dignity and perseverance as the norm. My father both complemented and supported this model of growth in me (Turner, 1984).

My parents, extended family, and significant other males and females in my community instilled a deep sense of African-American pride in me that has served as a cornerstone in my overall development. Connecting with the field of social work was a natural, highly valued extension of my upbringing and provided me with additional ways of giving something back to a community that had nurtured me ethnically, spiritually, emotionally, socially, and educationally.

In my undergraduate sociology classes at a historic Black university, I had an abundance of male mentors and professors who were African-American and Japanese. In my graduate school of social work, which was predominantly white, I had all white male and female instructors and supervisors. I felt highly educated, valued, and nurtured at college, but, although I was well educated in graduate school, I always felt I was kept at an "arm's length," professional distance. None of my teachers in graduate school shared my worldview. The other four African-American students and I often believed (although we did not state this) that we "didn't really belong," that our cultural norms were deviant and not highly valued, and that we were generally misunderstood. There was no overt racism, but the more

subtle forms of exclusion and a lack of cross-cultural theory or training had a strong impact on each of us. Sexism also existed in both of
these schools, but I was not as consciously aware of it or as reactive
to it as I was to racism. I was aware of and sorely missed the presence
of any African-American female teachers in my study of sociology
and social work. I have always been an avid reader of various women
writers, of both fiction and nonfiction works, especially if they were
women of color like me. Earlier in my life, I craved their written
words to compensate for and add to what I missed in the classroom.
Lately, reading has become more necessary, even vital, to helping me
feel nourished and whole.

A GLANCE AT MY PRACTICE

In my practice, I see individual women and men, couples, and families. They are white as well as people of color who are ethnically,
culturally, and socioeconomically diverse. They are heterosexual, lesbian, and gay, and range in age from 16 to 85 years. I have a warm,
inviting office in my home where my clients and I sit around a low
table (rather than separated by a desk) with the same style of seats for
all of us. I keep plenty of herbal teas, water, and decaffeinated coffee
on hand. My fee structure is based on a sliding scale, and I engage in
"barter" for services with those who cannot afford fees. About 80% of
my clients are female.

I also work with groups in a variety of settings—schools, churches, a
television studio, and community-based agencies—around a variety of
women's issues, cross-cultural concerns, and stress management. This is
done on a fee-for-service basis as well as a volunteer one. Formats include consciousness-raising groups, seminars, workshops, self-support
groups, and experiential groups. In addition, I occasionally teach, write,
and supervise social work students in their field practice as well as in
their postgraduate clinical practice as part of their credentialing process
for professional licenses.

EVOLVING SELF-DEFINITION

I do not define myself solely as a "feminist therapist," as I feel too
confined by the use of a label, and see myself still growing, developing,
and enhancing the ways in which I work. My work is and always has

been quite eclectic, borrowing from a number of theories: psycho-dynamic, Gestalt, cross-cultural, group, family, community organiza-tion, and feminist. Characteristic of all my work is a proactive, mutu-ally empathic, and empowering stance that is educational, systemic, and collaborative. I rely heavily on a variety of support systems, self-help groups, community organizations, family members, and signifi-cant others in the lives of clients, spiritual and religious organiza-tions, and other mental health and health care professionals, who can enrich the overall quality of my interaction with clients and who also serve the women clients directly. I utilize peer supervision, network interactively within and outside the social work field, make many re-ferrals throughout the community, and serve in an advocacy role whenever possible as a vital adjunct to my work.

FEMINIST INFLUENCE ON MY PRACTICE

I have always felt different from more traditional social work prac-titioners by virtue of my racial, gender-based, and class struggles within the patriarchal medical and conventional settings of a major psychiatric training hospital and a Big Ten university counseling clinic in which I have worked. In these settings, I was acutely aware that none of the social workers, psychologists, or psychiatrists with whom I worked had received any cross-cultural training. It was gener-ally assumed, and often stated, that part of my value to these teams rested in my availability to see and treat African-American clients (so the others would not have to). My first big fight with my first direc-tor, a white male psychiatrist, revolved around his wanting me to see only African-American clients. I insisted that I was on staff to see any clients regardless of gender, race, or socioeconomic status and I ex-pected other staff members to do the same, as long as we were help-ing and not harming clients. I further stated that we all needed train-ing to learn how to deliver these services in a more culturally sensitive, respectful, and mutually engaging and helpful manner.

I certainly did not have all the answers, and resented being typecast and polarized although, in reality, I felt I was "different" from the others in my work environments. I was the only person of color, and certainly the only African-American female on each of these staffs, and no one completely understood or affirmed my issues or those of our clients who were of color and "different." I sometimes felt as devalued as some of the clients; I felt deviant; I felt that both my sex and my color at times signaled danger if I looked or acted too nonconforming. I did know that, on some levels, I was liked and even respected by most of my colleagues; however, I utilized a healthy and highly functional "paranoia" as one of my best professional defenses. I remember, more often than not, hiding the most significant parts of my work and of my belief system from coworkers and those who supervised my work. But with my clients of color, especially the women, I felt bonded, emotionally creative, free to accept and give hugs, mutually empowered with them as we focused on their strengths and not solely on their problems. I felt free to affirm with them the impact of much of the society's pathology that systematically and insidiously was incorrectly projected onto them.

When I came to Wellesley College in 1977, I was the first social worker and the first African-American person to work in its counseling service. I had an opportunity for the first time in my career to help shape the philosophy, goals, and practice where I worked. We evolved a preventive, systemic, community-based outreach model utilizing an array of group approaches, collaborative programs, and long-term linkages with students, staff, faculty, and administrative groups throughout the campus. I was a team member of a counseling service that embraced psychiatry, psychology, social work, and pastoral counseling. We moved from a rigid medical model, which dictated that we see only individuals who would come in admitting to a problem, to a more fluid service-oriented, preventive, developmental model. In 1981, we hired Jean Baker Miller as our new director and changed our name from Counseling Services to the present Stone Center for Developmental Services and Studies to reflect more adequately our change in philosophy and direction. Dr. Miller added a research component to accompany our counseling and, in addition, brought into our ranks Alexandra Kaplan, another feminist author and pioneer.

At present, I feel most grounded in the feminist theory that is currently evolving at the Stone Center for Development Services and Studies at Wellesley College, where I worked for 9 years prior to my self-employed status 4 years ago. The approach of the Stone Center is often referred to as "self-in-relation" theory. The basic focus of this theory is on the "centrality and continuity of relationships" in women's development (Surrey, 1984); the premise undergirding the evolving theory was the belief that a closer examination of women and their development can lead to a new understanding of both women and men. Jean Baker Miller, the first director of the Stone Center, is one of my current mentors and role models. In 1976, she published the ground-breaking book, *Toward a New Psychology of Women*, which had a profound impact on me by validating much of what I previously believed and practiced.

The growing self-in-relation theory is the fruit of considerable collaborative work at the Stone Center that involved all of us in both joyous and painful growth spurts. We would unwittingly fall into patriarchal and hierarchical ways of relating to each other that would confound and distance us at times. Other times, we would engage in synonymous, focused, health-promoting collaborations that would help us all to feel as one and socially connected. We all worked *too* hard most of the time and would notice, in each other, our tendency to take better care of our clients than we did of ourselves. With each year, the relational theory that we all began to explore, write about, practice, and embrace assumed more shape.

I began to feel more valued and less deviant professionally. I actively and consciously began to understand and reclaim the female part of myself (which had been repressed) and integrated it more fully with the ethnic part of me. During this time, one of my African-American female role models and mentors, Elaine Pinderhughes, received great recognition and acclaim for courageous work in tracing her own family tree. I had then leaned—and still lean—heavily on Elaine's modeling and writing on cross-cultural interfaces, mutual empowerment, race, ethnicity, and systemic family interventions. She has helped others and myself to pay closer attention to how these issues affect the practitioner's own identity and all interactions with others—peers, subordinates, supervisors, or clients (Pinderhughes, 1984). My continuing development, personally and professionally, is dependent on my balancing and integrating these feminine and ethnic identities within a dynamic, healthy, whole self.

CLINICAL APPLICATIONS OF THE STONE CENTER THEORETICAL APPROACH TO MINORITY WOMEN

For purposes of clarity and focus, I will discuss these clinical applications in my work with African-American women only. There are far too many differences in traditions, family norms, beliefs, attitudes, styles, behaviors, and the like in various minority cultures in this country to try to lump them all together. However, in this country, racial oppression and being bicultural increase the possibilities for connectedness of women within a particular culture and often with other minority cultures different from their own. There will then be some common threads in applying the self-in-relation theory to all women of color that can be learned from working with African-American women. It is important to note that women in the same family within a particular culture vary greatly from one another in their individual traits, perceptions, personalities, and feelings, so there is no pat formula for clinicians to use in working with women of color. Instead, the purpose of these case illustrations and the theory undergirding them is to encourage greater awareness in readers of their own ethnicity and to increase their capacity, in clinical work, to care, listen, respect, and mutually engage in cultural worldviews that may be different from their own.

SELF-IN-RELATION THEORY

Women's experiences of self appear to contradict most developmental theories that emphasize the importance of disconnection from earlier relationships in order to achieve a separate and bounded sense of self (Surrey, 1984). Self-in-relation theory is intended to reflect more adequately the neglected complexities of human interconnection more commonly seen in women's experiences. The "relational self" concept is an evolutionary process, developing within (not outside of) mutually empathic relationships starting early in the mother-daughter dyad (Surrey, 1984). Rather than moving through a series of separations from mother and other significant family members, women add on relationships as they redefine primary relationships in age-appropriate ways. This type of development leads to self-awareness and understanding while serving to validate the "felt need" of women to understand and become better aware of the other. This is a dynamic, interactive, and flexible process rather than a static self-construct.

Self-differentiation is promoted and encouraged without a series of losses, occurring as it does within the context of remaining meaningfully connected to significant others. However, if the relational context in the family, in the surrounding society, and within the therapeutic alliance has been destructive, restrictive, or not conducive to growth-promoting relationships, women will experience considerable difficulty in feeling good about themselves and in building healthy connections to others. Kaplan (1984) has written in detail about some aspects of this phenomenon; she describes the resulting depressive features of women's vulnerability to loss and inhibition of action and assertion, as well as internalized anger and low self-esteem.

The Theory and Black Women

Self-in-relation theory represents, validates, and legitimates a large and important part of the African-American woman's maturation process. This maturation occurs as she strives to develop a balanced sense of self together with ethnic pride, in conjunction with an internalized affective and cognitive connection to her family and the African-American community. Too often this continued connection has been misconstrued as "deviant" or "dependent" and not valued for its growth-promoting qualities. The process of adding to and redefining significant relationships, instead of separating from them in order to achieve autonomy, can now be examined in a new light. Because this developmental process starts with the mother-daughter relationship before it spreads to others, we should take a closer look at African-American mothers and daughters.

As these women develop and grow, they simultaneously learn to redefine and differentiate their sense of self in relation to their concerns and feelings for significant others (mothers, fathers, siblings, other relatives, friends, authority figures, and the African-American community at large). Autonomy and separation may not be valued in the traditional ways psychologists have written and theorized about them. An African-American woman's connectedness to family and ethnic identity usually has been a source of love, strength, coping power, and stability that is vital and necessary for psychological survival and health. She does not cut off those important parts of herself if they have helped her to stay sane and negotiate the complexities of living in two cultural worlds, with all their mixed messages. She tends to see those connections as a base that she will augment over the course of time.

If African-American mothers are appropriately aware of their ethnic roots, they are constantly working in a "relational" context to instill in their daughters deeper feelings of positive self-esteem, awareness of both how to nurture and how to achieve more self-confidence, resourcefulness, and racial pride. In addition, these mothers are working to build within their daughters a sound base of inner strengths and coping mechanisms that they hope will fit well with the minority and majority cultures. Values are taught and continually reinforced, even though these daughters are being raised in a society that often devalues both them and their mothers at every stage of each other's development. These daughters are usually taught very early in life to rely on themselves as well as to care for others.

Empathic attunement between mother and daughter usually is learned and developed early in these relationships, often out of necessity. Depending on the socioeconomic level of the family, young Black women may become immersed quickly in the caretaking responsibilities in the home. Jordan and her associates have written about the complex cognitive and affective components of empathy and self-boundaries, and their centrality to the development of self and of relational capacities (Jordan, 1984; Jordan, Surrey, & Kaplan, 1982).

Black Women, Cultural Variations, and the Model

When African-American mothers raise their daughters, they have additional burdens and responsibilities due to the intertwining of the double binds of sexism and racism. For many of these mothers, there is also the added bind of classism. As the women move through the various developmental stages of childhood, latency, adolescence, and adulthood, the issues around closeness, trust, self-worth, caretaking, industry, achievement, and sexual intimacy are bound together in ways that are different from those of their white counterparts. A distorted, devalued image of African-American womanhood has been fostered too often via myths, stereotypes, misconceptions, media portrayals, and Westernized educational systems, as well as through legal, social, and political sanctioning in our society. There are those within majority and minority cultures, males as well as females, who work on correcting this image, but the damage is still there and, like a cancer, continues to fester. As a result of these harsh realities, African-American women are raised to be much more cautious than women in the majority culture. Discipline regarding what is acceptable behavior is more frequent and necessarily much stricter in these families because the consequences of doing something "nonacceptable" in the majority culture are usually more severe. Many times this "nonacceptable" behavior can affect one's family, job, residence—or even one's life in certain environments. This reality creates a set-up for tension and sometimes bitter arguments between mothers and daughters. These daughters are also taught and expected to perform many tasks at an earlier age than many of their white counterparts. As a result, they often experience themselves to be more "streetwise" and "grown-up" than their chronological ages imply.

Needless to say, it is difficult for these mothers to both protect and teach, while striving to be positive and loving in an overall atmosphere of being cautious. As they attempt to balance the realities of living in two cultural worlds, they are also trying to maintain calm, meaningful relationships with their daughters and significant others. Some of these mothers have been mislabeled as matriarchal, dominating, overly intrusive, and hysterical. Some of the daughters are labeled as aggressive, hostile, argumentative, and controlling when they each try to juggle their roles and expectations.

Conflicts, misunderstandings, and hurt feelings are likely among both the mothers and the daughters, along with hiding and cutting off their most vulnerable parts from others through defense mechanisms. This is often evident as these women relate to each other and, on a wider scale, to other men and women of various cultures. Complex and difficult issues arise between African-American women and men; among African-American women who befriend, date, and/or marry interracially and those who do not; between African-American women and white women; and among African-American women working with white men. There are also serious relational gaps among African-American women.

Developmentally, as has been implied earlier, African-American women have been socialized to integrate traditional male roles of achievement, autonomy, and independence with the more traditional female roles of caretaking and nurturing as a norm. For the majority of white women, this had been viewed as "deviant" or nontraditional until the women's movement helped to make it more acceptable. However, African-American women are affected by the remnants of racism in the women's movement and sexism in the civil rights movement, which often leave them caught in the middle.

Relevant to psychosocial barriers to African-American women's career development is a phenomenon I have referred to as the "chameleon syndrome" (Turner, 1984). This refers to these women "fine-tuning" and "adapting" themselves as they rotate alliances with various groups of men and women in order to pay attention to all parts of themselves that are important. It is well to note clinically that it is normal for African-American women to be conflicted about how to resolve these "splits" within themselves and to foster a "healthy paranoia" in relating to these groups. The nurturing, relational side will want to heal these splits while the assertive, achievement side will want to demand equality and support.

As clinicians, we need to listen to and validate these legitimate and conflicting realities, rather than deny, ignore, or just react to them negatively and/or noncommittally. These women need our support (not sympathy) and a verbalized, internalized willingness to work on a mutually empathic, "connecting" relationship with them. This can solidify the therapeutic alliance for both therapists and clients, and help these clients integrate the various sides of themselves.

Common Clinical Blind Spots and the "Relational Self"

Some therapists have misinterpreted the meaning of relational development as "dependent," "symbiotic," "deficient," or "weak." Any resulting therapeutic intervention based on this kind of mislabeling is harmful, and can interfere with the traditional acceptable and adaptive values of the Black family. It will also dilute and undermine the establishment of a healthy, productive alliance between the client and the therapist. A major task of the clinician is to learn to understand the client's functioning within her own cultural environment and value system (as well as how she functions within the majority culture) as a "norm." By doing so, the clinician is in a better position to determine mutually with the client the extent of conformity and deviation. To impose a traditional Westernized majority culture set of norms on this client will increase the probability not only of misdiagnosis, but also of mistreatment and a counterproductive therapeutic encounter.

Self-reliance is highly valued and encouraged in African-American families, *but* in a way that will not cut people off from their families, their ethnicity, and their culture. The more African-American families adapt and become upwardly mobile, the higher the probability that they will imitate majority norms. This can result in problematic issues around accommodation, homogenization, perfectionism, superiority, inferiority, and even "passing for white." African-American women will sometimes discriminate against one another based on skin color, hair type, facial contour, physical appearance, socioeconomic status, regional background, and the like. This discrimination is often a reflection of self-hatred, insecurity, and some "superiority." This pattern often mimics the majority culture's way of treating particular ethnic groups. Some Black people use it to elevate their "perceived" status in society.

Therapists must be aware of what I have labeled a "seesaw phenomenon" (Turner, 1984). This is a type of sibling-like rivalry between those inside a culture as well as those in other cultures who receive more "goodies" or favoritism at a given time from the majority culture. This phenomenon occurs among those in the majority culture and between the majority culture and various racial cultures. The rivalry often involves who gets accepted into schools, who gets government and state monies, or, more often, who gets the larger proportion of whatever is valued by both. Meaningful relationships and their consequences are then placed at high risk.

If there is mutual empathy and support from significant others, the related cultures, and society at large, the African-American woman's emotional development is greatly enhanced. A problem area exists, however, if support and validation do not come from these sources; this can cause self-doubts and can lead to the woman's putting herself down, labeling herself as too selfish, and developing insecurities, anxieties, suicidal and/or homicidal ideation, anger, hostility, and self-hatred.

It is not only good to try to understand African-American women in a relational and systemic context relative to their ethnicity, it is vital. If we can understand anything about the legacies of slavery, of African-American families being forcefully and legally torn apart, of the dehumanizing abuses and myths, and of the subtle forms of racism and sexism that are alive and well today, then we can appreciate more easily the necessity of developing and achieving within this relational context for our African-American women clients.

A student in a support group for African-American women that I facilitated a few years ago summed up her "relational self-awareness" this way:

> Whether my family and I are getting along or not, I always carry with me their belief in me and my ability to be whatever I want to be, with the unqualified belief that I will also be successful. I guess I realize how invaluable and important this is to my self-esteem and to my belief in myself that I will have a successful, meaningful life and career. This inner belief bolsters me when I

have a setback or encounter a putdown. I know that if I fail or bring shame in some way to myself, I also bring those negative behaviors onto my family and the African-American race in general. If I succeed, they in some way succeed too.

SUGGESTED CLINICAL GUIDELINES

There will be significant times in the therapeutic relationship when it will become necessary and appropriate to acknowledge the pathology and sickness that exist in our society (as opposed to inside the client) that contribute to additional stress for the African-American woman client. Doing so can help to create a more collaborative and proactive stance with her. In general, there are six important areas to explore as they relate to the woman's identified problem:

(1) how she feels about and experiences her ethnicity, along with her perceptions about how others feel about and experience her ethnicity

(2) her strengths and coping skills in negotiating the "two cultural worlds" in which she lives

(3) those parts of herself that are responding resourcefully to forces both within and outside her control

(4) those parts of herself and her experiences that cause her pain, hurt, and frustration, internally and externally

(5) the interactive parts of herself, family, employment, and social environment that work beneficially for her in fostering healthy growth and change, as well as those that interfere with this healthy process

(6) the extent to which she has acquired internalized and external meaningful connections and bicultural support systems (including the affective and therapeutic connection with the therapist as well as significant others, groups, organizations, religious affiliations, and the like)

These important areas can be missed easily if the therapist does not ask about them. Self-disclosure about these areas usually will not come easily, or at all in many instances. The client is usually aware if there is not a genuine quality of caring and resilience in the clinician and an ability to tolerate learning about these often well-insulated private and conflicting experiences. Too many times, bicultural stress is so time-consuming that these women have to decide if it does any good to share concerns and, if so, with whom. As a basic survival technique, they also learn to set priorities about which issues to put aside and which ones to take a stand on. Some elect to distance themselves from their Blackness and try to "fit in," forgetting that others can still see them as "Black" or African-American. The first case presented below is an example of this behavior.

EXAMPLES OF CLINICAL APPLICATIONS USING RELATIONAL THEORY

Ms. A is a young African-American woman college student who is dark complexioned, extremely bright, and an only child raised from the age of 4 by her upwardly mobile mother alone in a large northern city. She did not seek me out because I was an African-American female therapist; rather, she admitted she was assigned to me against her wishes. She was in a hurry to be seen, and my schedule was the only one that matched hers that particular day in the clinic.

She presented me with relational problems from an argument she had with her three best girlfriends, all of whom were white. They were reportedly "fed up with her arrogance, belittling of them and acting as if she were a Black princess" around them. In a nutshell, she was devastated that they dared to call her "Black," as she did not consider or see herself as Black or African-American, but as a person just like them. They had then stopped speaking to each other. She believed that if she denied her ethnicity, others would do likewise. She had no African-American friends then, nor had she ever been close to any in the past. Not surprisingly, her mother also lived this way and had maintained minimal and perfunctory ties to relatives and had had no contact with her husband since their divorce.

In the counseling clinic, I saw Ms. A eight times that year and four times the following year before she graduated. Since she elected not to have long-term therapy, I used the Stone Center short-term psychodynamic, interactive approach with her. Our time together was focused not only on reconnecting her to her friends, but also on reconnecting her to her ethnic sense of self in a way she had not valued nor taken time to do before. The interchange between us was critical in terms of increasing her ability to connect affectively with me, with other African-American women around her, and with other white women on her dormitory floor in a more appropriate manner. She and I created space in the therapy for her to express hostility directly at me, which she began to see was aimed also at herself. She was pleasantly surprised that I could both empathize with her experience and express my sadness about her ethnic denial without criticizing her. This experience led to a deeper awareness of the parts of herself she had cut off, and prompted her to call her mother one night to share her revelation. She was able to tell her mother directly of her realization that her supercritical attitude toward the behavior of others was due in great part to "not liking herself for being African-American." She and her mother cried together on the phone, and I believe this was a turning point for both of them to use their new "affective connection" to each other (as well as to me) as a lever for change.

In this case, a white clinician could have connected to Ms. A initially, and no doubt would have been seen as a more powerful and desirable person to engage with. I was an unwanted curiosity, but because I did not appear angry, nervous, or defensive, Ms. A began to engage with me. At the time, she perceived herself as "saving me the agony of rejection in front of my white coworkers at the clinic." She felt it would have embarrassed me professionally to have her refuse to continue working with me, as one Black woman rejecting another in favor of a white one. This also would have repeated her father's pattern of rejecting a Black woman for a white one. She had the ability to be humorous as well as hostile, but, more important, she could express a wide range of feelings with which I could begin to connect. The therapy probably could have proceeded with similar benefits with a white clinician who chose to deal with the ambiguities and self-hatred rather than ignore them. It might have been more tempting (and comfortable) to collude with the client and just treat the relationship issue, but the client would then not have had the opportunity to engage the cutoff parts of her reality. As this therapy progressed, it became clear to both of us that the early and unwanted loss of her father to a white woman contributed to her mother's feeling abandoned for "someone perceived to be better than she." It further led to her mother's feeling angry, vulnerable, and "blamed" by her family because she could not hold on to her husband.

It is important to note that African-American women of many hues, from light to dark, can suffer from self-hatred and can identify more strongly with the majority culture than their own for a variety of reasons. Ms. A's experience is neither unique nor isolated.

Ms. B is a young African-American woman in her 20s pursuing an advanced graduate degree. She had not had counseling previously, and, until recently, had not experienced any serious setbacks or difficulties. She is one of several siblings, and the younger daughter of a low-income intact family. One of her brothers has an advanced professional degree, but she will be the first woman in her family to earn one. She presented me with issues of deflated self-esteem, low grades, and the recent news from the dean that the school wanted to "counsel her out of the program" by the end of the current semester. She had failed all of her tests and did not seem to be making a good fit at the school, according to most of her teachers. She was shocked in light of her past achievement in college and her motivation to succeed. She appeared not only deflated but depressed and agitated. She was not suicidal, but very down on herself and very frustrated. She told me she studied religiously and knew her material, but just could not perform when expected to.

After a closer look, I discovered that Ms. B was cut off from any source of emotional, academic, or social support. She studied alone and *never* conversed with any of her teachers or school staff. She could not tell her family about her academic difficulties because she thought it would destroy them. In short, *no one knew what I knew* about this discrepancy between preparation and performance. She felt shame, embarrassment, and a profound sense of failure for letting herself and her family down. There were a handful of African-American women and men and a few more white women in her class, but she did not feel she could confide in any of them, and whenever anyone in her class asked how she was doing, she always responded, "Okay."

I saw Ms. B for a little over a year. I was able to connect with her around her profound isolation and guilt-laden feelings. This helped her to better see how she hid important parts of herself from people all around her. Basic to this was her feeling that she was not accepted as a legitimate member of her school environment. This feeling caused intense anxiety and somatic symptoms. She fostered a perception of not "belonging" or "being valued" that, as it turned out, was shared by a few at the school, but not by everyone. She did have to leave the school for a term; however, she is now re-enrolled there. This time, she has identified and sought out mentors, study groups, an active African-American organization, and a greater sense of "entitlement" to study there as an African-American woman. Fortunately, these activities are reflected in her profession and grades. She has learned to use a number of stress-reduction techniques to move past the anxiety and to relax more. She also knows now that her family loves and respects her, no matter what happens, because she freed herself up to share some of the pressure she felt about being the first woman in her family to achieve professional status. This pressure was tied in with her internal fears about losing her place with them and, in a sense, "leaving them behind." On an affective level, this fear contributed to her depressed feelings, while on a cognitive level, she wanted to believe that they would still love her as they always had. Because she felt vulnerable to the perceived loss of her family, her academic pursuits had been conflicted and inhibited.

This woman offers a prime example of the types of experiences I have seen in a large number of African-American women clients and associates in predominantly white academic and/or work environments. Most of them are very successful in their external achievements but feel diminished, devalued, unappreciated, and mainly "unknown," in a full sense, by those around them. They also fear being distrusted or not fully included in primary family and ethnic relationships since they feel more distanced from them because of their academic pursuits or jobs.

Many of these women report being treated at work or at school as if they are invisible, until someone wants or needs something they can provide. This is further complicated by internal and external perceived losses when prior significant relationships either accommodate to or change due to the women's achievements. The women's reactions range from complete compliance to the expected majority norms to uncontrollable rage because they cannot be their complete selves and do not feel they are vital, welcome additions to the school or organization. If they let these feelings build up inside them too long before expressing them, they are seen as inappropriate, "bad fits," troublemakers, complainers, "bad team players," and the like. It is vital that we provide safe, nonjudgmental environments for these feelings to be aired. Therapists can enhance and positively reinforce their work with these women and others by acknowledging clients' strengths, skills, and achievements, which will in turn strengthen the relational connection between therapists and clients. We also have to try harder to listen and respond in a way that will help empower these women to express to significant others a wide range of feelings and behaviors. This will, in turn, lead to proactive engagement and healthier connections rather than to more isolation and reactive disengagement. These women deserve the opportunity to bring all the meaningful parts of their experiences into processes where they can flourish and be fully accepted for who and what they are as human beings. This is good not only for the women and the clinicians, but also for the schools and organizations of which they are a part. It is the difference between individuals and organizations working together for mutual goals and working alone with separate goals.

The accompanying issue for many African-American women (and men) is the reality of "leaving others behind" and not being meaningfully connected. A struggle ensues to do well, meet new people, and move more comfortably into the majority world while deciding if and how one will give something back to the African-American community and also maintain cherished ties there.

A STRONG RECOMMENDATION FOR CROSS-CULTURAL TRAINING

If a clinician has never received cross-cultural training and decides to serve a racially diverse clientele, such training is a must. To help implement the self-in-relation theoretical approach, I rely quite heavily on strategies developed by other African-American clinicians as adjuncts and tools. Knowledge of cross-cultural counseling techniques is vitally important in working with this population as well as with women from other cultural backgrounds.

Pinderhughes (1982, 1984) has written about the cross-cultural interface among ethnicity, race, and power, and shares theories about knowing how power and powerlessness operate in human systems as keys to effective intervention. She has developed strategies for managing powerlessness constructively on individual, familial, and social systems levels to benefit client and worker. Further, clinicians can use a technique called "ethnotherapy," developed by Price Cobbs (1972), an African-American male psychiatrist based in San Francisco, to sensitize and raise levels of consciousness. This plan involves meeting in groups with others who are racially and ethnically similar to oneself as well as with others who are dissimilar to process feelings about one's own and others' ethnicity. If we can all learn to appreciate, value, and like ourselves—with our similarities and differences—we come that much closer to being receptive in mutually empowering ways to others who are different.

SUMMARY

The Stone Center self-in-relation clinical approach is very useful in working with African-American women as they develop and differentiate themselves in a relational, systemic context within two cultures. This model is a fluid one that sees maximum health as inclusive of all the experiences these women have without labeling their cultural uniqueness as deficient, pathological, or deviant. The process involves seeing development in African-American women in the context of relationships that emphasize being understood, as well as understanding others, in a mutually interactive model. This kind of interaction, in turn, leads to becoming empowered as well as being able to empower others. This dynamic has to occur in the therapeutic alliance if the client is to benefit in her life outside the alliance. It involves attending to this process, together with mutual goal setting, caring, listening, validating, and sharing observations, as well as taking risks in expressing feelings. The process is active, supportive, educational, and systemic. Psychosocial networking is highly encouraged, as this fosters more connections to others and utilizes support systems (including those that are bicultural) as healthy, desirable adjuncts to this type of therapy.

Attention to the organizations in which we work is also important. The sense of being part of relationships is central to all women's sense of self. Yet most institutions do not provide the kinds of relationships that speak to women's needs and experiences. The African-American woman may come from a history of having many ties to her African-American community; then she often encounters a lack of connection when she enters schools or workplaces that doubly devalue her because she is both African-American and female. By becoming aware of the societal, emotional, and institutional pressures that feed these disconnections, we can all be in a better position to address them.

REFERENCES

Cobbs, P. (1972). Ethnotherapy in groups. In L. Soloman & B. Berzon (Eds.), *New perspectives on encounter groups.* San Francisco: Jossey-Bass.

Jordan, J. (1984). *Empathy and self boundaries* (Work in Progress 16). Wellesley, MA: Stone Center for Developmental Services and Studies.

Jordan, J., Surrey, J., & Kaplan, A. G. (1982). *Women and empathy* (Work in Progress 2). Wellesley, MA: Stone Center for Developmental Services and Studies.

Kaplan, A. (1984). *Self in-relation: Implications for depression in women* (Work in Progress 14). Wellesley, MA: Stone Center for Developmental Services and Studies.

Miller, J. B. (1976). *Toward a new psychology of women.* Boston: Beacon.

Pinderhughes, E. (1982, June). Empowerment for our clients and for ourselves. *Social Casework: The Journal of Contemporary Social Work,* pp. 331-338.

Pinderhughes, E. (1984). Teaching empathy: Ethnicity, race and power at the cross-cultural treatment interface. *American Journal of Social Psychiatry, 4*(1), 5-12.

Surrey, J. (1984). *Self in-relation: A theory of women's development* (Work in Progress 13). Wellesley, MA: Stone Center for Developmental Services and Studies.

Turner, C. (1984). *Psychosocial barriers to black women's career development* (Work in Progress 15). Wellesley, MA: Stone Center for Developmental Services and Studies.

FEMINIST PRACTICE
IN A DAY-CARE SETTING

INTRODUCTION

NAOMI GOTTLIEB

The hallmarks of feminist social work practice include the need to demystify the professional relationship, to decrease the power differential between worker and client as much as possible, and, as stated in this book's introduction, to encourage the "practitioners' consciousness of their common ground" with the client. Implied in each of these ideals is that the worker has come to some increased understanding of women in society and then takes the initiative in making appropriate changes in practice to reflect that consciousness. With all of our good intentions, that stance conveys a subtle demeaning of the women with whom we work, as if we are always the teachers of feminism.

Bernice Liddie offers us another model. In her case study, she tells us of the learning she experienced in her work with the mothers of children in a day-care setting. As a result of that work, she gained a clearer appreciation for the strengths and survival powers of women even in the harshest circumstances. She also could see these women more clearly as individuals and not as persons in their prescribed roles. Also, acknowledging her own homophobia, she learned not only about accepting differences between lesbians and heterosexual women, but, more creatively, about celebrating those differences.

Liddie's chapter illustrates another dynamic as well. By empowering this group of mothers to be assertive with the day-care center staff, she found that the staff, in turn, learned assertiveness from them. Developing a sense of their own power, the staff used that assertiveness to improve their own working situation with the agency's administration. Learning can go in many directions, and empowerment, fortunately, appears to be contagious.

Rules for the Poor

Carie Winslow

Buy white bread.
Don't borrow money from friends.
If you borrow money;
                lie if you had fun with it.
                      Don't get angry.
Don't forget to feel guilty for being born poor and lazy.
Don't be too conspicuous when you get in for free.
Don't forget to grovel if someone pays for you.
Don't assume that you have a right to anything.
and . . .   Don't get angry.
Don't ever let your kids miss school
                have runny noses,
                or stained clothes.
Don't buy fresh fruit or vegetables.
Don't make any mistakes.
and . . .   Don't get angry.
Don't look too apologetic
                or arrogant
        Someone may suspect you of stealing something.
Don't talk about money.
Don't ever ask someone how much they make.
Don't talk to other poor people.
and . . .   Don't get angry!
Keep rubbing those pennies together.
Follow all of these rules for at least a year.
                BE SURE NOT TO GET ANGRY!
Soon,
        before you even notice it . . .
Bitterness will replace unease.
Fear will replace dreams.
You will forget who you were.
You will forget who you wanted to be.
You won't be a threat to anyone.

Chapter 6

RELEARNING FEMINISM ON THE JOB

BERNICE W. LIDDIE

If you asked a group of feminist social workers about the development of their feminist thinking and its effect on their practice, the chances are that most would say that the journey is an ever-changing one. Some readings or events or series of circumstances, often personal but sometimes professional, lead to additional insights about women in society and alter our work with women. However, even as we shift and deepen our thinking about women in society, it is infrequent that we clearly acknowledge the direct impact of women clients on the development of our professional thinking. Usually, the direction is the other way—our new insights, developed in other arenas, are then applied to professional work with our clients.

This chapter describes my learning more about feminism and diversity from a group of women clients in a professional setting, with the potential now of carrying that learning into more informed work with other women. A description of the setting for those changes and my prior development as a Black professional woman are the starting points of the description of my journey. My interactions with a group of moderate- to low-income mothers whose children were in a day-care setting are the context for the movement in my thinking about women and diversity. I will describe that interactive process of learning from clients as well as the long-term effects on my continued work with other women clients.

The description of the group's activities is the other major purpose of the chapter. A group of women who saw themselves as disempowered, fearful, and inadequate moved to a very different self-perception and, in the process, implemented several social action projects to improve their own circumstances.

THE SETTING

Union Child Day Care Center, Inc. (Union, to most) was in its twelfth year of operation when I came on as a social worker. Union is located in suburban upstate New York, in a predominantly Black community. It was organized to provide professional day care for young children from infancy through the early elementary years. The majority of the children's mothers have always had to work and leave their children during their working hours. Establishment of a day-care center was one of the first major projects undertaken by the people living in this small community. The purpose was twofold: to provide a needed service and to help raise the community out of neglect and despair. The service was available to all the area's families, and the day-care population represented a wide range of ethnic and socioeconomic backgrounds.

My previous work experience had been in a residential treatment center and in foster care. The children in those settings had also been left by their parents for daily care, but sometimes some of those parents had been either unwilling or unable to pick them up at the end of the day. The faces of those children almost always appeared sad and angry—few smiles, even fewer words—just sad, angry faces. Somehow, being at the Union day-care center felt different and better for me. This program was not aimed at replacing the parents; rather, it was designed to help parents care for their children while they worked, went to school, or were otherwise unable to be at home during the day. The mission statement proposed that the center "provide good group day care services to strengthen family life through the integration of education, social services and health programs to serve the best interests of children, parents and the community."

The particular setting for my work at Union was the Parent Participation Project for Effective Family Living (PPPEFL), the aim of which was to provide a dimension of help that went beyond the scope of the traditional goals of the day-care program. The context of my enhanced learning about feminism and diversity was my work with a white female coleader for one of the groups of women in this project.

PERSONAL AND PROFESSIONAL BACKGROUND

My entry into this setting was part of my life as a Black woman raised by a very caring, supportive mother, whose ideas and behavior closely resembled those of a feminist. I have lived in a community where women worked together for the good of the neighborhood and the community in a supportive, nonhierarchical, noncompetitive manner. Two professional relationships were particularly useful to my growth. In the late 1970s, during my graduate education at Columbia University, I worked with a white female field instructor who exhibited the sensitivity, insight, and commitment needed to tackle the tough issues related to women and children (intellectually and behaviorally, individually and institutionally). I did not have this kind of experience in the classroom. I also worked with a Black male physician who fostered an atmosphere of egalitarianism in the workplace as well as in the community. Important changes were possible also from other personal and professional relationships with women of several ethnic, religious, and sexual orientations throughout my career.

The work at Union represented another opportunity for me to assess continually my own circumstances, including the opportunities, choices, and benefits I have achieved as results of all these and other experiences. Writing now about my feminist practice experience is yet another context for reassessment. As I do this, I am also sadly reminded of the fact that while I have had the good fortune of personal and professional growth, there are still far too many women who have faced tremendous barriers in their efforts toward self-actualization.

For me, oppression has a double meaning, both as a female and as a Black woman in a society that has often been insensitive, often hostile, too often racist. Both in work with others and with clients, I approached my practice with a focus on women. It has been possible for me, both at "home" and in Africa, to identify and address issues that prevent a fulfilling life for all, especially for women. I have done this at the grass-roots level by incorporating community organization and consciousness-raising activities with groups in Kenya, Ethiopia, and

Ghana, where I worked in mother-child health programs. These same approaches have been applicable in my professional employment in this country as a clinician, administrator, and educator. My training in two traditional professions, nursing and social work, also played some part in my definition of feminism as it related to the pervasive oppression of women and people of color in the United States.

As an active registered nurse, I was taught that my role was to help the sick patient. Then as a social worker, I learned to be concerned about and involved in the interactions between people and social institutions that can affect people's ability to accomplish life tasks, realize their aspirations, live by their values, and alleviate distress (Pincus & Minahan, 1973). All of these relationships, events, and experiences and some aspects of my professional education are important to the meaning of feminism in my life and practice.

THE GROUP'S PURPOSE AND MEMBERSHIP

The project with the day-care mothers as part of the PPPEFL at Union grew out of a need identified by a group coleader, parents, day-care teachers, and myself. My coworker had worked at a local psychiatric center and was a day-care consultant to parents and day-care teachers. The new program was to be a nontraditional group that would meet the needs of the women and enhance the various roles fulfilled by them (i.e., mothers, wives, lovers, daughters, wage earners, church members, and unrecognized cowriters of dissertations). Members would be encouraged to express their unmet needs and to use self-help as a coping strategy. Techniques of consciousness-raising were to be introduced and utilized at various points.

Specific objectives of the PPPEFL were to provide the following supports:

(1) supportive opportunities to increase self-awareness, including awareness of the individual's value systems and cultural strengths, which would heighten the ability and willingness to take greater responsibility for self and family members and would ultimately benefit the community

(2) social and educational opportunities to alleviate social isolation and increase the range of resources available to enhance individual and family functioning, as well as the functioning of the larger community

   (3) identification of underused/unavailable community resources in re-
     sponse to unmet needs, including strategies for social action and com-
     munity change

   (4) for group members in crisis situations, time-limited individual counsel-
     ing not appropriate for the group

   (5) formation of a food co-op to be managed by group members (a project
     funded in full through a grant from the New York State Division for
     Youth for one year, with the understanding that subsequent funding
     would require matching funds)

Many, although not all, of the families who used the Union day-
care services were headed by women solely responsible for arrang-
ing and supporting their child care. Others were sharing parenting
with spouses, significant others, and extended family members.

I remember well the many faces rushing past me each morning as I
greeted parents, mostly women, bringing their children to the day-
care program. The faces were of many shapes, shades, and hues, although most wore the same expression—one of stress. The mothers
usually greeted me quietly. Their smiles to me disappeared all too
quickly as they raced down the hallways to deliver their children to
the day-care workers, equally as stressed, who would take over the
children's care for the next 10 hours.

The children all seemed to be running, their little legs and feet not
quite able to keep up with the big steps taken by their mothers—their
agendas so very different. Mom would be off to take another bus on
her journey to work, while her children were off for another day of
"self-discovery." There seemed little time during this morning rush
for anything other than quick messages: Behave yourself today, Patty;
Remember the tissues in your pocket, Omar; You listen to the teacher
today, Yolanda; Make sure you eat all your lunch, Hans; Yes, I'll be
back to pick you up tonight, Mary.

The messages were given to the children, who were by now out of
earshot, some at the water table, talking with their friends, or sitting
in their "cubby space," some caught up in their own sorrow of being
without mom for another day. The mothers' messages seemed more
for the teachers than for the children—messages left in the hopes that
they conveyed the love they felt for the children they had to leave for
the day. The routine was the same, the process ever changing.

These were mothers struggling, day after day, to respond to the
many demands in their lives. Many began their days by responding to

alarms ringing at 5:30 a.m. and pre⟩ aring themselves and their children for the demands of day care, the workplace, and domestic chores in the evening, as well as meeting demands of the larger community. All of these demands left very little opportunity or energy to reflect on and meet their own needs in a meaningful way.

The rewards for these women in the workplace continued to be elusive and were not tied to their efforts. Most often, they received minimum salaries; few, if any, opportunities for upward mobility, security, or stability within the job; and a great deal of stress attributable to their position, gender, and/or race. For some, when upward mobility occurred, it came at great expense, because it often meant a slight increase in salary and a large decrease in day-care "scholarship awards." For example, an increase in pay of $500.00 per year most often raised the cost of day care from $25.00 to $75.00 per week. Trying to surmount rising costs of living and gaps in support from family networks, these women were struggling with problems that threatened their individuality, their families, and their lives in the community.

THE GROUP'S ACTIVITIES

Over a 3-year period, an average of 25 women participated actively at any given time in the formal group structure. Meetings were held each Tuesday from 5:30 to 8:30 p.m. The women's presence at these meetings, in light of the myriad pressures they encountered, was clearly an indication of the importance of this experience to them. The group was diverse and included several ethnic and religious groups, approximately 60% women of color, and 4 lesbian women. The economic situations of the group members also varied: Some received supplementary income maintenance, while others' salaries supplemented their husbands' incomes.

As members moved to the point where they felt able to leave the group or left for other reasons, such as job relocation, pregnancy, or educational opportunities, new members were added through outreach to other mothers of the day-care center community who could use the services.

All the women expressed feelings of being overwhelmed with the struggles of meeting daily basic needs for themselves, their children and partners, their work, and, often, the needs of others in the "extended family," including nonfamily members in the community.

They felt "inadequate," "inferior," "frustrated," "helpless," "alone," and "spiritually drained." Although these women exhibited many strengths, they were also in need of additional supports, such as family planning, job training and placement, counseling about personal and professional situations, opportunities to develop additional parenting skills, and a basic understanding of their individual strengths and needs, and their roles in relation to self, family, and community. We felt it was crucial to help them understand the oppressive systems operating in their lives, preventing or intruding on their efforts toward greater control and self-fulfillment. Techniques of consciousness-raising were introduced and utilized at various points throughout the project.

We intended to provide a dimension of help that went beyond the scope of the traditional goals of the day-care program, particularly by reinforcing the concept of empowerment. As I will later describe, this emphasis on specific empowerment practices, particularly for social action, appeared to have a more profound impact on these women's lives than a more traditional approach to individual problems would have had.

The friendships that developed both within and outside of the group seemed to be based on the many similarities shared by the group members. Each was struggling with handling home and work and meeting family needs with very few resources. Differences were also identified and initially broached in a cautious, superficial manner. These differences covered many issues, such as conflicts over the direction the group would take, the size of the group, forms of discipline with children, and, for heterosexual women, attitudes and stereotypes of self and lesbian members. Over time, these issues and others became a natural part of our discussions. While consensus or changes in attitudes were not always easy to come by, a level of respect translated into a supportive group process.

Fear of rejection was a major theme in the early stages of the group. Members expressed feelings of rejection time and time again. Members and leaders spent considerable time in the beginning sessions relating and exploring situations that had contributed to and reinforced those feelings, including the experience of rejection from the day-care staff. Throughout all of the meetings, the need for acceptance of words and behaviors became a focal point in moving the group toward personal and collective growth.

A particular focus of concern was interaction with the day-care staff. The women were bothered by what they perceived as the staff's expectations for their parenting skills and life-styles. They reacted to decisions being foisted on them and their children by the staff and felt labeled as "troublemakers," "irrational," and "uncooperative" if they questioned staff members. We saw evidence that staff frustrations were sometimes inappropriately vented on these women and their children.

Group members frequently said that day care was a necessary and valuable resource. However, they often felt overburdened by the expectations of the staff. Staff members kept after them about drop-off and pickup schedules, criticized the way the children were dressed, reprimanded the mothers about overdue accounts, and recounted their children's unruly behavior to the mothers. Story after story revealed the same concerns, and the response was usually the same: I'm doing the best I can, but I'm always expected to do more.

Mothers also felt left out of the program's decisions. Directives regarding what was needed in the program, what should be done about those needs, and where children should be placed in the program were being made without serious input from the mothers. They expressed fears of being oppressed when not allowed to participate in the planning for the children. Child-care staff, on the other hand, many of whom had worked at the day-care center for several years, felt that they were "the authority" in terms of child care and parenting, and should be in a position to have the final word.

In view of the mothers' pervasive sense of lack of control over their major life circumstances and these particular concerns about powerlessness vis-à-vis the day-care staff, several strategies to encourage empowerment were implemented. As we initiated these strategies, I made connections to other experiences in my life and my own learning about women was enhanced.

STRATEGIES FOR EMPOWERMENT

As I listened to these women, I realized that their concerns were similar to those of other women with whom I had worked and socialized. In fact, their expectations were very much like those that many women, including my mother, had attempted to meet all their lives. These expectations required women to respond continually to the needs of others, often to the exclusion of their own needs.

The women in the group, as well as others I have known, expressed a need for self-development. However, most felt this was inconsistent with the expressed norms within the culture and within the larger society. None felt that they would receive consistent support for these feelings from significant persons in their lives. All seemed to be locked into gender roles that had been prescribed for them at a very early age, some more subtly than others. For many of the Black women in the group, these stereotypes, their perceptions of the prescribed identity, and the expectations others had for them seemed to have a profound effect on their self-identity, aspirations, and expectations. bell hooks (1981) states:

> Racist stereotypes of the strong, superhuman Black woman are operative myths in the mind of many white women (and men), allowing them to ignore the extent to which Black women are likely to be victimized in this society and the role white women (and men) may play in the maintenance and perpetuation of that victimization. (p. 13)

White women in the group, similarly victimized by the oppressive practices within our society, also expressed their dissatisfaction with their life situations. Many said they felt overburdened with the traditional demands of the wife/mother role and the experiences of sexism in their daily lives. Often they described these roles as conflicting and irreconcilable.

The victimization and stereotyping inherent in traditional expectations of all women, but especially limiting in the vulnerable status of women of color and poor women, caused these women to question consistently their own worth. When we would point out their strengths to them, they would say, "That's nothing." Yet they would talk with admiration about similar abilities shown by other women in the same circumstances. It seemed that they could not accept their own strengths—not would not, but could not. Their self-perceptions were skewed, despite evidence to the contrary. If we commented on some actions they took in light of the few options offered to them, we discovered that they could not acknowledge the strengths inherent in their actions, despite the odds, nor did they feel that they had a right to protest the very limiting hostile environment. If we asked them about themselves, they would respond by describing something about their roles—mother, wife, partner. If we persisted by asking about their own needs and their own dreams, a typical response was: "I don't have dreams. I have no time for them." Keller (1974) notes that "sex roles become firmly locked into the psychic system, forming a permanent screen through which to perceive and experience the world" (p. 412). The experiences with this group of women enabled me to see the debilitating effects of restrictive gender roles more clearly than I had before.

Underlying the planning and implementation of the group's activities was the goal of promoting individual growth while engaging in group action. We believed, and acted on the belief, that each member had something to offer that would result in her own growth, contribute to that of others in the group, and ultimately result in some positive changes in the community, including the day-care program itself. Many of the strategies we developed in the group were intended to increase the women's sense of self and their autonomous actions. We placed emphasis on the women's taking concrete steps to improve their life situations, not just expressing their feelings in the group.

My coleader and I initiated a series of exercises designed to enable the women to move from the helplessness they felt at the outset toward some successful accomplishments. For this purpose, we used a combination of cognitive- and task-oriented work. We examined with them where their self-beliefs and frustrations came from. We continually emphasized that they were worthy and had a right to confront and change a hostile environment. We consistently pointed to their strengths and used those identified strengths to teach them techniques to negotiate the system differently. We used role play extensively in planning, rehearsing, and later evaluating particular tasks, and we tried to instill hope in the possibility of change.

We suggested ways for the women to avoid people who made them feel less than they were. If they were stuck in blaming the racist society, we practiced with them ways to confront racism openly and not to be afraid of anger. In becoming more assertive, the women also talked about their fear of reinforcing the "Black bitch" stereotype, which they considered dangerous. We tried to help them see the origin of this stereotype and reinforced their right to meet their own needs for autonomy.

In our own behaviors, we tried to reduce the status differentials between ourselves and the women. We joined them in some community activities, such as church attendance. I needed to confront my own assumptions about the backgrounds of these women, and worked to reduce the social distance between us, partly by being aware of the particular experiences that informed their views. One way to do this conversationally was to refer to the TV programs they knew, rather than to plays I had seen.

For several of the members, this program was their first opportunity to work in a collaborative effort. Several of the group's efforts were noteworthy. First, they were successful in establishing a food cooperative. Out of this experience, the women could see and appropriately respond to the exploitative, sexist, and patronizing behavior of the merchants (male) we encountered weekly at the market. At first, the women felt it was all right for me but not for them to confront the merchants because I was educated and could "use the right words." With practice of their assertions and confrontations, they were able to act on their own. Through the food co-op experience, they also gained an increased sense of independence, which was accepted and supported by others, and a sense of power as they gained greater control over how and where they spent their money.

The other collaborative effort was the successful organization of 500 community members to march on city hall to protest cuts in day-care funding. Other projects, such as a food fair, a job fair (which resulted in nontraditional jobs for some members), theater parties, children's shows, yearly picnics, and several fund-raisers to continue the project, were entered into with equal enthusiasm and confidence.

Another major area of the group's assertion and action focused on the day-care staff. As noted earlier, the women had felt intimidated by and resentful of the day-care program staff. In group discussions, plans were made for several meetings, mutually agreed upon, with the day-care staff. This was an effort to move toward a more workable relationship, and the mothers were enabled to speak about their feelings of powerlessness and inadequacy vis-à-vis the staff.

Initially, there was some resistance among the women to expressing their concerns, particularly about staff behavior and performance. Comments such as "I don't want this to get back to her and have her take it out on my child" reflected this apprehension. Assurances that teachers were concerned about their ability to work more effectively within the classroom seemed to allay the mothers' fears and allowed them to express concerns as well as possible solutions, including a mutual working relationship. The result was a much more satisfactory experience for the workers, the mothers, and the children.

As a latent function of these interactions with the staff, the group's input served as an impetus for staff members themselves to confront the director and the board members regarding issues directly related to their work within the program. This increased the staff's sense of empowerment vis-à-vis the administration and, in turn, the day-care staff recognized the strengths of the mothers to a greater extent.

The process within the mothers' group was intended in itself to be empowering. During the course of the weekly meetings in which all these activities were planned, members would make their own decisions about various group activities: planning the next week's agenda, inviting guest speakers, preparing dinner, assigning cleanup chores, devising fund-raisers and other income-generating projects. They would decide about attendance in day-care board meetings, participation in food co-op activities, plans for social and educational events for members and their children, participation in outreach efforts, meeting with local politicians, working with day-care staff on mutually agreed-upon activities, and speaking to other day-care programs regarding PPPEFL.

LEARNING FROM THE WOMEN

I have long been familiar with some of the earlier writings about oppression and feminism (e.g., Friedan, 1963; Giddings, 1984; Hooks, 1981; Ladner, 1971) and have debated, redebated, and sometimes resolved some issues related to various forms of therapy and gender-role stereotyping. I have become strongly committed to several points of view espoused by many feminist therapists I have encountered, though my approaches have varied somewhat according to the population I am working with; the issues, needs, and choices presented; the social context; institutional realities reflecting oppression in various forms; and the adaptive strengths of each individual in responding to his or her particular circumstances. I have also tried to integrate feminist theory with the traditional concepts of systems theory.

Analyses of women in society and challenges to traditional therapies had been part of my orientation before I started to work with these women. Existing literature testifies to the oppression of women and other groups in American life (Block, 1973; Chesler, 1972; hooks, 1981; Kravetz, 1976b). Social workers, too, have maintained the norms of the larger society, viewing many individual behaviors as "sick," including those behaviors that are used to deal with life pressures. If the norms are oppressive (i.e., institutional racism, sexism, ageism, homophobia, and classism), then social work can be seen as oppressive or, at the very least, as an agent of oppression if it follows those norms. As Kravetz (1976a) points out regarding the oppression of women, many popular and professional journals "have criticized mental health professionals for helping to perpetuate an adjustment-oriented system that severely limits women's opportunities for personal growth and participation in society" (p. 422). Traditional methods of interacting with clients limit practitioners in their efforts to change women's situations personally, socially, and economically.

Social work has often adopted sexist theoretical frameworks upon which to base its array of services. Psychoanalytic theory, the basis for most caseworkers' orientations, has for a number of years been questioned for its gender bias, sex-role stereotyping, and class bias, coming as it did from the European middle-class male perspective. Women are consistently presented in the theory as innately passive, dependent, anatomically inferior, and emotionally immature (Kravetz, 1976a, 1976b; Sturdivant, 1980). The values and premises inherent in such theoretical ideas fail to take into account women's realities and perpetuate the current state of discrimination against women.

Situations in which the client is viewed as being the "owner" of his or her behavior and therefore responsible for his or her life circumstances often focus on changing that individual's behavior. This negates the impact of external factors that impinge on the individual's efforts to cope. Many critics of traditional theories and practice point out that we need to look beyond the individual client to the roles of those institutions that are responsible for, or at the very least perpetuate, the debilitating pressures on women's lives.

In working with families who are living in marginal conditions, professionals often find it easy to focus on the problem areas while ignoring environmental factors. This prevents clients from feeling empowered enough to recognize their own strengths to change the systems around them. We were also taught that although institutional change was necessary, it took a long time, so that, in the meantime, we were to use strategies and interventions to help people adapt to their current conditions. However, to alter the client's oppressive personal, social, and economic situation in a positive way, social workers can use methods to produce institutional changes in the near future, preferably through encouraging clients to exert pressure for those changes themselves.

There is considerable literature about how Black community members have done much to help themselves in altering the status quo. Authors such as Billingsley (1968), Hill (1972), McAdoo (1981), Sudarkasa (1981), Stack (1974), and Martin and Martin (1985) have written about the reality of Black families, demonstrating the myriad strengths inherent in individuals and communities that have been utilized in a positive manner to better their social, economic, and environmental situations. The many empowering, self-actualizing actions engaged in by Black women have included moving from the welfare rolls into the work force, forming women's groups for mutual support, forming and supporting informal child-care activities, and organizing in the community for improved educational and health services.

All of these convictions—about the need to change oppressive conditions, the inadequacy of previous explanations for the condition of women, the challenges to those explanations, and the need for empowerment strategies—were part and parcel of my approach to the women at Union as we began our work. Interactions with these women deepened my understanding of women in society and strengthened my convictions about an even more conscious use of feminist principles in my practice.

I became more acutely aware of the strengths of women who survive in extremely debilitating circumstances and still cannot see and take credit for those strengths. Two aspects of these experiences will be useful in my future work with women clients. The first is the importance of eliciting a clear accounting of these strengths from women, despite their disclaimers and hesitancies. This may mean probing for specifics, perhaps with repeated playback to them so that they can see and incorporate the meaning of their accomplishments. Women may then be able to redefine their behaviors so that they can see their value. Second, it will be important to encourage women to use those strengths to change their circumstances. In the process, they may have the experience of working collaboratively with others as well as understanding how changes in institutions and policies can, in turn, alter their personal conditions.

Another aspect of learning for me was an increased ability to see women not just in their prescribed roles, but as individuals. Gender-role stereotyping, which is ingrained in all of us, encases women in their roles, particularly family roles, and is very difficult to escape.

A woman is always someone's daughter, or wife, or mother. As we questioned the women in this group to look to their own needs and consider their own dreams, I was more impressed than I had been both with the need for women to do this and with the inherent difficulty of doing so. Many women come to us because of their difficulty in relationships and in fulfilling society's expectations of them in their roles, and it is easy for us to see them primarily in those roles. It takes special effort to see the women as separate individuals whose ideas and wishes for themselves may go beyond, as well as encompass, the lives of those close to them.

Another very important part of my learning concerned the lesbian women in the group. Like most people, I had been affected by this society's homophobia, but as I began the work on this project, I felt I could acknowledge and accept the "differences" in these women compared with heterosexual women. In the process of encouraging the heterosexual women in the group to deal with their homophobia, and as we all listened attentively to the experiences of the lesbians, an important change occurred for me. I found I could move from the simple acceptance of difference to the more important valuing of the differences that the lesbian women represent. This moved me from a stance of tolerance closer to one of true respect.

CONCLUSION

The practice experience I have described within one day-care setting suggests many applications for transforming child-care programs into a feminist environment beneficial to mothers, children, and personnel who work in centers. Child care, a paramount issue in the feminist movement, must not only become available to all women who need this service, but it should be provided within a feminist model. That model has the potential for changing women's consciousness and enabling women to take part in collaborative social action to change their environment as they empower themselves.

This practice experience is also an example of the possibility of renewal and change in one's own feminist thinking and the power of the women with whom we work to have such an impact on us. We tend to think of the empowerment of clients only in terms of their individual thinking and behavior. We may need a greater appreciation for their empowerment to change us.

REFERENCES

Billingsley, A. (1968). *Black families in white America*. Englewood Cliffs, NJ: Prentice-Hall.

Block, J. (1973). Conceptions of sex roles: Some cross-cultural and longitudinal perspectives. *American Psychologist, 28*, 512-526.

Chesler, P. (1972). *Women and madness*. New York: Avon.

Friedan, B. (1963). *The feminine mystique*. New York: Norton.

Giddings, P. (1984). *When and where I enter: The impact of black women on race and sex in America*. New York: Bantam.

Hill, R. B. (1972). *The strengths of black families*. New York: Emerson Hall.

hooks, b. (1981). *Ain't I a woman: Black women and feminism*. Boston: South End.

Keller, S. (1974). The female role: Constants and change. In V. Franks & V. Burtle (Eds.), *Women in therapy* (pp. 411-434). New York: Brunner/Mazel.

Kravetz, D. (1976a). Consciousness-raising groups and group psychotherapy: Alternative mental health resources for women. *Psychotherapy: Theory, Research and Practice, 13*(1), 66-71.

Kravetz, D. (1976b). Sexism in a women's profession. *Social Work, 21*, 421-426.

Ladner, J. (1971). *Tomorrow's tomorrow: The black woman*. Garden City, NY: Anchor.

Martin, J., & Martin, E. (1985). *The helping tradition in the black family and community*. Silver Spring, MD: National Association of Social Workers.

McAdoo, H. P. (Ed.). (1981). *Black families*. Beverly Hills, CA: Sage.

Pincus, A., & Minahan, A. (1973). *Social work practice: Model and method*. Itasca, IL: F. E. Peacock.

Stack, C. B. (1974). *All our kin: Strategies for survival in a black community*. New York: Harper & Row.

Sturdivant, S. (1980). *Therapy with women: A feminist philosophy of treatment*. New York: Springer.

Sudarkasa, N. (1981). Interpreting the African heritage in Afro-American family organization. In H. P. McAdoo (Ed.), *Black families*. Beverly Hills, CA: Sage.

Social Security

Barbara Bolz

She knows a cashier who
blushes and lets her use
food stamps to buy tulip
bulbs and rose bushes.

We smile each morning as I
pass her—her hand always
married to some stick
or hoe, or rake.

One morning I shout,
"I'm not skinny like
you so I've gotta run
two miles each day."

She begs me closer, whispers
to my flesh, "All you need,
honey, is to be on welfare
and love roses."

Previously published in Sandra Martz
(Ed.), *When I Am Old I Shall Wear Purple*, 1987. Reprinted by permission of
Papier-Mâché Press and the author.

FEMINIST PRACTICE
IN RURAL COMMUNITIES

INTRODUCTION

NAOMI GOTTLIEB

Joanne Mermelstein's chapter accomplishes a number of purposes. She reminds us that rural social work practice is an important part of our profession, although it has often received short shrift in our professional deliberations. She demonstrates needed sensitivity to the core of such practice—the recognition that rural communities have distinctive norms of living. Those norms require respect at all times, but especially so during the current farm crisis, which is the context of Mermelstein's work.

She makes the creative connection between rural social work practice and a feminist approach, illustrating, as did Garry as well as Rathbone-McCuan and her associates in earlier chapters, that feminist practice can be instituted and can thrive in a diversity of settings, each with its own conventions and restrictions. Mermelstein also details the commonalities between rural and feminist practice, enlarging the possibilities for their coexistence. She describes and advocates the potential for developing the strengths of women in the milieu of the farm family with traditional gender norms.

Mermelstein's additional contributions include discussion of the responsibility of feminist social workers for the education of other professionals about the needs and potential of women and a detailed description of the implementation of such education.

Those Womyn

Marilyn Mesh

She was a farmer
organic farmer of watermelons
peas
potatoes
beans
squash
sometimes five or six or seven womyn farmed
sometimes fewer.
There were men also.
Four or five men
But background, they were background
Like the gnats that buzzed around her legs.

It was the womyn
who pulled her
shaped her
as the tractor shaped
the hills and rows for planting
planting
planting her love of womyn
in thick rich soil of solid bodies
strong arms
tender tears
in the sandy soil loaded with chicken shit
and days of heat
pungent bodies
and loose dirt between her bare toes.

It was that farm
fields surrounded by oaks and pines
pecans and chinaberry trees,
watermelon rows stretched long   thin
their end distant
to the tired arms holding hoes
hoes that sharpened
sharpened against the coffee weed
sharpened against her grain
raised on men
raised on TV
raised to marry
sharpened her longing for womyn into movement
as the martins dip and swoop
eating twice their weight in mosquitoes daily,
sharpened her longing for womyn into awareness
as the hands
that tossed melons
dug potatoes
drove a tractor
yearned to touch
those womyn.

Chapter 7

FEMINIST PRACTICE
IN RURAL SOCIAL WORK

JOANNE MERMELSTEIN

PRACTICE SETTING

Rural social work was not my planned career choice. Rather, a series of personal decisions, beginning with the selection of a rurally located state university for my graduate education, changed my ideas about the alien but appealing rural world. Subsequent events kept me "outstate," the sociological descriptor for locales outside metropolitan areas. When one is outstate and outside, employment-pattern deviance seems logical as well. In contrast to the predominant employment pattern of professional mobility, the institutional sanction and auspices for the 30 years of my professional practice has come from one source: the state land-grant university referred to above. The University of Missouri legitimated my entry into a diverse range of practice settings, including the medical and psychiatric service units of the university hospital and medical school; the chronic wards of a rural state hospital; inpatient and outpatient services of a rural public acute mental health facility; a rural community mental health center; the training units of the state child welfare and probation/parole agencies; the personnel office of state government; and, most recently, the Rural Crisis Task Force of the University of Missouri Extension Service.

The chronology of these settings reflects two themes in my personal/professional evolution as a feminist and social worker. The first theme is my commitment to rural people. Rural residents three decades ago, as now, were systematically disadvantaged by economic and social policies and processes predicated on an urban society. My growing appreciation of what that meant in the daily lives of people paralleled and frequently overlapped the second theme, which is the effort to apply an emerging feminist worldview to the assessment of rural social phenomena.

In trying to find solutions to the problems I confronted early in my career in clinical mental health settings, I became aware of the weaknesses of a single-method approach to practice. Institutional and societal preconditions that led to many of the behaviors that we were to control or treat were never addressed. The second theme inherent in the sequence of practice settings then was the development and implementation of a new practice model that fit the context. Since rural residents generally, and rural women particularly, formed an oppressed population, the practice model had to be attentive to that concern. My particular brand of rural generalist practice evolved as the contextually specific answer to the need for a "better way." Once I grasped the fundamentals of this practice model and observed its efficacy, I chose to enter practice settings where it could be fully exploited.

The practice model of the rural generalist is capable of embracing any goal appropriate to empowerment of people; it is applicable to both feminist and general rural issues. My personal integration of feminism and rural social work practice was further enhanced by the fact that both became social movements in their own rights (granted, the latter in a far more modest way than the former), illuminating at a societal level the essential similarities of the value systems they espoused.

This chapter is an attempt to demonstrate the interface of feminism and rural social work. The conclusion that they interface and overlap derives from my personal experience with both as intellectual streams and as social movements. From that unique frame of reference, I will briefly trace their historical and developmental parallels, highlighting their converging value positions. Based on these similarities, I will argue that the practice model of rural generalist can be employed to serve the goals and purposes of both. Drawing on my current practice endeavors in Missouri's rural crisis, the chapter will conclude with a case example demonstrating the integration of feminism and rural social work.

The reader is cautioned that rural social workers of my generation do not come to feminist practice from the same place, psychologically or

experientially, that younger or urban-oriented clinicians do. Both the
rural and the historical contexts in which we matured professionally
irretrievably altered the route. What follows underscores that distinction as well.

FEMINISM: THE PERSONAL TERRAIN

I believe that modern feminism is essentially a philosophy, or
value constellation, that upholds the freedom of a woman to choose
her own life path to self-actualization, to create and inhabit her own
dreams of the desirable, to discover and reconcile the consequences
of life choices for herself (Bricker-Jenkins & Hooyman, 1984;
Friedan, 1963; Mander & Rush, 1974; Van Den Bergh & Cooper,
1987; Wetzel, 1986). To achieve this ideal in a society in which social
and economic policy, political power, accepted history, tradition, and
many social conventions restrained, conditioned, or forcefully prevented it, a social movement was required. The feminist movement is
thus the translation of a worldview and an ideology into the means of
social change (Berg, 1978; Cott, 1986; Delmar, 1986; Freeman, 1987;
Friedan, 1981).

Part of the social revolution focused on development of a theoretical
base for feminism (Kantor, 1975; Rosenberg, 1982). Contemporary feminist theory rendered topsy-turvy the prevailing understanding of *why* social
structures are the way they are. Applying economic and political explanations to what were formerly classified as biological and cultural
phenomena, feminist theory not only disassembles but competes with
the basic paradigm of how society *should* be structured, implicating immediately the supraordinate system of any society, the family (Beard,
1946; Kingston, 1977; Millett, 1970; Rich, 1976). The altered perception of *why* women and men are interrelated in particular societal patterns spawned previously unthinkable concepts that centered on the
notion of women as an oppressed minority, savaged by the very societal
institutions and processes that purport to protect, value, and enhance their
well-being (Ballou & Gabalac, 1985; Brownmiller, 1975; Dworkin,
1974).

This political and intellectual ferment was the backdrop for my professional development. As a neophyte academic and beginning professional social worker during the rise of feminism in the 1960s, I
relished the burgeoning intellectual ferment and found comfort in resis-

tance to the old stereotypes. Affective learning, through what later was termed "consciousness-raising," had begun for me in the 1950s when my father's death at an early age left my mother socially and economically devastated. Men whom my father trusted to care for his family sacrificed honor for personal gain. The experience became the central lesson of my adolescence and the single most crucial motivator of my young adult life choices. Those choices, for economic self-sufficiency, were deviant in the cultural context of that period. Combining marriage, motherhood, and a profession was not the norm in a conservative Catholic environment. Ironically, I was helped by the double-bind communication experience of my education in exclusively female schools, where an ambivalent faculty modeled self-sufficient (deviant) roles in contradiction to the socialization pattern of female dependency inherent in the dominant paradigm of society. In school, I learned to live with ambiguity.

By the 1963 publication of Friedan's *The Feminine Mystique*, marking the beginning of modern feminism, I was launched in a demanding social work career and in a marriage characterized by modification of traditional roles, and had begun a family that would include three children before the decade ended. Along the way, personal economic pragmatism forced me as an individual to contest organization policies that modern feminism would later target as sexist social injustices (Firestone, 1970; Freeman, 1987; Valentich, 1986). On my own agenda were forced, lengthy pregnancy leaves without pay, differential insurance coverage for women and men employees, differential salaries for women and men in the same positions, and exclusion from decision making at work because of gender. These and many more became the routine frustrations and fights of my life and helped to raise my consciousness further than I had ever wanted it to go. They painfully contributed to my understanding of the personal, familial, collegial, and professional costs of "just" trying to support myself and my family "like men do." I tried to rely on an ever-increasing work load and demonstration of competence to overcome prejudice. I learned early why some women gave up (Norman & Mancuso, 1980).

But there was a built-in counterforce in my world. The rural women—and men—whom I encountered as clients in those days were struggling against economic and social barriers to survival and quality of life that both contrasted with and mirrored my own (Burdge & Rogers, 1972; Flora & Johnson, 1978; President's National Advisory Commission on Rural Poverty, 1967). Rural people were pervasively disadvantaged in making their needs known and in exercising choice as to where and how they would be helped for a number of reasons: rural America's unfamiliarity with bureaucracy (and concomitant inability to negotiate it); the strictures of a strongly patriarchal, traditional society; and the educational, cultural, experiential, and communication differences between rural clientele and urban-based and -trained providers of care (Ferrill, Ferrill, & Jenkins, 1973; Munson, 1980; Rodefeld, 1978). Their attempts to be self-determining were often interpreted within the paradigm of the medical model as "resistance," "instruction noncompliance," "cultural deficiencies," or other demeaning descriptions (Ballou & Gabalac, 1985).

I could not help but notice the striking similarities in the social service and medical institutional responses to rural people and to women generally. Feminist values and the resulting behavioral interpretations had invaded my professional assessments. I no longer believed in the "standard" explanations of human behavior that guided social treatment in the practice settings I inhabited. In abandoning traditional wisdom, I was acutely aware that potential rural clients viewed me as a threat to freedom of action. From their cultural perspective, they were suspicious of my offers of help, just as I was suspicious of others from my feminist perspective. This forced me to have to share enough of myself and of what I knew about the specific barriers to their goals and the risks in confronting those barriers that they could feel the same commonality of struggle that I felt. Only then could they drop their stoicism, guardedness, and fear and admit to feeling defeated, depressed, or uncertain about their wants and the routes to achieving them.

So it was that I learned what "partnership" with the client system entailed. And I saw how the interconnectedness of these people's will and strength with my knowledge and determination changed us both. Social work with rural people and feminist principles had begun to merge in my life.

RURAL SOCIAL WORK AND
THE GENERALIST MODEL OF PRACTICE

There are historical parallels in the reemergence of the rural social work movement in the United States in the 1960s and the rise of feminism. Both developed essentially along the lines of a social movement, hearkening back to the societal/environmental change tradition in social work (settlement house/social activism orientation) far more than the case-work tradition. From similar developmental paths, feminism and rural social work arrived at very similar principles of producing societal change. These principles dictated the employment of change technol-ogies directed toward institutional and societal targets, not change di-rected solely, or even predominantly, toward the individual. Individ-ual change was viewed as a prelude, as a sometimes necessary but not sufficient condition for instituting societal change. Thus the rural so-cial worker who would integrate the worldview of the rural generalist with feminism does not have far to travel.

Rural social work, analogous to the feminist movement, had been without a theory base, a reported history, an organized constituency, recognition by professional and academic leadership, and visibility in national forums. Then, in 1969, from the podium at the National Con-ference on Social Welfare, Leon Ginsberg, dean of the West Virginia University School of Social Work, issued a declaration of the exis-tence of rural social work and a rallying cry to those who shared his commitment. The call was heard by many of us who, in abject isola-tion from and ignorance of one another and with little to draw upon but our own experience and creativity in adapting urban-assumed so-cial work theory to rural environments, joyfully created a social movement of our own as a means to effect social change (Martinez-Brawley, 1981; Mermelstein & Sundet, 1976). In the two decades since, rural social work has developed a strong national visibility and identity, a literature, status as a concentration or emphasis in degree programs, and an expanding theoretical base.

Beyond the similarities described above, what rural social work shared with feminism was the essential belief in the right and respon-sibility of all people to choose for themselves a way of life, fortified by community structures and processes nurturant of their needs (Cox, Erlich, Rothman, & Tropman, 1979; Griffith & Libo, 1968; Martinez-Brawley, 1986; Morrison, 1976). Rural people are removed geograph-ically and culturally from federal and state centers of social planning. They are subjected to the arrogance and ignorance of urban-trained professionals who fail to discover or appreciate the uniqueness of the rural world but attempt to ply their trade regardless of context. As a consequence, rural people are often voiceless and powerless in affairs that profoundly affect their personal lives (Lynch, 1983; Margolis, 1979; Rosenblatt & Anderson, 1981; Sachs, 1983).

Cognizant of these realities, many rural social workers had independently arrived at some notion of "generalist" practice as the appropriate model to guide intervention at all four systemic levels: individual, family-group, organization, and community (Davenport & Davenport, 1984; Martinez-Brawley & Munson, 1981; Southern Region Education Board, 1976). Unfortunately, in mainstream social work theory, the term *generalist* became almost exclusively associated with the baccalaureate level of professional education, unwittingly denigrating its importance and leveling its meaning to a kind of "jack of all trades, master of none" (Johnson, 1983; Vice-Irey, 1980). Some schools, in an effort to rescue the concept, created "advanced generalist" concentrations at the master's level (Hernandez, Jorgenson, Judd, Gould, & Parsons, 1985).

In my own school, we conceptualized generalist social work as an approach to, or philosophy of, social work. It is an approach that employs a coherent blend of change roles and technologies, mastered in a sequential, planned, career-developmental design (Mermelstein & Sundet, 1978). The description of the generalist social worker is deceptively simple:

> The generalist is a social worker who, within the framework of social work values, identifies and assesses social phenomena in all their systemic ramifications, and based on that assessment, identifies and intervenes at whatever level is efficient and effective within her/his resources to bring about the desired social change. (Boettcher, 1978, p. 6)

Not a new method or any unique combination of methods, generalist practice is derived from the totality of social work. The rural generalist is guided by the ultimate values of the profession and its historical dedication to vulnerable and oppressed populations, and draws strength from the holistic practice tradition, with twin emphases on societal change and individual change. In its ideal form, this model focuses on the creation of a competent and empowering community, one that is nurturant of individual *and* collective potential.

Harriet Bartlett (1970) taught us that our values determine our goals: What we believe tells us what we want to do. What we want to do determines what we need to know. And what we know determines what we can do. This succinct interpretation of the relationships among values, knowledge, and intervention in social work is embodied in our version of generalist.

Assessment is crucial and comprehensive. If we want to do more than treat or rehabilitate the casualties of an ism-infested society, we must generate the social assessments that suggest where to intervene. The specific employing agency's purpose and goals and the social worker's predilections for role and strategy must not limit the assessment.

The assessment is requisite to identification of societal and organizational influences on human behavior and thus societal and institutional injustice. That assessment cannot be limited by any prejudgment proscribing the ultimate choice of social work client, target, change role, or change strategy. Competent assessment calls for knowledge of systems theory and scientific method, and understanding of the essential interrelatedness of the social environment as foundation knowledge for the practice of social work.

Once an assessment is complete, then and only then does the professional examine "her or his resources to identify and intervene at whatever level is efficient and effective to produce the desired social change" (Boettcher, 1978, p. 6). The resources subject to examination include *all* sources and means of power and influence accessible to the social work change agent. The knowledge, experience, and training of the social worker are resources. The familial, social, and professional networks through which the social worker can gain entry to community subsystems or organizations are resources. The employing agency's mandate or purpose and what it is allowed and not allowed to do are resources/constraints. The social worker's unique status and position within the agency is a resource or constraint, depending often on the credibility, tenure, and experience of that individual professional. The social worker's specific knowledge of the community and/or institutional context, appraisal of the leadership in those contexts, and sensitivity to their current "readiness" for change are resources.

In short, provided with a comprehensive, systemic assessment of a social phenomenon (whether it be unwanted pregnancy, grinding poverty, women's chemical dependency, racism, family violence, school dropout, or whatever), the generalist social worker, within the resources at her or his disposal, ideally seeks to intervene at many levels to alter the conditions contributing to creation and maintenance of that phenomenon. When the assessment implicates community processes, intervention will need to be multitargeted. If the social worker confines intervention to the individual or family/group level of change but the assessment indicates the target should be organization or community change, the generalist is faced with a dilemma. He or she must reconcile values and ends with means in the short run. But as personal/professional power, agency sanction/auspices, knowledge, and/or community context alter over time, the original assessment may become the impetus for intervention at a higher level of change. Professional longevity in the community is thus transformed into an asset in generalist practice. What cannot be done today may become possible tomorrow.

Another characteristic of rural society, its relative smallness, supports the practice model of generalist. The social worker is highly visible and plays multiple community roles that permit entry to multiple community systems. Relationships with the county commissioner and the factory owner may originate through parent roles in the PTA or membership in the Rotary Club. Overlapping roles permit access to decision makers that is often denied to the frontline social worker in an urban locale. Rural generalist social work exploits that capability.

Credibility as a generalist is facilitated by the communication networks that spread the details of the social worker's interventions throughout the community. Success in implementing a subrole of the generalist—educator, for example, or consultant, negotiator, mediator, broker, technical expert, advocate, therapist—is communicated through the ubiquitous rural grapevine, opening opportunities and invitations to perform other subroles or the same role in another community subsystem. This transfer of credibility drastically shortens the time frame for acceptance into many corners of the community. Community tolerance and support of a practitioner who sometimes *does* advocate contra-normative community change (such as the solution to identified injustice) becomes possible because of the "good" that he or she does. The generalist model supports trade-offs. The community soon understands that its sanctioning of the social worker to serve *manifest*, acknowledged community need (the residual function of social services) carries a risk that it may not have expected. That risk is the discovery of pathological or insidious *latent* community processes that are frequently encountered in the course of this kind of work.

Examples abound. One was a health task force in a rural community that was created to develop a viable transportation system to the regional hospital/clinics 50 miles away. The social worker who joined the task force did an assessment of the community's health care needs that inadvertently revealed a long-established pattern of referral of all African-American patients to one physician. Overworked and out-of-date with medical science in many areas, he, in turn, sent many patients out of the community for routine care. Transportation *was* a problem for the community. Part of the "transportation" problem, however, was an unacknowledged community intention to retain the status quo of institutional racism in the health system. In this instance, the assessment reframed the problem and forced community leaders to confront an ugly dimension of community life that they would have preferred to ignore. Risk is an element in producing change—how much risk becomes clearer in generalist assessment.

CONGRUENCE OF FEMINIST AND RURAL GENERALIST PERSPECTIVES

What rural generalist practice and feminism require of their adherents is the central life commitment to work for social justice. This shared value determines the preferred goal. *Efficient* intervention to achieve that goal normally requires macro-level change (Jacobson, 1980; Morrison, 1976). Institutionalized discrimination is the target. But the professional social worker is judged by an equally high standard of *effective* intervention. The change process begins with a shared awareness of injustice among the change partners, but the effort cannot plateau there. The rural feminist social worker must possess the interventive repertoire required to produce such change. This is a professional, developmental task with no shortcuts. Skill building requires the willingness to risk, zest for lifelong learning, lots of humility, and a strong bent for discipline and perseverance. And the obligation to produce change requires even more. Knowledge is rendered impotent when there is no opportunity to employ it. That opportunity, as the second stage of feminism has revealed (Friedan, 1981), rests on the change agent's credibility with the institutional gatekeepers. The hard lesson of feminism and rural generalist social work, in my experience, is that the professional is first judged acceptable on the *existing* (male-oriented, societal) criteria for the professional role attempted. Once he or she is accepted as "part of" the community or organization structure, the auspices and sanction for change exist.

This is a controversial point within feminist circles. Some feminist professionals eschew existing societal criteria for role enactment, taking the position that a professional who can provide concrete, useful help in a difficult situation will be accepted and used despite her different value system. My experience has shown that the rural community's judgment about the professional's competence is made relatively quickly. It is often based on superficial knowledge of performance augmented by impressions of the individual's professional persona. If the professional's presentation of self and initial performance do not correspond to community expectations, he or she may never be given the opportunity to help in difficult situations. Achieving credibility, as the foregoing suggests, is intrinsically an intellectual activity (Mermelstein & Sundet, 1980) buttressed by self-confidence and emotional security (Murty, 1984)—and a measure of physical stamina does not hurt!

Both the feminist and rural social work movements have innovated mechanisms for the dissemination of new knowledge, the building of self-esteem/confidence, and the facilitation of support systems consonant with this understanding of the demands of the change role. Networking, mentoring, and bartering of mutual assistance are common to both, while both vehemently reject the guild mentality currently enveloping mainstream social work and competing disciplines. Guilds elevate form over substance to emphasize status, elitism, and endless credentialing, characteristics foreign to feminist and rural social work practice. Celebration of diversity, joy in shared values, and generosity in giving of oneself are the hallmarks of feminist and rural social workers who have "grown up" in one or both of these movements.

CASE OF THE RURAL ECONOMIC CRISIS
IN NORTH MISSOURI:
THE COMBINED PRACTICE APPROACH

Since the early 1980s, the American grain belt has been in the throes of the most devastating economic crisis since the Great Depression of the 1930s (Drabenstott & Duncan, 1985). The convergent forces that created this upheaval include the international political economy, U.S. foreign and domestic policy initiatives that created negative policy spillover into the agricultural sector, adverse weather over a period of several years, pursuit of an all-out production philosophy in agriculture in the 1970s, and the negative impacts of U.S. farm policy, lowered inflation, and high interest rates (Briemeyer, 1977;

Samuelson, 1983; Sinclair, 1985). A domino-effect type of collapse spread from the farm failures to the rural business economy, seriously threatening a treasured way of life. Emotional and psychological reactions to such stress have been evident in the elevation of many social indicators: clinical depression, suicides, family violence and breakdown, and teenage pregnancies. National and international news media sensationalized the "farm crisis" for a while in the mid-1980s, reveling in the visual feasts of tractorcades on the Washington Mall, marches on the Chicago Board of Trade, and queues of hungry farmers in the richest agricultural nation in the world waiting in line for free federal commodity foods. Media attention faded when the news diminished to a monotonous litany of bankruptcies, foreclosures, soaring unemployment, family breakups, out-migration, and relinquishment of hope. As far as urban America was concerned, the farm crisis was over.

The frontline human service providers in rural Missouri concurred. The so-called crisis was a misnomer, because no short-term, reversible period of community disequilibrium existed. Instead, insidious forces of dramatic, long-term economic and social decline were in process and were causing waves of human casualties. With each new planting season and harvest, survivors of prior years were forced out of farming and/or the rural economy. Whole communities were being abandoned by those young enough or educated enough or rich enough to get out. Starved of leadership, communities were adrift and at sea. What had started in the agricultural economy as an acute farm crisis was now a rural transitional period of unknown destiny.

AUSPICES FOR
MY PROFESSIONAL PRACTICE

The Cooperative Extension Service is the arm of the land-grant university that extends new knowledge gained through research into the state where it can be put to use in improving the quality of life. Vertically integrated with the U.S. Department of Agriculture, the Extension Service is traditionally associated with farming and rural life, although today it also serves urban populations. It extends a university presence throughout the state.

During the 1980s, the Extension Service was in the forefront of the rural crisis in north Missouri. The traditional disciplines that it employs—home economists, livestock specialists, agronomists, soil and water experts, community developers—were the professional groups in the most direct, daily interaction with the agricultural community and the collapsing rural infrastructure. All of them were doing crisis intervention with their clientele, and the contagion of the generalized upset hit them hard.

The Rural Crisis Task Force was created in the Extension Service late in 1984 in response to staff demoralization and fatigue. It had a dual purpose: to channel and focus the fragmented and haphazard efforts of rural Extension field staff in addressing the accelerating devastation caused by the farm economic crisis; and to provide concrete technological and emotional support to these staff, some of whom were near physical and/or emotional collapse under the unrelenting stress of their locales (Ashley, 1986; Fetsch, Flashman, & Jeffiers, 1984; Hughes, 1988; Patterson & McCubbin, 1984). Invitations to volunteer in the Rural Crisis Task Force were extended to campus faculty drawn from agriculture, rural sociology, home economics, youth 4-H programs, business, vocational/technical education, community development, career planning, and preventive health and social work. This range of disciplines reflected the complex, multidimensional phenomena that had to be addressed in the rural crisis. Along with a male colleague/partner in social work, I volunteered to join the change effort.

Our initial work incorporated both purposes of the task force. We had to provide visible proof of its existence and a substantive show of support for rural extension staff as quickly as possible. As social workers, we were the only members of the task force representing a traditional mental health discipline. Respecting that uniqueness, the task force let us design and implement a 2-week series of interdisciplinary "stress-management" workshops, delivered to all Extension staff in the eight regions of the state. To demonstrate competence and build the credibility we would later need for reconnaissance (obtaining a systemic assessment of the phenomenon of the farm crisis as it currently affected the target populations), we plotted the "road show" very carefully.

We two social workers were joined by a rural sociologist and a public health specialist and a van load of sophisticated teaching hardware with which we aimed to impress our audiences. (Extension agents, after all, are community educators par excellence.) Consistent with the task force mission, the 7-hour team-teaching days were designed to provide substantive content on stress management to field staff so that they, in turn, could put it to immediate use in their communities. Moreover, the format and structure were conducive to a second important function: consultation to workshop participants desperately needing to ventilate to someone who understood.

While one of us was onstage, teaching, the rest of the team separated and casually lounged in the hallways outside the conference room, creating unannounced "corridor confessionals." We stayed very busy; lines formed as individuals nervously awaited their turn to ask "a few questions" about how to help "a friend."

During the nightly several-hour drives to the next site, we shared our individual experiences of the day. Our collective assessment of the operating condition of the Extension Service and of the specific rural communities we toured then provided the basis for the next phase of intervention. We had identified the locales and the staff who needed immediate and more sustained help. We had an appraisal of workability—motivation, capacity, and resource/opportunity—of our potential target systems, and of ourselves (Ripple, 1955). The four of us became a strong, mutually supportive subgroup of the task force.

One of the most striking findings of our community reconnaissance was the severe stress that women field agents and rural women generally were experiencing as their families, way of life, community institutions, and emotional security collapsed around them (Norem & Blundall, 1988; Rosenblatt & Anderson, 1981; U.S. Congress, 1986; Van Hook, 1987; Weigel, 1981). Men's pain was more visible, as farming earned the dubious distinction of the occupation with the highest rate of male suicide in Missouri; but women were struggling to comfort their men, to make up for lost income through their own off-farm labor, and to salvage "communities" from towns rancorously divided by debtors and lenders (Wilhelm & Ridley, 1988). In rural America, personal economic failure is often universally perceived as a violation of core rural values of self-sufficiency and traditional morality. Because moral "goodness" is associated with success, failure generates shame and guilt. These attitudes stifle mutual self-help in a time of trouble (Heffernan & Heffernan, 1986; Wright & Rosenblatt, 1988).

Our later research study, drawn from a series of public workshops focused specifically on rural women's stress, added empirical documentation to our early anecdotal impressions (Sundet &

Mermelstein, 1988). Findings showed significant gender differences in perception of the residents' sense of and belief in community, and—*crucial* for community organization—differences in a stated willingness to work on community revitalization. Women far outdistanced men in expressing the motivation to try to save their way of life, whereas men's dismal outlook on the future conditioned their belief that it was already too late.

Our intervention plan had to build on strength. Potential community strength was evident in the attitudes of these rural women. Potential female leadership was evident in the Extension Service. We assumed that the role modeling of female Extension personnel in these distressed communities would assist in overcoming the traditional, internal barriers to public leadership that rural women impose on themselves. Empowering and sustaining women to confront their sad burdens with effective problem solving eventually encompassed the following strategies and techniques.

(1) We worked on identifying and sustaining individual women—potential leaders—who with backup and consultative support could build the structures needed for community revitalization and development. Starting with women in the Extension Service, we encouraged them to draw women partners with demonstrated community commitment into the endeavor. Taking full advantage of our task force prerogatives, we brought women field agents onto campus regularly to participate in task force operations. Because men are in the majority in the Extension Service, this visibility boost provided organizational recognition of women's talents and growing experience in combating the farm crisis. As a central resource bureau, the task force then was easily able to introduce female talent from one corner of the state as "expert" consultants/trainers to a fledgling effort in another locale. As the experience of community successes multiplied, we used our professional and scholarly networks to feature these women's work in regional and national conferences and in a special edition of the rural social work journal, *Human Services in the Rural Environment* (Mermelstein & Sundet, 1986a; Parsons, 1986).

As the farm crisis rolled inexorably across the grain belt, and as women's farm organizations such as Women in the Farm Economy (WIFE), American Agri-Women, and Rural American Women, Inc., mobilized at regional and national levels, we encouraged all our consultees to affiliate. The written materials, conferences, personal and network camaraderie, and resource sharing that occurred through these organizations were invaluable aids to the organizing effort in Missouri.

(2) A second strategy involved the design of educational vehicles specifically geared to address problems of stress faced by rural women, but capable of being used generically in rural communities. One of our workshops focused on an analysis of the sources of stress in the rural crisis, the continuum of stress-crisis behaviors, and the anatomy of crisis resolution (Golan, 1978; Parad, 1965). This workshop promoted social support as essential in coping with unrelenting stress but advocated that the best antidote to stress produced by social injustice is social action. Two commercially available videos drove home the message. One demonstrated the influence of support systems for women confronting divorce, college entry, aging, and cattle ranching upsets (MTI Teleprograms, 1982), while the other featured three farm women who were transformed into "radical" and enormously successful social activists by the rural crisis (Minnesota Public Radio, 1985). We leveraged the potential influence of this workshop by accepting invitations to give it only in cooperation with Extension personnel who would treat it as a first step in the long-term process of building community strength and leadership. If the extension staff were willing to commit themselves to organizing and staffing a community effort, then we were willing to help them initiate and sustain it. That forged a true change partnership in a quid pro quo exchange for our teaching, a departure from the traditional campus offerings that require no further obligation. As full-time, campus-based social work faculty, we were volunteers in the Extension work. Our time to devote to the field was in our control. When this was circulated through the field grapevine, it enhanced our ability to negotiate with the field staff for a cooperative commitment.

When the workshops in a particular county did, in fact, produce the desired effect—encouraging participants to undertake our recommendation for management of stress and crisis, that is, to work for social justice at the community level—we then became co-consultants with local field staff.

(3) During the course of all our field activity, many rural women confided personal/familial problems with which they needed ongoing professional help. In attempting to arrange such help through our extensive networks of social workers and mental health practitioners throughout the area (alumni, field agencies, colleagues in former service activities), we discovered a severe shortage of viable resources for farm stress-related problems (Mermelstein & Sundet, 1986b).

Although these problems had very visible legal, economic, medical, employment, spiritual, and emotional dimensions, mental health facilities were not serving this unfamiliar and unknown target population, nor were some even aware of the mounting toll of human casualties (Mermelstein & Sundet, 1988). Many confessed that these problems outstripped their knowledge and skills. It was clear that some of these professionals, living in the midst of the community crisis, were themselves victims of stress overload. Our efforts had to turn to the formal community mental health system.

We arranged a meeting between the CMHC (community mental health center) directors of North Missouri and Extension regional directors, the first meeting of its kind ever held in the state. Using emotionally charged case material drawn from our consultations with Extension staff and rural workshop participants, we tried to motivate these two delivery systems to combine their respective needs and expertise into a shared, mutually strengthening change effort. Eventually, federal funding was obtained, under the 1985 Farm Bill and the subsequent 1987 Rural Crisis Recovery Act (P.L. 100-219, Section 1440) to implement a demonstration project of mental health service delivery in the rural crisis. Experienced mental health social workers, employed and supervised by the CMHCs but salaried by Extension, operated from Extension offices. They became immediately available to provide generalist assistance to extension agents and rural communities and to sidestep the stigma that mental health care has in farming communities.

(4) Once advocacy and program development had opened the gate to traditional brokerage functions in addressing individual/family problems, we taught Extension staff and community residents how to identify and access needed resources. We provided technical expertise and consultation to help them construct resource directories for their communities, including both formal and informal resources. The task force provided the materials and human resources in every county for publication of these brochures. Data collection procedures forced the residents to evaluate resource extent and quality, thereby also contributing to the needs assessment facet of community organizing. The whole strategy had a secondary goal: By transferring our linkage work to local staff and community residents, we accomplished some abatement of their negativism toward utilization of certain kinds of resources. For example, when they were in the position of trying to convince a neighbor or friend to use a needed resource, the friend's

resistance was lowered. Most particularly, referrals for food stamps, AFDC, and mental health services were increased. We encouraged Extension staff to support women who actually used the resources by urging them, in turn, to broker those resources for others. Their courage in taking the first step to change was a tool for empowering others.

(5) The strategy of action research was used to persuade colleagues on the task force to support the change processes outlined above. The use of action research is another point of congruence between feminist practice and rural social work. It is designed to produce knowledge for a specific purpose (programming, for example), not just for the sake of knowing. This research gained unanticipated attention on the national rural crisis scene as one of the few bodies of cumulative, empirical data on the emotional and psychological ravages of the farm crisis. Through it, we were able to give voice to rural Missourians at national levels of policy-making (Bergland, 1988).

DISCUSSION

Generalist practice in the case described above involved all four levels of social change: individual, group, organization, and community. Using the single role by which the task force knew me (and that held credibility in their eyes)—that of educator—I forged it into an instrument designed to impress the gatekeepers (Extension field staff) and to open the gates to rural communities wherein generalist practice would be appropriate and allowed. Once "inside," I could gradually adopt an array of the subroles of the rural generalist, required by the emergence of new phenomena in the ongoing intervention process.

Among those roles, my feminist commitment is most apparent in the choices of consultee-centered consultant (of women Extension staff and potential women leaders), social broker, client and policy advocate, program planner, and researcher. Preferable always in dealing with rural women (and men) is the professional role that best supports their efforts to take responsibility for their community and affirms their essential strength and ability (Weick, Rapp, Sullivan, & Kisthardt, 1989).

In a context of such overwhelming stress, it is easy to see weaknesses before strengths and to assess first impressions as though these were continuous behaviors. Notable by its absence in the above vignette is the role of therapist, which, in my experience in rurality, is too frequently applied when a different role would have accomplished the purpose better. I consciously chose not to be a therapist to these people. For them to perceive that choice as an affirmation of their strengths, they needed to know that I can be and am a therapist in other contexts. One way I conveyed that message was through case consultation focused on their own "clients" (who may have been neighbors or colleagues). Drawing on an extensive knowledge base in psychopathology and familiarity with psychiatric nomenclature, I shared dynamic assessments with them in some depth. Sometimes this interaction led to revelations of their own personal problems. When it did, I did not alter my role. Even though social work theory does not distinguish well between therapist and "consultant on personal problems," there is a boundary. Consultation never requires the forced intimacy of therapy, but does not preclude intimate disclosure—at the consultee's discretion and pace. The control is in the consultee's hands.

In summary, the level of generalist practice at which I engage is unique to my personal and professional resources, consistent with the credibility accrued from long service in one institution. My feminist convictions are interwoven with my identity as a rural change agent. The integration of both perspectives is facilitated by the values, dedication to societal change, and appreciation of the impact of that commitment on self that both feminism and rural generalist social work share. The above example has demonstrated the influence of this value constellation in one change process.

REFERENCES

Ashley, A. (1986). From the front line: Perspectives on rural stress. In *Summary report of the Policy Forum of the Council of State Governments and the National Institute of Mental Health: The personal stress problems of farmers and rural Americans*. Lexington, KY: Council of State Governments.

Ballou, M., & Gabalac, N. W. (1985). *A feminist position on mental health*. Springfield, IL: Charles C Thomas.

Bartlett, H. (1970). *The common base of social work practice*. New York: National Association of Social Workers.

Beard, M. K. (1946). *Women as a force in history*. New York: Macmillan.

Berg, B. (1978). *The remembered gate: Origins of American feminism*. New York: Oxford University Press.

Bergland, B. (1988). Rural mental health: Report of the National Action Commission on the mental health of rural Americans. *Journal of Rural Community Psychology, 9*(2), 25-40.

Boettcher, R., (Ed.). (1978). *Self-study report* (Vol. 1) (Report submitted to the Council on Social Work Education, Commission on Accreditation). Columbia: University of Missouri, School of Social Work.

Bricker-Jenkins, M., & Hooyman, N. (1984, March). *Not for women only: Teaching for feminist practice in the 1980s.* Paper presented at the annual program meeting of the Council on Social Work Education, Detroit.

Briemeyer, H. F. (1977). The changing American farm. *Annals of the American Academy of Political and Social Science, 429,* 16-22.

Brownmiller, S. (1975). *Against our will: Men, women and rape.* New York: Simon & Schuster.

Burdge, R. J., & Rogers, E. M. (1972). *Social change in rural societies.* New York: Appleton-Century-Crofts.

Cott, N. (1986). Feminist theory and feminist movements: The past before us. In J. Mitchell & A. Oakley (Eds.), *What is feminism?* (pp. 47-85). Oxford: Basil Blackwell.

Cox, F., Erlich, J., Rothman, J., & Tropman, J. (Eds.). (1979). *Strategies and tactics of community organization* (3rd cd.). Itasca, IL: F. E. Peacock.

Davenport, J., & Davenport, J. A. (1984). Josephine Brown's classic book still guides rural social work. *Social Casework, 65,* 413-419.

Delmar, R. (1986). What is feminism? In J. Mitchell & A. Oakley (Eds.), *What is feminism?* (pp. 14-46). Oxford: Basil Blackwell.

Drabenstott, M., & Duncan, M. (1985). Another troubled year for U.S. agriculture. *Journal of the American Society of Farm Managers and Rural Appraisers, 49*(1), 58-66.

Dworkin, A. (1974). *Woman hating.* New York: E. P. Dutton.

Ferrill, M. Z., Ferrill, O. C., & Jenkins, Q. (1973). Social power in a rural community. *Growth and Change, 4*(2), 3-6.

Fetsch, R. J., Flashman, R., & Jeffiers, D. (1984). Up tight ain't right: Easing the pressure on county agents. *Journal of Extension, 22,* 23-28.

Firestone, S. (1970). *The dialectic of sex: The case for feminist revolution.* New York: Bantam.

Flora, C. B., & Johnson, S. (1978). Discarding the distaff: New roles for rural women. In T. Ford (Ed.), *Rural U.S.: Persistence and change* (pp. 182-201). Ames: Iowa State University Press.

Freeman, M. L. (1987). Beyond women's issues: Feminism and social work. In J. Lantz & M. Coleman (Eds.), *Women's issues, poverty, and human service organizations* (pp. 136-151). Columbus: Ohio State University, College of Social Work.

Friedan, B. (1963). *The feminine mystique.* New York: Dell.

Friedan, B. (1981). *The second stage.* New York: Summit.

Golan, N. (1978). *Treatment in crisis situations.* New York: Free Press.

Griffith, C., & Libo, L. (1968). *Mental health consultants: Agents of community change.* San Francisco: Jossey-Bass.

Heffernan, J., & Heffernan, W. (1986). When farmers have to give up farming. *Rural Development Perspectives, 2*(3), 10-14.

Hernandez, S. H., Jorgenson, J. D., Judd, P., Gould, M., & Parsons, R. J. (1985). Integrated practice: Preparing the social problem specialist through an advanced generalist curriculum. *Journal of Social Work Education, 21,* 28-35.

Hughes, R. (1988). Burnout among county extension staff involved in the rural crisis. *Human Services in the Rural Environment, 12*(1), 23-28.

Jacobson, G. M. (1980). Rural communities and community development. In H. W. Johnson (Ed.), *Rural human services: A book of readings* (pp. 196-202). Itasca, IL: F. E. Peacock.

Johnson, L. (1983). *Social work practice: A generalist approach*. Boston: Allyn & Bacon.

Kantor, R. M. (1975). *Feminist perspectives on social life and social science*. Garden City, NY: Anchor.

Kingston, M. H. (1977). *The woman warrior*. New York: Vintage.

Lynch, M. M. (1983). A social development perspective on the inequality of women. *Social Development Issues, 7*(3), 45-52.

Mander, A., & Rush, A. (1974). *Feminism as therapy*. New York: Random House.

Margolis, R. J. (1979). The quest for rural equity. *Human Services in the Rural Environment, 1*(2), 19-24.

Martinez-Brawley, E. E. (1981). *Seven decades of rural social work: From country life commission to rural caucus*. New York: Praeger.

Martinez-Brawley, E. E. (1986). Beyond cracker barrel images: The rural social work specialty. *Social Casework, 67*, 101-107.

Martinez-Brawley, E. E., & Munson, C. (1981). Systemic characteristics of the rural milieu: A review of social work related research. *Arete, 6*(4), 23-34.

Mermelstein, J., & Sundet, P. (1976). And that's the way it was. *Human Services in the Rural Environment, 1*(1), 1-4.

Mermelstein, J., & Sundet, P. (1978). The social work generalist. In L. Hulen (Ed.), *Educating for practice in rural areas* (pp. 21-37). Fresno: California State University, School of Social Work.

Mermelstein, J., & Sundet, P. (1980). Worker acceptance and credibility in the rural environment. In H. W. Johnson (Ed.), *Rural human services: A book of readings* (pp. 174-178). Itasca, IL: F. E. Peacock.

Mermelstein, J., & Sundet, P. (Eds.). (1986a). Notes from the field. *Human Services in the Rural Environment, 10*(1), 30-37.

Mermelstein, J., & Sundet, P. (1986b). Rural community mental health centers' response to the farm crisis. *Human Services in the Rural Environment, 10*(1), 21-26.

Mermelstein, J., & Sundet, P. (1988). Factors influencing the decision to innovate: The future of community responsive programming. *Journal of Rural Community Psychology, 9*(2), 61-76.

Millett, K. (1970). *Sexual politics*. New York: Avon.

Minnesota Public Radio. (Producer). (1985). *Dairy queens* [Videotape]. (Available from producer, Minneapolis, MN)

Morrison, J. (1976). Community organization in rural areas. In L. Ginsberg (Ed.), *Social work in rural communities* (pp. 57-62). New York: Council on Social Work Education.

MTI Teleprograms. (Producer). (1982). *Learning to cope* [Videotape]. (Available from producer, 3710 Commercial Ave., Northbrook, IL 60062)

Munson, C. (1980). Urban-rural differences: Implications for education and training. *Journal of Education for Social Work, 16*(1), 95-103.

Murty, S. (1984). Developing the trust of a rural community. *Human Services in the Rural Environment, 9*(2), 15-20.

Norem, R., & Blundall, J. (1988). Farm families and marital disruption during a time of crisis. In R. Martoz-Baden, C. Hennon, & T. Brubaker (Eds.), *Families in rural America: Stress, adaptation and revitalization* (pp. 21-31). Minneapolis: National Council on Family Relations.

Norman, E., & Mancuso, A. (Eds.). (1980). *Women's issues and social work practice*. Itasca, IL: F. E. Peacock.

Parad, H. (1965). *Crisis intervention*. New York: Family Service Association of America.

Parsons, C. (1986). Poem: The auction of a man and his family. *Human Services in the Rural Environment, 10*(1), 4.

Patterson, J. M., & McCubbin, H. I. (1984). *Minnesota county extension agents: Stress, coping and adaptation.* St. Paul: University of Minnesota, College of Home Economics.

President's National Advisory Commission on Rural Poverty. (1967). *The people left behind.* Washington, DC: Government Printing Office.

Rich, A. (1976). *Of woman born: Motherhood as experience and institution.* New York: Norton.

Ripple, L. (1955). Motivation, capacity and opportunity as related to the use of casework service: Plan of study. *Social Service Review, 29*(2), 172-193.

Rodefeld, R. (1978). *Change in rural America: Causes, consequences, and alternatives.* St. Louis: C. V. Mosby.

Rosenberg, R. (1982). *Beyond separate spheres: Intellectual roots of modern feminism.* New Haven, CT: Yale University Press.

Rosenblatt, P., & Anderson, R. (1981). Interaction in farm families: Tension and stress. In R. Coward & W. Smith (Eds.), *The family in rural society* (pp. 82-109). Boulder, CO: Westview.

Sachs, C. E. (1983). *The invisible farmer women in agricultural production.* Totowa, NJ: Rowman & Allanheld.

Samuelson, R. J. (1983, August 20). Farm folly. *National Journal*, p. 1744.

Sinclair, W. (1985, January 27). Farm failures threaten to reshape rural U.S.: Long predicted crisis seems at hand. *Washington Post,* Sec. V, p. 1.

Southern Region Education Board, Manpower Education and Training Project, Rural Task Force. (1976). Educational assumptions for rural social work. In L. Ginsberg (Ed.), *Social work in rural communities* (pp. 41-46). New York: Council on Social Work Education.

Sundet, P., & Mermelstein, J. (1988). Community development and the rural crisis: Problem-strategy fit. *Journal of the Community Development Society, 3*(3), 63-78.

U.S. Congress, Senate, Committee on Governmental Affairs. (1986). *Governing the heartland: Can rural governments survive the farm crisis?* (Report of the Subcommittee on Intergovernmental Relations, 99th Congress). Washington, DC: Government Printing Office.

Valentich, M. (1986). Feminism and social work practice. In F. J. Turner (Ed.), *Social work treatment* (pp. 564-589). New York: Free Press.

Van Den Bergh, N., & Cooper, L. B. (1987). Feminist social work. In *Encyclopedia of social work* (18th ed., pp. 611-618). Silver Spring, MD: National Association of Social Workers.

Van Hook, M. (1987). Harvest of despair: Using the ABCX model for farm families in crisis. *Social Casework, 68,* 273-278.

Vice-Irey, K. (1980). The social work generalist in a rural context: An ecological perspective. *Journal of Education for Social Work, 16*(3), 36-42.

Weick, A., Rapp, C., Sullivan, W. P., & Kisthardt, W. (1989). A strengths perspective for social work practice. *Social Work, 34,* 350-354.

Weigel, R. (1981). *Stress on the farm.* Ames: Iowa Cooperative Extension Service.

Wetzel, J. (1986). A feminist worldview conceptual framework. *Social Casework, 67,* 166-173.

Wilhelm, M., & Ridley, C. (1988). Stress and unemployment in rural nonfarm couples: A study of hardships and coping resources. In R. Martoz-Baden, C. Hennon, & T. Brubaker (Eds.), *Families in rural America: Stress, adaptation and revitalization* (pp. 40-46). Minneapolis: National Council on Family Relations.

Wright, S., & Rosenblatt, P. (1988). Isolation and farm loss: Why neighbors may not be supportive. In R. Martoz-Baden, C. Hennon, & T. Brubaker (Eds.), *Families in rural America: Stress, adaptation and revitalization* (pp. 208-215). Minneapolis: National Council on Family Relations.

Family Secrets

Gail Atkins

the following piece is dedicated to all the wimmin who are in the process of healing from child sexual abuse. As i wrote this piece, i was particularly happy about the lack of pain i experienced around the memories that surfaced to make the writing possible. My incest incidents happened years ago, and i feel the healing is complete. i felt no anger, fear or pain during the process of writing this piece.

Grandmother,
i remember your strong farm woman hands,
holding your saucer of coffee to your mouth,
elbows propped on the kitchen table.
i remember how small
i seemed
beside your strong thick farm woman's body,
strong enough to carry two 5 gallon buckets
of slop to the hogs.
i remember you,
solid, strong,
staring far out over the fields outside the kitchen window.
i was small,
so small
i'd have to get up on my knees in my cane bottom chair
to see what you were looking at . . .
so hard, so long,
your eyes squinted
sometimes lids fluttering a bit.
maybe it was grandpa, or uncle tump
behind the mules plowing the back field,
but when i looked,
there were only the hills of west tennessee
glorious in the after breakfast morning.

sitting back in my chair,
i'd look up at you again,
so strong, so intent.
finally,
a small squirmy 4 year old curiosity
would push me shy and stumbling up to this big strong farm
woman
and i'd ask,
"mema, what're ya lookin at?"
your thick calloused hand would pat my small thigh gently
and you'd say,
"mema's studin, hon, just studin."
with that explanation you'd take another sip
of your coffee from the saucer
and go back to "studin."

i remember the winter nights under loads and layers
of homemade quilts,
snuggled in a featherbed
you and your sisters had made together,
the winter colds brought pungent smelling poultices,
warm from the kettle on the wood stove,
you'd put on my small chest.
in the morning i'd feel better,
laughing with the family around the breakfast table
piled with fresh scrambled eggs i'd gathered from the
chicken house the day before and those delicious homemade
biscuits made by those thick calloused hands
kneading that dough, rocking, singing.

some notion you'd drop into the
morning talk
about aunt emma might come today
(no phone, you couldn't know)
and later she'd come!
i'd be amazed!
"how'd you know?" i'd ask.
"mema's a witch, baby," you'd laugh and say.
and all the women would laugh and say
"it's so Estelle, you are."

I remember the day i came in from bringing in the cows
with uncle tump, 7 years older than me.
you were sewing in the living room,
rocking back and forth as you
pumped the treadle on your white sewing machine,
again in front of a window
looking out over the pond and side pasture.

i watched you, listening to your soft humming
in rhythm with the treadle.

i was afraid to tell you what
uncle tump had made me do
in the deserted share croppers' house
on the way back from the pasture

But you were strong
and you could stop it.
i had to tell you.

i did and you were angry!
but not at him!
at me!

Part II

CORE CONCEPTS

INTRODUCTION

NAOMI GOTTLIEB

The themes of the chapters in Part II have appeared in different contexts in previous chapters, but they are now set in a separate section because we want to give them clear emphasis. Certain aspects of feminist analysis are central to all feminist social work practice, and we believe that the three chapters here represent the most prominent of these—acting on the principle that the personal is political, empowering women, and celebrating the strengths of women as survivors.

The woman Marilyn Wedenoja writes about is the mother of a seriously emotionally disturbed adult son. She is therefore one of a group of women who have had a particular societal albatross hung around their necks. We know that all women are held responsible for the mental well-being of family members, but in the field of mental illness that responsibility is carried to extreme lengths. Family and mental health professionals believe that mental problems, particularly schizophrenia, are, in Wedenoja's words, "the mother's fault, her responsibility to solve, or both." The mother with whom Wedenoja worked believed all of that, and Wedenoja describes how she helped her understand where her responsibility began and ended. She raised this mother's consciousness about societal issues—about the caregiving imperative for all women and the lack of supportive social programs. Wedenoja's translation of "the personal is political"—of making the connections between private troubles and public issues, of depathologizing—is but one of many versions possible in work with women.

Lorraine Gutiérrez's chapter describes the possibilities of transformation when women develop the skills and attitudes necessary for personal and political empowerment. Within a year, a group of low-income women of color moved from the immobility resulting from a multitude of pressures to a social action confrontation with a large city bureaucracy. Gutiérrez's contribution is more than a case study, however. She offers us an analysis of different aspects of empowerment and leads us through possible steps to action by women, individually and in groups. In so doing, she provides us with the tools for our own empowerment as a vehicle for the empowerment of the women with whom we work.

Wawa Baczynskyj's personal essay is a poignant example of the strengths of refugee women in the face of terror, starvation, and political upheaval. Her own refugee experience has enabled her to understand those survival skills in a special way and to build relationships with these women through their common experiences. I believe it will not diminish our respect for the survival capabilities of the Southeast Asian women Baczynskyj describes to say that we are all survivors. Her own experiences and those of the refugee women are far more than most of us have had to endure. However, through her commentary, she helps us to see the survival strengths we all have and the value of sharing the commonalities of survival among women.

In the introduction to this book, Bricker-Jenkins states that one of the important aspects of feminist practice is that these are all "works in progress." A corollary is that core concepts are also open to continual scrutiny. At a later time, the core concepts emphasized here may be replaced or modified, as we learn from our further work with women and our own deliberations.

PMS

Carie Winslow

PMS, manic depressive, schizophrenia, multiple personality, hysteria
                                                                BITCH . . .

These are just words
            about women
                  women who remember pain
                  and scream about it!

Women who hang onto yearnings
                  and scream about it

                                    when they are ripped to shreds.

Women who will fight to the death
                  and scream about it

                              when they win.

Women who know no shame
            no limits
            make no apologies
                  and scream about it

                                    when asked to sit down.

Women who kill their husbands . . . for no apparent reason.
Women who refuse to endure
                  and scream about it

                              when they aren't listened to.

Women who have been drugged, raped, beaten, defined, caged, lied
about, tortured

                                    and scream about it!

Chapter 8

MOTHERS ARE NOT TO BLAME
Confronting Cultural Bias in
the Area of Serious Mental Illness

MARILYN WEDENOJA

As a feminist social worker working with family caregivers of persons with serious and prolonged mental illness, I have over time made links, both conceptually and in practice, among feminism, social work, and the situations of family caregivers, many of whom are mothers. This chapter charts my own evolution in developing a feminist social work approach; it defines what I have found to be the key elements of feminist practice and attempts, with hindsight, to identify the factors that have contributed most to my integrating feminist practice principles with my work as a social worker. The second part of the chapter describes my work with family caregivers of mentally ill persons, presenting a clinical example as well as a comparative analysis of a feminist social work approach with both conventional and collaborative approaches.

"Mother-blaming" is deeply rooted in our culture. The culture as a whole, and human service delivery systems in particular, share a belief that problems in families and of individual family members are the mother's fault, her responsibility to solve, or both (Imber-Black, 1986, 1988, 1989). Mothers tend to be held accountable for any emotional ills that befall their children (Anderson & Holder, 1989; Walters, 1988); this has been particularly true in the history of schizophrenia. Ranging from earlier psychoanalytic theories, which held that either a cold and uncaring or overinvolved and smothering "schizophrenogenic mother" was the primary cause of this psychotic disorder (Fromm-Reichmann, 1948), to the family systems theories that portray psychotic symptoms as a result of "double-bind" communication or an inappropriate "enmeshment" on the part of the mother (Bateson, Jackson, Haley, & Weakland, 1956; Haley, 1980; Wynne, Ryckoff, Day, & Hirsch, 1958), mothers of persons with schizophrenia continue to be held accountable for this condition. This view prevails in spite of growing evidence that identifies biological and, in some instances, genetic factors as primary in the etiology of severe mental illness (Andreasen, 1985; Taylor, 1987; Torrey, 1983). These blaming attitudes continue to be prevalent in the professional literature; for example, a survey of major clinical journals found 72 different kinds of psychopathology attributed to mothers (Caplan & Hall-McCorquodale, 1985). Reflective of this cultural double bind of both blaming mothers and holding them responsible for solutions is the current state of care for those with psychiatric disabilities. As service delivery systems have shifted their emphasis from institutions to the community, home care of persons with mental illness has fallen heavily on families, and particularly on women: "As an extension of their culturally appointed nurturing role, they unavoidably have filled the vacuum left by the unmet promises of community care" (Thurer, 1983, p. 1162).

The cultural bias of blame toward mothers of persons with serious mental illness is reflective of the dynamic of woman blaming identified by feminists in other areas, such as rape and battering. It has resulted in both social and internalized responses of stigma and devaluation. As a result, generations of mothers who have witnessed their children's pain and suffering caused by unexpected and unexplained chronic psychotic disorders have then at times been blamed for those disorders and shunned by mental health professionals, other family members, and the public at large. Due to the stigma associated with mental illness, it is only in the last 10 years that family members as a whole have publicly identified themselves and created a national organization, the National Alliance for the Mentally Ill, for the purposes of education, support, and advocacy. This process of empowerment that family caregivers and persons with mental illness are themselves embarking on is similar in spirit to the feminist movement. Both advocate for the rights and recognition of an oppressed minority-status group, value collective support and consciousness-raising, and attempt to dispel and correct social myths and misinformation. The feminist experience shares and parallels their sense of awakening, their questioning and their challenging the lack of dignity, respect, and resources afforded them that, up to this point, has been socially acceptable.

DEVELOPING A FEMINIST SOCIAL WORK PERSPECTIVE

Feminism initially occupied a distinct corner of my mind and heart, viewed more as a personal interest and not yet integrated, as a way of understanding the world, into my personal and professional philosophy and value base. My eventual career in psychiatric social work began with a volunteer experience at a state psychiatric institution in the early 1970s, when writers such as Laing and Esterson (1964) and Szasz (1974) popularized the notion of the "myth" of mental illness, explaining psychotic symptoms as understandable reactions to a "crazy" and oppressive society/family/mother. Later, as a helper in a therapeutic community in London that was based on these principles, I viewed my role as "rescuing" those considered emotionally distressed from their families and from psychiatric institutions. The mothers of the residents were often viewed as the problem, and little contact was sought or maintained with family members.

During this same period, I became more involved in feminist consciousness-raising groups. It was unsettling to become aware of what was always there, yet unnamed and mysterious. With an increasing understanding of sexism, its links among racism, classism, and other forms of oppression and discrimination became more evident on an institutional as well as on a personal level. I became sensitized to the way in which a mind-set of splitting the world into dominant and subordinate, powerful and powerless, primary and secondary classes of people was dehumanizing and unjust (Miller, 1976). Feminism offered a means for analyzing the dynamics of this process of oppression as well as a vision of personal and social relationships rooted in equality.

Despite the now obvious links between feminism and the situation of the mothers of those with severe mental illness, and even with an evolving feminist consciousness at that time, the mother-blaming bias was so entrenched that these traditional views still predominated. The incongruence of this form of mother-blaming in the therapeutic community setting was not yet apparent to me.

My weaving of feminist values into social work practice occurred while I was working on a masters degree in social work.
Following a course on gender issues in social work practice, a
number of us formed a feminist social work study group that continued for the next 3 years. We used the group as our base for de-
bating and analyzing, from a shared feminist perspective, what we
were learning from our courses, internships, and later our employment. Through support, disagreement, and passionate dialogue, the
group fostered our development of feminist ways of working within
our diverse "mainstream" settings, which ranged from community
mental health centers and adolescent group homes to services for the
elderly. With the variety of practice and theoretical approaches represented in this group, we came to see feminist social work more as a
core set of values from which to operate than as defined by specific
techniques or particular populations.

Walters, Carter, Papp, and Silverstein (1988) report a similar experience in a peer group of feminist family therapists, describing how
such a group led to "defining a shared viewpoint, a value system, that
would be strong enough to permit us to break through our commitments to various methodologies" (p. 16). The common values and
principles that surfaced in our group were influenced by our readings
on feminism and exposure to feminist culture through music, literature, political organizing, and social events. The viewpoint that
emerged from our discussions centered around the principles of (a)
the personal as political, (b) empowerment as both the goal and the
means to the goal, and (c) valuing and reclaiming those aspects of
women (and other groups subject to social oppression) that have been
devalued, hidden, and unacknowledged. These principles formed our
core foundation for practice and are reflective of the basic tenets of
feminist theory as well as inclusive of some of the key characteristics
of feminist practice that were identified in the NASW Feminist Practice Project survey (Bricker-Jenkins & Hooyman, 1986).

The link between the personal and the political, and between the individual experience and the broader social structure, was facilitated
by the composition of our group. We were a mix of clinicians, political organizers, and administrators, and our discussion topics ranged from
individual case examples to broader social issues and organizational dynamics. We shared our individual interests by rotating as presenters
and as facilitators of the group discussion. Through this process, we
learned to analyze an issue or clinical situation from a perspective that

integrates the continuum between micro-level and macro-level practice. In an atmosphere of respect and trust, we were able to cross the boundaries separating different types of social work practice.

Empowerment, and sensitizing ourselves and others to the dynamics of power at the interpersonal, social, and organizational levels, became central to our goal of practice, our means of practice, and our way of conducting our own group. As a collective, we struggled with the tensions between individual and group goals, with definitions and expectations of commitment, and with balancing the more active and more reserved styles of participation. We moved back and forth between discussing planned topics and case presentations and taking time to learn from our own group dynamics. Empowerment in this sense became a process of identifying, examining, and asserting our individual needs and wants within the context of our commitment to a valued collective of feminists. This challenge ran parallel to that of our clients, who wrestled with identifying and valuing their own needs and interests within the context of their intimate relationships and their employment and community commitments. Recognizing and valuing women's work and unique qualities, such as caregiving, that have been devalued and unsupported played a powerful role in our own consciousness-raising with regard to both clients and ourselves as practitioners.

After social work training, teaching in an undergraduate women's studies program solidified my identification with feminism. Working within a feminist environment meant experiencing, struggling with, and becoming socialized in feminist culture in all its complexity. Moving from feminism in the abstract and as an ideal to a more applied feminism carried with it both the exhilaration of putting into practice a vision for social and personal transformation and the disillusionment of realizing that feminism was neither an instant cure-all nor problem free.

One particular classroom experience gave me a fuller understanding of the nature of women's anger toward oppression and enabled me to know firsthand the effects of being a target of blame—an experience that came into play in my later work with the mother of a mentally ill son. Idealistically expecting an automatic sense of feminist community in the classroom, I was caught off guard by expressions of anger and mistrust directed toward those in leadership positions, including myself. The classroom atmosphere of permission, safety, and encouragement to express feelings and opinions directly, supplemented by the emotionally

charged content highlighting the oppression of women and the importance of empowerment, served to open a floodgate of intense feelings
and strong opinions that previously had been suppressed.

The struggles within feminist groups regarding formal and informal
leadership have been noted since the early literature on women's
groups (Freeman, 1972-1973). In this situation, the role of teacher or
group leader became a prime target for the stored anger toward social
injustice and authority. It was difficult to distinguish these social projections of blame and criticism directed toward me as a leader from
feedback about my actual attitudes and behaviors. It was necessary to
sort out this complicated interaction of reality and projection in order
not to personalize the distortions. At first I viewed it as "part of the
job" to allow this anger from previous experiences of unjust leadership to be vented toward me. But I later realized that in so doing, I
was modeling a woman who allowed herself to be scapegoated in the
name of trying to meet others' needs rather than engaging in a process
of mutual growth, responsibility, and empowerment. Even though this
situation was contained and time limited, the experience of being the
target of blame and projection by a group helped me later to relate to
and empathize with the experience of mothers who were being
blamed for their children's mental illness and being held responsible
for the subsequent stresses affecting their families. It is difficult not
to personalize and internalize these social projections, especially
when they are constant and consistent over time.

The change in my view of family caregivers came with increased
contact with these families while working as a psychiatric social
worker on an inpatient unit. With the shift of research and treatment
of serious mental illnesses, I came to understand such illness as a brain
disease, and observed the significant positive effects of psychotropic
medications, when used thoughtfully. It was increasingly obvious that
the whole family was under considerable stress in coping with the effects of the mental illness of a family member and was receiving little
support, understanding, or services for their care of relatives.

This growing recognition of the situation of these families led to
my current involvement as an activist and ally with the National Alliance for the Mentally Ill. It is here that my professional social work
interests and feminist orientation have become better integrated
through collaborative working relationships with family members, a
collective striving toward empowerment, and a linking of the personal
and the political with regard to those with mental illness and their

families. This perspective has also influenced my clinical work in more traditional settings. The following description of my work with a mother who was coping with a son with mental illness highlights more fully these mothers' experiences and provides more detail about how a feminist approach differs from other approaches to this situation. As background to that work, the phenomenon of mother-blaming needs to be understood and acknowledged.

CASE ILLUSTRATION

The woman in this example contacted me for services in my role as a social work clinician at a local outpatient mental health clinic. She came to the clinic originally to seek help for depression and anxiety, citing difficulties with sleeping, depressed mood, lack of interest in social activities, constant worrying, a feeling of isolation, and ongoing health problems that had been identified as stress related. She blamed herself for "not being able to pull myself together" and felt very alone, feeling "relatives and friends are tired of hearing about my worries."

The primary focus of her worrying was the welfare of her 26-year-old son, who had schizophrenia and who had been in and out of psychiatric hospitals over the previous 10 years. Since the onset of her son's illness, she had been his primary and most consistent caregiver in terms of support and assistance. Over the years he had had numerous doctors and case managers because of frequent turnover of staff, the episodic nature of his condition, and the lack of continuity and connection among various services. He had lived with his mother and her second husband for periods of time, yet even when he was living in the nearby community he would continue to need her help on a weekly and at times daily basis. This help would include receiving late-night phone calls when he was anxious, accompanying him to appointments for psychiatric or medical care, providing assistance in dealing with the social security benefit system, and making arrangements for hospital care when he became acutely psychotic. Her son was a client at the local community mental health center, and he attended his appointments regularly and took his prescribed antipsychotic medication. However, he was one of 60 clients assigned to his caseworker, and he had an appointment scheduled only once every 4 to 6 weeks. The case manager refused contact with the mother,

citing confidentiality issues and lack of time. The one initial interview
she did have with the case manager focused on questions regarding her
treatment of her son as a child. She was then told that currently she appeared to be overinvolved with her son and that it was probably making his condition worse. No additional services, however, were offered
as a means for her to reduce her involvement, nor was she given any
assurances that his special needs would in fact be met.

This woman felt alone and isolated in her concern for her son. Her
other children were angry and resentful toward her, feeling that her
attention was unequally focused on one child and that his "bad behavior" was a result of her catering to him. Her second husband referred
to her son's condition as "her problem" and would become angry with
her when he felt it took time away from their time together. Her son's
father provided intermittent financial support, but was not involved in
day-to-day caregiving, and he questioned what she had done wrong as
a mother for their son to "turn out like this." She had also reached a
point of no longer mentioning her son's condition when speaking with
friends or new acquaintances, weary of the awkward silences, judgments, and insensitive advice, and fearing herself that his ongoing
problems reflected some deficiency in her mothering.

Her son's condition was most certainly cause for concern. When experiencing a psychotic episode, he would hear voices, become withdrawn
to the point of rarely leaving his room, and neglect regular eating and
self-care; sometimes he would disappear without warning while in this
condition and then reappear in another part of the country, confused and
without any resources. He had also talked of suicide during times of
frustration and despair. Between episodes, he would try to work and live
independently, but with each episode and subsequent hospitalization he
would need again to begin looking for new work and a new place to live.
Despite his numerous problems and difficulties over the previous 10
years, his mother continued to remember vividly what he was like while
growing up, prior to the onset of the illness, when he was symptom free.
She feared something must be terribly wrong with her to have somehow
caused such problems for him now.

CONVENTIONAL APPROACHES

The common conventional approaches used by social workers in
this situation can be summarized primarily by the three different

problem definitions and subsequent interventions depicted in Table 8.1. In an individual treatment approach, the client is diagnosed as depressed and anxious and the primary focus of intervention is to reduce these presenting symptoms. Psychotherapy then centers on an exploration of the client's individual dynamics that are hypothesized to be the cause of the presenting symptoms. The severity of the symptoms is assessed to determine if a psychiatric consultation is indicated to evaluate the need for medication.

In the second approach listed in Table 8.1, the family system is considered to be both the unit of attention and the source of the problems, and the whole family is encouraged to participate in the treatment. The symptoms of the individual family members would be expected to decrease when the underlying conflicts in the family system are addressed. Intervention centers primarily on reducing the more acute symptoms of the son, identified as the *family scapegoat*. Even though the family systems approach is centered around this process of projecting onto a single family member the problems of the family as a whole, the intervention itself remains narrowly focused on the *identified patient* with psychotic symptoms and neglects exploring how this dynamic operates in the family system, and how the mother is the target of these projections.

In the third conventional approach, the woman is viewed as exacerbating her own problems and those of her son by her caregiving relationship, defined in pathological terms with labels such as "overinvolved," "enmeshed," or "enabling." Interventions are directed toward decreasing her contact and caregiving behaviors, yet often without solutions or services for her son's concrete and urgent needs. This approach is the equivalent of telling a family caregiver to cut back caregiving activities for a relative with Alzheimer's disease or cancer, but without providing any alternative services to meet the very real needs for care.

There may be situations in which some of these conventional approaches are relevant at some point in time for some family caregivers. Certainly out of the whole population of these families there are mothers, in comparable numbers to the general population, who have preexisting depressive disorders in need of treatment. Or there may be family caregivers who, even with reliable services and a remission of their family member's psychotic symptoms, have difficulty reducing their caregiving role. As an exclusive and initial response, however, these conventional approaches provide a very

Table 8.1
Conventional and Collaborative Approaches With Caregivers

Problem Definition	Goals	Interventions
Conventional Approach (level of primary attention: micro)		
client depresed and anxious	reduced depression and anxiety	individual treatment: psychotherapy and medications
client or family system causing or precipitating son's mental illness	improvement of son's condition	family treatment
client overinvolved, emeshed with adult son	reduction of family pathology	services directed toward son's needs
	reduced overinvolvement; acceleration of delayed separation-individuation process	encourage client to decrease contact with son
Collaborative Approach (level of primary attention: micro)		
client experiencing burden of inadequately supported caregiving role in relation to a family member with biogenetically based psychiatric illness	improved coping with a traumatic and chronic situation	family consultation and supportive counseling for the family member
	increased access to information, support and services for both person with the mental illness and the family member	psychoeducation regarding mental illness

referral and case management |

limited and narrow assessment of the situation, without taking into account the wider context of the social environment and the interactions among the family, the mental health service system, and the community at large. In some circumstances, these conventional approaches have been used to perpetuate the process of mother-blaming by interpreting the behaviors and attitudes of these mothers solely within the framework of individual psychopathology. Practitioners may attribute the cause or relapse of psychotic symptoms to the mother's behavior without acknowledging the biological origins, the lack of services and social supports, and the erratic and unpredictable course of these psychiatric conditions.

COLLABORATIVE APPROACHES

Collaborative approaches with family caregivers of persons with mental illness have developed in response to the recognition of this condition as an illness and the need for supportive, consultative, and educational interventions to support and strengthen family coping (Bernheim & Lehman, 1985; Hatfield & Lefly, 1987). These approaches acknowledge the social stigma that family caregivers face (Lefly, 1989); the interventions aim to reduce internalized blame and guilt through education for family caregivers about mental illness. Family caregivers are viewed as collaborators in the caregiving process, and referrals to self-help groups, such as the Alliance for the Mentally Ill, are encouraged.

In contrast to the conventional approaches, collaborative approaches are more in tune with a feminist philosophy. With an emphasis on a democratic relationship between professional and family caregiver and the sharing of information and education, family caregivers are explicitly valued and empowered. There are, however, areas of concern to feminists that this approach has not yet addressed. The focus of this approach to date has been primarily on family caregivers as a whole, for example, without further exploration into how this experience may be affected by gender differences and sexist assumptions regarding the role of women. Although the supporters of this model are themselves quite active in public education and advocacy, the importance of these activities for professionals working with families of persons with mental illness has not been included and emphasized in the literature describing the collaborative or consultative approach. The focus has remained at an individual family problem-solving level and does not incorporate a broader analysis of the links between an individual's personal situation as a caregiver and political, economic, and cultural structures.

Table 8.2

Feminist Approach With Caregivers (level of primary attention: micro/macro)

Problem Definition	Goals	Interventions
women client overwhelmed as caregiver trying to "fill in the gaps" of inadequate community services and low involvement by other family members	*client/family/society:* increased awareness of sexist nature of societal expectations of and dependence on women as primary caregivers; increased assuming of responsibility by other family members and the community at large for individuals in need	*with client/community/ policymakers:* consciousness-raising regarding (a) unmet needs of persons with mental illness and family caregivers, (b) defining social responsibility regarding these needs, (c) identifying sexist expections regarding female caregiving
	society: improved community support services for those with severe mental illnesses	*with community/policy makers:* advocacy for improved services; public education
	client: recognition of own limitations; increased ability to set limits and challenge the underresponsibility of others/society	*with client:* support for setting limits; advocacy skill training
client as a mother being blamed and held responsible for problems of her adult child; client internalizes blame and views her son's problems as a result of her own weakness or deficiency	*client/family/society:* understand biogenetic research regarding severe mental illness and recognize the traumatic impact of this condition for all involved	*with client/family/society:* public education; psychoeducation; referral to self-help and support groups for family caregivers
	client: reduced self-blame and guilt as a mother regarding son's condition	
influenced by female socialization, client devaluing and neglecting own needs and wants in face of extensive and on-going unmet needs of adult son with a prolonged psychiatric illness	*client/family/society:* value and attend to the needs of both the person with a mental illness and the family caregivers	*with client/family/society:* consulation and support; explicit valuing of and concern for client's individual needs and interests

(continued)

Table 8.2 (continued)

Problem Definition	Goals	Interventions
	client: increased valuing and identification of own needs and growth in balance with concern for ill family member	
client socially isolated and stigmatized by association with an oppressed group (e.g., persons with mental illness)	*client/family/society:* increased awareness of the larger social context and shared collective nature of discrimination against persons with mental illness and their family members	*client/family/society:* consciousness-raising and education regarding the historical and current trends in social policy, research, mental health service delivery, and public attitudes regarding those with mental illness and their families
	client: identification with and compassion for others in similar situations; decreased shame; increased self-acceptance and more open self-disclosure regarding being a mother of an adult child with a severe mental illness; participation in advocacy on an individual and collective level	*with client:* self-help support groups; individual and collective advocacy; identify links between client's situation and that of (a) women in similar situations as caregivers, (b) comparable groups subject to discrimination

FEMINIST APPROACH

A feminist approach, as outlined in Table 8.2, draws these links between the micro and macro, between the individual situation and the larger social context. Advocacy on an individual and on a systems level is encouraged for both the client and the worker. The discrimination and stigma associated with mental illness and the family, as well as the sexist nature of mother-blaming, are overtly labeled and actively resisted. In my work with this client, from a feminist social work approach, the interventions described below formed the primary focus.

Functioning as an alternative reference point to the projections of blame. It was important to state explicitly to this woman that she was not the cause of this condition (e.g., "You are not to blame for your child's mental illness") and to reinforce this perspective by providing education about the current knowledge about these conditions as brain illnesses. Sharing with her the history and theories of how mothers have been blamed for mental illness helped her to counteract the messages she had been receiving from others, including mental health professionals and other family members, and strengthened her resolve to identify and challenge such attitudes rather than to personalize them.

Referral to a self-help group for family caregivers of persons with a mental illness. By accepting my referral and participating in the local chapter of the Alliance for the Mentally Ill, this mother had the opportunity to meet with other family caregivers and to realize that she was not alone in her struggles. In such a group setting, she was able to hear from others how they, too, had blamed themselves and had accepted the blame from others, but were no longer feeling guilty or ashamed after learning more about these illnesses. Through presentations and discussions in this group, she also became more aware of how the lack of services for and social stigma toward mental illness affected her own situation. She began to feel angry about the poor treatment her son was receiving, especially compared with the services and benefits available for those with other types of illnesses. Through this experience of consciousness-raising, she began to take a stronger stand with his community mental health worker, advocating for improved services and questioning his refusal to include her in joint meetings with her son on occasion. She also began to feel more identified with other family caregivers, whom she had come to respect. Rather than trying to hide these issues from others, as she had done previously, she became more open to sharing that she had a son with a mental illness. Through this process of coming out of the closet and being ready to talk about these issues, she found others in her network of acquaintances who were then more willing to talk about similar situations in their own families.

Referral to a family psychoeducation series on mental illness. This was an additional means by which this mother could meet other family caregivers and learn specific information about mental illness.

This information further reinforced the idea that she was not to blame for this condition and offered practical suggestions for coping with the symptomatic behavior of a family member, dealing with the mental health service system, and learning more about the various treatment approaches. She reported that being more informed about these areas helped her feel more confident discussing these issues with others and gave her additional tools for facing problems as they arose.

Explicitly valuing and acknowledging caregiving efforts that have been socially devalued and taken for granted, and at the same time challenging the current neglect of social responsibility. When an adult member of our society is unable to care for his or her own basic needs due to a chronic disabling condition, whose responsibility is it to provide and manage the care that is needed? During the first half of this century, care for persons with serious mental illness was provided primarily by state institutions and was assumed to be a social responsibility. The shift toward deinstitutionalization was originally intended to be a means of better integrating those with psychiatric disorders into the community, but the continuing reduction of both institutional and community care have instead resulted in major gaps in meeting even basic needs, such as housing, medical care, day-to-day support, and, when necessary, protective supervision. The overt neglect of these services is evidenced not only by statistics but by the increasing numbers of persons with mental illness who are homeless and living on the streets of our cities, openly hallucinating or severely withdrawn.

Although the homeless psychiatrically disabled are certainly the most glaring example of societal neglect of the mentally ill, family caregivers have also borne the burden of this neglect by being expected, with little support or respite, to "fill in the gaps" of an inadequate system of care and services. Approximately half of the mentally ill persons in this country live with their families (Carpenter & Keith, 1986). As with home care of persons with other types of chronic illnesses and disabilities (Polansky, 1980), the family caregivers are primarily women (Cook, 1988; Thurer, 1983). The implicit assumption is that full-time caregiving of a person with a disability is a maternal or marital obligation (Polansky, 1980) rather than a position that should be balanced with social and government responsibility and support. This expectation for caregiving has no sense of limits. In the case of severe disability, such care may be necessary for prolonged periods of time.

Within this social context of unrealistic and limitless expectations upon mothers of persons with mental illness, the focus of intervention with this woman was (a) to support and encourage her to identify and honor her own personal limitations and needs, and therefore set realistic expectations for herself about the extent of the caregiving she can offer; (b) to encourage her to challenge both individually and collectively the lack of services and support currently being provided for her son; and (c) to acknowledge and recognize explicitly the value of the caregiving she is providing, for which she has received little feedback or appreciation and that has been taken for granted. In response to these approaches, she showed signs of becoming more protective of herself; for instance, she established a schedule with her son for phone calls and visits that allowed some time for herself. She also disagreed with the critical comments of other family members regarding her involvement with her son, gave them educational reading material on mental illness, and encouraged them to accompany her to the family support and educational meetings. She began to challenge the lack of services available, by becoming more assertive with the community mental health case manager. Although the improvement of services so far has been minimal, her approach now is to keep informing the case manager of problems as they arise rather than feeling it is her responsibility alone to bear. She no longer speaks with shame or embarrassment about her caregiving efforts. Yet she continues, at times, to ask for reassurance that she is, in fact, doing enough for her son and that it is indeed all right for her to take time for her own care and nourishment.

Work as an advocate and public educator in order to reduce the stigma and myths associated with mental illness, heighten community awareness regarding the impoverished state of services, improve the training of mental health professionals, and encourage a sense of responsibility and compassion on the part of the community toward those afflicted with brain illnesses and their family caregivers. To date, this type of macro approach for me has included working closely with the local chapter of the Alliance for the Mentally Ill as a resource person; participating on a countrywide public education committee on mental illness that has been providing educational presentations, information fairs, and displays for the community; teaching a community-based family education series on mental illness; presenting at numerous conferences and in-service training workshops on new approaches for families of persons with mental illness; and teaching social work courses specific to this topic. By working side by side with family caregivers in these various settings, and by facing with them the common challenge and goal of transforming an inadequate service system and reducing the stigma of mental illness, I have fostered and cultivated a sense of a working partnership. The development of this sense of alliance, and the respect that accompanies it, carries over into my individual work with family caregivers. This work of public and professional education is a step toward creating a more supportive environment for persons with mental illness and their family caregivers.

SUMMARY

In working with women who have relatives with serious mental illness, a multilayered feminist approach that bridges both the micro and macro spheres of practice best reflects the principles of empowerment, the understanding of personal experience within the context of the political and social environment, and the valuing of those who have been socially devalued through a process of discrimination and stigmatization. These women have historically been the targets of blame for an unpredictable condition with unclear causes. As research points toward an understanding of serious mental illness as a brain disease, and as the collective voice of family caregivers begins to be heard through self-help organizations, the needs and strengths of these women are now more apparent. Information about serious mental illness and its impact on the family needs to be integrated into the professional training of social workers. Social workers need to learn how to be supportive of caregivers and not further perpetuate prior patterns of blaming.

REFERENCES

Anderson, C. M., & Holder, D. P. (1989). Women and serious mental disorders. In M. McGoldrick, C. M. Anderson, & F. Walsh (Eds.), *Women in families: A framework for family therapy* (pp. 381-405). New York: Norton.

Andreasen, N. (1985). *The broken brain: The biological revolution in psychiatry.* New York: Harper & Row.

Bateson, G., Jackson, D. D., Haley, J., & Weakland, J. H. (1956). Toward a theory of schizophrenia. *Behavioral Science, 1,* 251-264.

Bernheim, K. F., & Lehman, A. F. (1985). *Working with families of the mentally ill*. New York: Norton.

Bricker-Jenkins, M., & Hooyman, N. R. (1986). Grounding the definition of feminist practice. In M. Bricker-Jenkins & N. R. Hooyman (Eds.), *Not for women only: Social work practice for a feminist future* (pp. 25-33). Silver Spring, MD: National Association of Social Workers.

Caplan, P., & Hall-McCorquodale, I. (1985). Mother-blaming in major clinical journals. *American Journal of Orthopsychiatry, 5*, 345-353.

Carpenter, W. T., Jr., & Keith, S. J. (1986). Integrating treatments in schizophrenia. *Psychiatric Clinics of North America, 9*(1), 153-164.

Cook, J. A. (1988). Who "mothers" the chronically mentally ill? *Family Relations, 37*(1), 42-49.

Freeman, J. (1972-1973). The tyranny of structurelessness. *Berkeley Journal of Sociology, 17*, 150-164.

Fromm-Reichmann, F. (1948). Notes on the development of treatment of schizophrenics by psychoanalytic psychotherapy. *Psychiatry, 11*, 263-274.

Haley, J. (1980). *Leaving home: The therapy of disturbed young people*. New York: McGraw-Hill.

Hatfield, A., & Lefly, H. (1987). *Families of the mentally ill: Coping and adaptation*. New York: Guilford.

Imber-Black, E. (1986). Women, families, and larger systems. In M. Ault-Riche (Ed.), *Women and family therapy*. Rockville, MD: Aspen.

Imber-Black, E. (1988). *Families and larger systems: A therapist's guide through the labyrinth*. New York: Guilford.

Imber-Black, E. (1989). Women's relationship with larger systems. In M. McGoldrick, C. M. Anderson, & F. Walsh (Eds.), *Women in families: A framework for family therapy* (pp. 335-353) New York: Norton.

Laing, R. D., & Esterson, A. (1964). *Sanity, madness, and the family: Families of schizophrenics* (Vol. 1). London: Tavistock.

Lefly, H. (1989). Family burden and family stigma in major mental illness. *American Psychologist, 44*, 556-560.

Miller, J. B. (1976). *Toward a new psychology of women*. Boston: Beacon.

Polansky, E. (1980). Women and the health care system: Implications for social work practice. In E. Norman & A. Mancuso (Eds.), *Women's issues and social work practice* (pp. 183-199). Itasca, IL: F. E. Peacock.

Szasz, T. H. (1974). *The myth of mental illness: Foundations of a theory of personal conduct*. New York: Harper & Row.

Taylor, E. H. (1987). The biological basis for schizophrenia. *Social Work, 32*, 115-121.

Thurer, S. L. (1983). Deinstitutionalization and women: Where the buck stops. *Hospital and Community Psychiatry, 34*, 1162-1163.

Torrey, E. F. (1983). *Surviving schizophrenia: A family manual*. New York: Harper & Row.

Walters, M. (1988). Mothers and daughters. In M. Walters, B. Carter, P. Papp, & O. Silverstein (Eds.), *The invisible web: Gender patterns in family relationships*. New York: Guilford.

Walters, M., Carter, B., Papp, P., & Silverstein, O. (1988). Toward a feminist perspective in family therapy. In M. Walters, B. Carter, P. Papp, & O. Silverstein (Eds.), *The invisible web: Gender patterns in family relationships*. New York: Guilford.

Wynne, L. C., Ryckoff, I., Day, J., & Hirsch, S. (1958). Pseudomutuality in the family relations of schizophrenics. *Psychiatry, 21*, 205-220.

All the Time

Michael Andrews

It was 93 degrees.
She wore 3 sweaters,
a sweatshirt,
some long pants,
a few dresses,
rolled down nylons,
sneakers,
a feather boa,
and a 47 year old mink.
She bought the mink
for consolation
the day she outlived
her last husband.
One eyelid
was in a flutter
of perpetual motion.
Lipstick
ran all over her face
like a map of Chicago.
She was as crazy
as a 5 o'clock commuter.
Went to the Safeway
twice a week
with molding dollars,
social security checks,
and food stamps.
Stole Tootsie Rolls
and ate them before
she left the market.
Walked to the intersection.
Waited for the light
to turn red,
hunched low, knees high,
lurched out in front
of oncoming traffic,
waved madly at
the skidding cars,
her wire basket
with coffee, doughnuts
and smoked oysters
bouncing right behind her,
chuckling and muttering
about insane drivers,
one eyeball rotating
in an orgasm of fear.

It was her little joke.

Once a policeman stopped her.
She kicked him in the shin,
scattered his citations
all over the street,
yelled rape
in her reed-piped voice
and scurried home
muttering about cops.
After that
the police left her alone,
but sometimes they
spoiled the fun
by stopping the traffic
at her favorite crosswalk.

Her house buzzed
with ticking clocks.
She didn't trust the electric ones.
Wound all 217 of them every day,
but never set the time.
She considered the random firing of alarms
a form of music.
She kept the smoked oysters
for the dog in the freezer
with her third husband's appendix,
which the dog greatly desired.
But the old lady kept it
in memory of the surgeon
she married after he performed
the appendectomy in which
her third husband died
of cancer of everything.
Sometimes at night
she beat on the windows
across the airshaft
with a broom handle,
shouted obscenities and yelled
"You keep quiet in there.
You keep quiet."

After a while
they sealed up the windows.
It was getting harder
all the time
to get someone's
attention.

Previously published in Sandra Martz (Ed.), *When I Am an Old Woman I Shall Wear Purple*, 1987. Reprinted by permission of Papier-Mâché Press and the author.

From *Les Guerilleres*

Monique Wittig

There was a time
when you were not
a slave,
    remember that.
You walked along,
    full of laughter,
you bathed barebellied.
You may have lost
all recollection of it,
    remember . . .
You say there are not
words to describe it,
you say it does not
    exist.
But remember,
make an effort
    to remember,
Or, failing that,
    invent.

Chapter 9

EMPOWERING WOMEN OF COLOR
A Feminist Model

LORRAINE GUTIÉRREZ

Although the feminist social work literature expresses a commitment to eliminating racism and recognizing the experiences and contributions of all women, the needs, issues, and contributions women of color have often been overlooked (Kopasci & Faulkner, 1988; Schechter, 1982; Withorn, 1984). Consequently, women of color have not benefited fully from developments in feminist social work that have the potential of addressing how women of color have been affected by the interaction of racism, sexism, and classism in our society. This chapter, drawing upon my experiences as a feminist social worker with women of color and from the empowerment literature, suggests one way in which feminist social work can be carried out with women of color.

Women of color—African-American, Latina, Asian-American, and Native American—make up 20% of the total female population of the United States (Lin-Fu, 1987). Although the groups encompassed by this term differ in many respects, together we share similarities in terms of status and power. As women we are directly affected by sexist structures and practices that limit the opportunities of all women. As people of color, we are also limited by racist practices that have resulted in average earnings lower than those of white women, overrepresentation in low-status occupations, and an average low level of education (Gordon-Bradshaw, 1987; Kopasci & Faulkner, 1988; Lin-Fu, 1987). In spite of affirmative action laws, women of color continue to be underrepresented in positions of power in government, corporations, and nonprofit institutions (Gordon-Bradshaw, 1987; Zambrana, 1987). These facts suggest that effective social work practice with women of color needs to address how our marginalized and less powerful position in this society contributes to individual problems.

The lack of direct access to structures of power has very direct and concrete effects on the lives of women of color, especially in relation to their socioeconomic status. The poverty rate of women of color is more than double that of white women (Wilson, 1987). Accordingly, women of color are more likely than white women to suffer from conditions of poor or no housing, insufficient food and clothing, and inadequate access to health and mental health services (Gordon-Bradshaw, 1987).

Even for women who are not poor, social marginalization can contribute to poor mental health outcomes. Women, poor people, and members of ethnic and racial minority groups have, on average, much higher rates of mental illness than do men, whites, and the more affluent (Moos & Billings, 1982; Pearlin & Schooler, 1978; Thoits, 1983). Most researchers who have studied this connection have focused on the stressful life circumstances of these groups and the resulting strain on their coping capacity (Pearlin & Schooler, 1978; Silver & Wortman, 1980). This relationship can also be analyzed from the perspective of power and the effect marginalization has on reducing the ability to exercise personal control, on the development of negative stereotypes toward women of color, and on access to necessary social and material resources.

In my work with women of color, I have found that most models of direct social work practice underestimate how the social conditions related to powerlessness affect their problems and opportunities. Consequently, the focus of practice is often on assisting women of color to cope with or accept difficult situations rather than on working actively to change them (Gould, 1987b; Morell, 1987). Many social workers may recognize that a client's problem is rooted in insufficient power, but increasing the client's power is rarely the primary goal of practice. This observation led me to explore alternative models, such as feminist social work and the empowerment approach, in an effort to find ways to work more effectively with this population.

The feminist and empowerment perspectives assume that issues of power and powerlessness are integral to the experiences of women of color. Researchers, activists, and practitioners in this field propose concrete and specific methods for use in the resolution of the personal problems of women of color by increasing their power on a number of different levels. This chapter outlines the assumptions of these perspectives, the psychological changes they involve, and specific techniques for empowering women of color. As women of color make up one of the fastest-growing segments of the American population (Lin-Fu, 1987), skills to work with this group will be of increasing importance for us all.

DEFINING EMPOWERMENT

Empowerment is a process of increasing personal, interpersonal, or political power so that individuals can take action to improve their lives. Empowerment theory and practice are rooted in many fields, such as community organization, adult education, feminist theory, and social psychology. Empowerment is one of the critical concepts of feminist social work, and one that differentiates it from a nonsexist or women's issues approach to practice (Bricker-Jenkins & Hooyman, 1986; Nes & Iadicola, 1989; Van Den Bergh & Cooper, 1986).

Empowerment theory assumes that societies consist of separate groups possessing different levels of power and control over resources (Fay, 1987; Gould, 1987a). It views individual problems as arising not from personal deficits, but from the failure of the society to meet the needs of all people. The potential for positive change is thought to exist within every individual, but negative behaviors and symptoms can emerge from attempts to cope with a hostile world (Pinderhughes, 1983). Although individuals can be helped to develop less personally destructive coping strategies, changes in the power structure of society are considered crucial if individual problems are to be prevented (Albee, 1986; Rappaport, 1981; Solomon, 1982).

To understand empowerment, we must understand the role power can play in social relationships. Feminist theory has moved beyond negative views of power, which present it as an exploitative and scarce resource, to a perspective that assumes that power can be a positive force (Bricker-Jenkins & Hooyman, 1986; Katz, 1984). It assumes that power is not finite because it can be generated in the process of social interaction. Within this perspective, power can be defined in the following three ways: the ability to get what one needs; the ability to influence how others think, feel, act, or believe; and the ability to influence the distribution of resources in a social system such as a family, organization, community, or society.

Empowerment theory focuses on increasing three different kinds of power (Dodd & Gutiérrez, in press):

Personal power involves experiencing oneself as an effective and capable person. One means of increasing personal power is to identify and understand the power one already has. This is the basis of all other kinds of empowerment.

Interpersonal power is the ability to influence others through the use of social power. Social power derives from such things as social position (e.g., as a supervisor), role (e.g., as a parent), interpersonal skills (e.g., conversational ability), credibility (appearing knowledgeable), and attractiveness (either physical or personal); (Feld, 1987; French & Raven, 1968). Some of these bases of power are ascriptive—based on race, gender, or class—but others can be achieved as an individual develops social skills or attains new social positions. Therefore, identifying skill deficits and learning new skills is a key element of the empowerment process.

Political power is the ability to influence the allocation of resources in an organization or community through formal or informal means (Parenti, 1978). Political power is most commonly gained through collective action and collaboration with others.

Empowerment practice with women of color can involve any of these kinds of power or combinations of them. Often it involves multiple levels of practice and can require skills for working with individuals, groups, families, and communities. It requires combining a sense of personal control with the ability to influence the behavior of others, focusing on enhancing the existing strengths in individuals or communities, and establishing equity in the distribution of resources (Biegel & Naperste, 1982; Katz, 1984; Kieffer, 1984; Rappaport, 1986; Van Den Bergh & Cooper, 1986). A feminist perspective on empowerment focuses specifically on how individual women have been affected by forces such as racism, ethnocentrism, and sexism and on ways in which social structures can be challenged. Because women of color are at the bottom of our social hierarchy in terms of political power, social workers must look at ways to work toward the interpersonal and political levels of empowerment. Gaining a sense of personal power must be viewed as only the first step toward the ultimate goal of changing oppressive structures (Bricker-Jenkins & Hooyman, 1986; Gould, 1987b; Gutiérrez, 1990).

THE PSYCHOLOGY OF EMPOWERMENT

Research and practice in feminist social work suggest that in order for women to be empowered, they must both understand the connections between personal and political issues and see themselves as capable of engaging in change. Four psychological changes have been identified that seem crucial for moving women of color from apathy and despair to action; these are discussed in turn below.

Increasing self-efficacy. Self-efficacy stems from beliefs about one's ability "to produce and to regulate events in one's life" (Bandura, 1982, p.122). This involves strengthening ego functioning, developing a sense of personal power or strength, developing a sense of mastery, developing client initiative, and increasing the client's ability to act (Fagan, 1979; Garvin, 1985; Hirayama & Hirayama, 1985; Mathis & Richan, 1986; Pernell, 1985; Shapiro, 1984; Solomon, 1976; Stensrud & Stensrud, 1982).

Developing a group consciousness. Group consciousness is the awareness of how political structures affect individual and group experience. It results in a critical perspective on society that redefines individual, group, or community problems as emerging from a lack of power. The development of a group consciousness creates within the individual members of a group or community a sense of shared fate and a belief in the collective basis for change (Gurin, Miller, & Gurin, 1980; Klien, 1984). This allows individuals to focus their energies on the causes of their problems, rather than on changing their internal subjective states (Bricker-Jenkins & Hooyman, 1986; Burghardt, 1982; Friere, 1973; Gould, 1987a; Keefe, 1980; Longres & McLeod, 1980; Solomon, 1976; Van Den Bergh & Cooper, 1986).

Reducing self-blame. By attributing the cause of their problems to the existing power arrangements in society, clients are freed from feeling responsible for their negative situation. As self-blame has been associated with feelings of depression and immobilization, this shift in focus allows clients to feel less defective or deficient and more capable of changing their situation (Brickman et al., 1982; Garvin, 1985; Hirayama & Hirayama, 1985; Janoff-Bulman, 1979; Keefe, 1980; Longres & McLeod, 1980).

Assuming personal responsibility. Assuming personal responsibility for change counteracts some of the potentially negative results of reducing self-blame. Clients who do not feel responsible for the cause of their problems may not feel invested in developing solutions unless they assume some personal responsibility for future change. This process is similar to Friere's (1973) notion of becoming a subject, or active participant, in the social world rather than remaining a powerless object (see also Bock, 1980). By taking personal responsibility for the resolution of problems, clients are more likely to engage in active efforts toward improving their lives (Brickman et al., 1982).

Although these changes have been described in a specific order, the empowerment process does not occur in a series of stages. Instead, different aspects of the process often occur simultaneously and work to enhance one another. For example, as women develop self-efficacy, they may be more likely to assume personal responsibility for change. Those who have studied the process closely also suggest that one does not necessarily "achieve empowerment," but that it is actually a continual process of growth and change that can occur throughout the life cycle (Friere, 1973; Kieffer, 1984). Rather than being a specific state, empowerment is a way of interacting with the world.

EMPOWERING METHODS

As stated previously, social workers may be aware of how a lack of power affects women of color, but may not know how individuals can gain power, especially in the context of individual practice. When working with women of color who may be overwhelmed by their particular situation, this lack of knowledge can lead to feelings of frustration and can be disempowering for individual social workers. Fortunately, the literature on empowerment suggests specific techniques and methods that social workers can use to increase client empowerment.

Context: The Helping Relationship

At the basis of empowering practice is a *helping relationship based on collaboration, trust, and the sharing of power*. It is critical that the worker perceive him- or herself as an enabler, organizer, consultant, or compatriot with the client in an effort to avoid replicating the powerlessness that the client experiences with other helpers or professionals. The interaction between worker and client should be characterized by genuineness, mutual respect, open communication, and informality. The interaction presumes that the worker does not hold the answers to the client's problems, but that in the context of collaboration the client will develop the insights, skills, and capacity to resolve the situation (Bock, 1980; Bricker-Jenkins & Hooyman, 1986; Fagan, 1979; Schechter, Szymanski, & Cahill, 1985).

Along these same lines, workers can assist women to *experience a sense of personal power within the helping relationship.* This technique is based on the assumption that the experience of personal power can be generalized to feelings of power in the larger social environment. Methods include having clients role-play and practice powerful behaviors, engaging clients in roles in which they help others, and having clients take control of the helping relationship by setting the agenda, coleading groups or meetings, and researching resources (Pernell, 1985; Pinderhughes, 1983; Schechter et al., 1985; Shapiro, 1984; Simmons & Parsons, 1983a, 1983b; Withorn, 1980).

Actively involving the clients in the change process is another aspect of the helping relationship that encourages empowerment. According to Solomon (1976), empowerment is a "process whereby the social worker engages in a set of activities with the client or client system that aim to reduce the powerlessness that has been created by the negative valuations based on membership in a stigmatized group" (p. 19). Like other authors, she describes empowering methods as involving activities ranging from the exploration of a problem to the development of alternative structures in a community (Beck, 1983; Checkoway & Norsman, 1986; Fagan, 1979; Kahn & Bender, 1985; Pinderhughes, 1983; Solomon, 1976).

What is common to all of these activities is praxis: the wedding of reflection and action. If clients' active involvement in change is to contribute to empowerment, they should be encouraged to reflect upon and analyze their experience. The results of this analysis can then be integrated into the development of future efforts (Bock, 1980; Burghardt, 1982; Friere, 1973; Resnick, 1976; Rose & Black, 1985).

Suggested Modalities

The literature on empowerment describes interventions on individual, group, family, and community levels. Practitioners are advised to develop skills on all of these levels of intervention and to feel comfortable moving from one modality to another. However, *small group work is presented as the ideal modality for empowering interventions* because it is an effective means for integrating the other techniques. It can be an ideal environment for raising consciousness, engaging in mutual aid, developing skills, problem solving, and experiencing one's own effectiveness in influencing others (Coppola & Rivas, 1985; Garvin, 1985; Hirayama & Hirayama, 1985; Sarri & du Rivage, 1985). This emphasis on small group work holds true regardless of whether the initial goal is to empower individuals or to change institutions.

In the same spirit, *involvement of clients in mutual-aid, self-help, or support groups* is recommended. These groups are formed by women who are experiencing similar problems to provide them with emotional and concrete assistance and support (Garvin, 1985; Kahn & Bender, 1985; Sherman & Wenocur, 1983; Withorn, 1980). Support groups facilitate empowerment by creating a basis of social support for the process of change, a format for providing concrete assistance, the opportunity to learn new skills through role modeling, and a potential power base for future action (Gutiérrez & Ortega, 1989; Solomon, 1982). They can also provide the context for developing group consciousness by involving clients in dialogue with others who share their problems.

Specific Techniques

Within this context of a collaborative helping relationship and a small group work modality, some specific techniques are suggested for empowering clients. The first of these is *accepting the client's definition of the problem.* By accepting the client's definition, the worker is communicating that the client is capable of identifying and understanding the situation. This also places the client in a position of power and control over the helping relationship (Beck, 1983; Fagan, 1979; Shapiro, 1984).

By *identifying and building upon existing strengths*, the empowering practitioner gets in touch with the client's present level of functioning and sources of individual or interpersonal power (Mathis & Richan, 1986; Shapiro, 1984; Sherman & Wenocur, 1983). This is most effective if the worker can recognize that many women of color have been involved in a process of struggle against oppressive structures and that this has required considerable strength. By analyzing elements of the struggle, client strengths can more easily be identified, communicated to the client, and then utilized as a basis for future work.

Engaging in a power analysis of the situation is a critical technique for empowering practice. This involves, first, analyzing how conditions of powerlessness contribute to the situation. A second crucial step is then to identify sources of potential power. One indirect technique is dialogue between the worker and clients aimed at exploring and identifying the social structural origins of their current situations (Keefe, 1980; Longres & McLeod, 1980; Resnick, 1976). Another more direct technique focuses clients on specific situations, either their own or from vignettes developed for the intervention, on which they can focus their analysis (Bock, 1980; Schechter et al., 1985; Solomon, 1976). Clients and workers should think creatively about sources of potential power, such as forgotten skills, personal qualities that could increase social influence, members of past social support networks, and organizations in the community.

An effective power analysis requires that social workers themselves fully comprehend the connection between the immediate practice situation and the distribution of power in society as a whole (Garvin, 1985; Mathis & Richan, 1986). This may require consciousness-raising exercises to look beyond the specific situation to problems shared by other women of color. It is also crucial that workers not adopt feelings of powerlessness from clients, but learn to see the potential for power and influence in every situation.

Teaching specific skills is one means of helping women to develop the resources to be more powerful (Mathis & Richan, 1986; Pernell, 1985; Shapiro, 1984). The skill areas most often used when working with women of color include problem solving; skills for community or organizational change; "life skills" such as parenting, job seeking, and self-defense; and interpersonal skills such as assertiveness, social competence, and self-advocacy (Fagan, 1979; Garvin, 1985; Schechter et al., 1985; Simmons & Parsons 1983a, 1983b; Withorn, 1980). The social worker's role when teaching these skills should be that of a consultant or facilitator, rather than instructor, so as not to replicate the power relationships that the worker and client are attempting to overcome (Schechter et al., 1985; Sherman & Wenocur, 1983; Solomon, 1976).

Mobilizing resources or advocating for clients is also suggested if worker and client together lack adequate resources for empowerment. In this case the worker gathers concrete resources or information for clients, as well as advocates on their behalf when necessary. Although some have argued that advocacy can be in conflict with the goal of empowerment because it may reinforce feelings of powerlessness

(Rappaport, 1981; Solomon, 1976), it can be carried out in a collaborative way that includes the client and involves learning new skills.
Through advocacy and resource mobilization, the worker and client
together ensure that the larger social structure provides what is necessary to empower the larger client group (Checkoway & Norsman,
1986; Pinderhughes, 1983; Solomon, 1982).

CASE EXAMPLE

How can these techniques be integrated into social work practice in
a clinical setting? An example of my work with African-American
and Latina single mothers in a community mental health center suggests how this relationship can be established in a traditional setting.

The Setting

The Center for Child Development (CCD) is a municipal agency
located in a low-income minority neighborhood in a large East Coast
city. Families and children are referred to the center, primarily by
teachers, when the children exhibit behavioral or learning problems.
All families are seen by a multidisciplinary team that includes a social worker, pediatrician, psychologist, speech therapist, and educational consultant. Many of the children are found to have specific
learning or behavioral problems that require additional counseling or
therapy at another agency.

Caseloads at the CCD are large, and the problems presented by
most families are quite complex. Most of the children are members of
African-American or Latino female-headed, single-parent households
receiving Aid to Families with Dependent Children (AFDC). The
learning or behavioral problems found through the diagnostic assessment are for many families another complication to lives characterized
by low income, inadequate housing, poor services, and experiences of
racism and sexism. Social workers and other staff at the CCD view their
roles as case managers who can only carry out an assessment of a case
and then make referrals to other agencies. This is communicated to staff
by the administrators of the mental health center, who often have more
concern about the compilation of client statistics and Medicaid reim-
bursement than about the quality of services. Social workers frequently
spend more time on the phone advocating for clients than in interaction
with the women and their children.

Designing the Intervention

Bringing a feminist approach to this setting required a new perspective on the role of the social worker and other helping professionals. The program coordinator and another psychologist, both white, and the two social workers, both Latina, began to talk about ways in which the clients of the agency could begin to confront the conditions of powerlessness in their lives and learn to advocate for themselves. One of our initial concerns was to find ways in which clients could follow through on referrals so that they could receive the services they needed; therefore, our first focus was on developing a sense of personal empowerment. A long-term goal was to encourage the clients to work together and mobilize toward the improvement of resources. In discussing our cases and the common problems experienced by these families, we determined that a group approach would be the most effective use of our skills and agency resources, would encourage group support and interaction between the women, and would help clients to make the connections between personal and political issues.

The Intervention Phase

Four groups were run over a 9-month period. The first group provided was a *support group* for Latinas offered by the social workers in English and Spanish. We first explored with the women how they viewed their situation—why did they think their children were not doing well in school? This led to an exploration of the concrete realities of these women's lives: They often defined the presenting problem of school failure as resulting from family stress, dangerous neighborhoods, and an inadequate school system. These issues, then, became the focus of the group. Together we generated ways to work on these particular concrete problems. As group facilitators, we presented ourselves as resources to the women. In some cases this meant providing specific information on their legal rights in the public schools or with the welfare system; in other cases, it involved providing the women with the opportunity to learn from one another. For most of the women, this engagement toward changing concrete issues worked toward the resolution of personal problems as well.

This experience led us to the development of *skill-building groups*, formed primarily to focus on parenting issues. In the first group, most women voiced a number of concerns related to raising young children alone in a stressful urban environment. Therefore, with the women, we established a group with goals of teaching specific parenting skills, increasing personal sense of power and self-esteem, and encouraging the universalization of experience and social support.

This group was short term and structured. We focused on learning techniques for effective parenting based on behavior modification and social learning theory. The women defined the specific problems they wanted to work on and selected methods for change that could fit into their family systems. Group support and problem solving were encouraged. Pre- and posttests indicated that the women experienced fewer problems with their children and felt more in control of the family at the end of the group sessions (Schaeffer & Gutiérrez, 1980).

After the initial 12-week cycle was completed, many women wanted to continue. They became the core of a parenting group to which new members were invited. These graduates acted as *mentors* to the new women, helping them to develop new skills and sharing their new insights.

The final group was client led and focused on *social support and social action*. When the second group cycle was completed, these women began setting the agenda for the group. They maintained a focus on parenting, but selected the specific topics for discussion and skill building. Some of these topics included how to budget their welfare allotment, how to make toys and gifts for children, understanding their children's behavior, and sex education. Concerns regarding the educational system came up repeatedly. As a group they invited a representative from the local school board to hear their concerns. When they remained dissatisfied, we invited an attorney who initiated a class action regarding the lack of appropriate special education services in their community. The case was won a few years later, improving conditions for all children in the city.

This example indicates how in less than a year, these women moved from feeling overwhelmed by their young children to feeling capable of confronting the city board of education. Critical elements of this case example were our willingness as social workers to have the clients set the agenda, the use of skill-building techniques, the group modality, our willingness to act as consultants and resource people to the women, and the women's involvement in peer and self-help efforts. Although these women initially set out to learn how to become more effective parents, they quickly became interested in having an impact on those external conditions that made their role so difficult. Equally important was our ability as workers to understand realistically our power and ability to determine the type and form of services we provided as long as we met the agency's goal to serve a specific number of clients. In this way, our empowerment as workers contributed to the empowerment of clients.

SUMMARY

The techniques described here form the basis for empowering practice with women of color on personal, interpersonal, and political levels. They suggest that in order for social workers to have an impact on conditions of powerlessness, we need to rethink both the mode and focus of practice. These techniques require us to move beyond work with individual clients and problems and to think of ways to engage women of color in group efforts toward both individual and community change.

If feminist practice is to be effective, it calls for some changes in the current structure and content of social work practice and education (Gould, 1987a; Hasenfeld, 1987; Morell, 1987). Attention must be paid to the effects of powerlessness and oppression on clients' lives and ways to overcome them. Social workers will also need to develop skills in small group work and community practice if they are to work in empowering ways. And the workplace needs to support the efforts of social workers to engage themselves in the social context of their clients and to move among levels of intervention. These changes and others are critical for the implementation of feminist practice.

Working with women of color can be challenging and gratifying. The literature on empowerment suggests very specific ways in which social workers can move individual women from feelings of hopelessness and apathy to active change. When these techniques are applied effectively, they can contribute to the empowerment of individual women and to their involvement in solving the problems of all women of color.

REFERENCES

Albee, G. (1986, August). *Powerless, politics, and prevention.* Paper presented at the annual meeting of the American Psychological Association, Washington, DC.

Bandura, A. (1982). Self-efficacy mechanism in human agency. *American Psychologist, 37*, 122-147.

Beck, B. (1983). *Empowerment: A future goal of social work*. New York: CSS Working Papers in Social Policy.

Biegel, D., & Naperste, A. (1982). The neighborhood and family services project: An empowerment model linking clergy, agency, professionals and community residents. In A. Jeger & R. Slotnick (Eds.), *Community mental health and behavioral ecology* (pp. 303-318). New York: Plenum.

Bock, S. (1980). Conscientization: Paolo Friere and class-based practice. *Catalyst, 2*, 5-25.

Bricker-Jenkins, M., & Hooyman, N. R. (Eds.). (1986). *Not for women only: Social work practice for a feminist future*. Silver Spring, MD: National Association of Social Workers.

Brickman, P., Rabinowitz, V., Karuza, J., Coates, D., Cohn, E., & Kidder, L. (1982). Models of helping and coping. *American Psychologist, 37*, 368-384.

Burghardt, S. (1982). *The other side of organizing*. Cambridge, MA: Schenkman.

Checkoway, B., & Norsman, A. (1986). Empowering citizens with disabilities. *Community Development Journal, 21*, 270-277.

Coppola, M., & Rivas, R. (1985). The task-action group technique: A case study of empowering the elderly. In M. Parenes (Ed.), *Innovations in social group work: Feedback from practice to theory* (pp. 133-147). New York: Haworth.

Dodd, P., & Gutiérrez, L. (in press). Preparing students for the future: A power perspective on community practice. *Administration in Social Work*.

Fagan, H. (1979). *Empowerment: Skills for parish social action*. New York: Paulist Press.

Fay, B. (1987). *Critical social science*. Ithaca, NY: Cornell University Press.

Feld, A. (1987). Self-perceptions of power: Do social work and business students differ? *Social Work, 32*, 225-230.

French, J., & Raven, B. (1968). The bases of social power. In D. Cartwright & A. Zander (Eds.), *Group dynamics* (3rd ed., pp. 259-269). New York: Harper & Row.

Friere, P. (1973). *Education for critical consciousness*. New York: Seabury.

Garvin, C. (1985). Work with disadvantaged and oppressed groups. In M. Sundel, P. Glasser, R. Sarri, & R. Vinter (Eds.), *Individual change through small groups* (2nd ed., pp. 461-472). New York: Free Press.

Gordon-Bradshaw, R. (1987). A social essay on special issues facing poor women of color. *Women and Health, 12*, 243-259.

Gould, K. (1987a). Feminist principles and minority concerns: Contributions, problems, and solutions. *Affilia: Journal of Women and Social Work, 3*, 6-19.

Gould, K. (1987b). Life model vs. conflict model: A feminist perspective. *Social Work, 32*, 346-351.

Gurin, P., Miller, A., & Gurin, G. (1980). Stratum identification and consciousness. *Social Psychology Quarterly, 43*, 30-47.

Gutiérrez, L. (1990). Working with women of color: An empowerment perspective. *Social Work, 35*, 149-154.

Gutiérrez, L., & Ortega, R. (1989). Using groups to empower Latinos: A preliminary analysis. In *Proceedings of the Eleventh Annual Symposium*. Akron, OH: Association for the Advancement of Social Work with Groups.

Hasenfeld, Y. (1987). Power in social work practice. *Social Service Review, 61*, 469-483.

Hirayama, H., & Hirayama, K. (1985). Empowerment through group participation: Process and goal. In M. Parenes (Ed.), *Innovations in social group work: Feedback from practice to theory* (pp. 119-131). New York: Haworth.

Janoff-Bulman, R. (1979). Characterological versus behavioral self-blame: Inquiries into depression and rape. *Journal of Personality and Social Psychology, 37*, 1798-1810.

Kahn, A., & Bender, E. (1985). Self help groups as a crucible for people empowerment in the context of social development. *Social Development Issues, 9*(2), 4-13.

Katz, R. (1984). Empowerment and synergy: Expanding the community's healing resources. In J. Rappaport, C. Swift, & R. Hess (Eds.), *Studies in empowerment: Toward understanding and action* (pp. 201-226). New York: Haworth.

Keefe, T. (1980). Empathy skill and critical consciousness. *Social Casework, 61*, 387-393.

Kieffer, C. (1984). Citizen empowerment: A developmental perspective. In J. Rappaport, C. Swift, & R. Hess (Eds.), *Studies in empowerment: Toward understanding and action* (pp. 9-36). New York: Haworth.

Klien, E. (1984). *Gender politics: From consciousness to mass politics.* Cambridge, MA: Harvard University Press.

Kopasci, R., & Faulkner, A. (1988). The powers that might be: The unity of white and Black feminists. *Affilia, Journal of Women and Social Work, 3*, 33-50.

Lin-Fu, J. (1987). Special health concerns of ethnic minority women. *Public Health Reports, 102*, 12-14.

Longres, J., & McLeod, E. (1980). Consciousness raising and social work practice. *Social Casework, 61*, 267-277.

Mathis, T., & Richan, D. (1986, March). *Empowerment: Practice in search of a theory.* Paper presented at the annual program meeting of the Council on Social Work Education, Miami.

Moos, R., & Billings, A. (1982). Conceptualizing and measuring coping resources and processes. In L. Goldberger & S. Breznitz (Eds.), *Handbook of stress: Theoretical and clinical aspects.* New York: Free Press.

Morell, C. (1987). Cause is function: Toward a feminist model of integration for social work. *Social Service Review, 61*, 144-155.

Nes, J., & Iadicola, P. (1989). Toward a definition of feminist social work: A comparison of liberal, radical, and socialist models. *Social Work, 34*, 12-22.

Parenti, M. (1978). *Power and the powerless.* New York: St. Martin's.

Pearlin, L., & Schooler, C. (1978). The structure of coping. *Journal of Health and Social Behavior, 19*, 2-21.

Pernell, R. (1985). Empowerment and social group work. In M. Parenes (Ed.), *Innovations in social group work: Feedback from practice to theory* (pp. 107-117). New York: Haworth.

Pinderhughes, E. (1983). Empowerment for our clients and for ourselves. *Social Casework, 64*, 331-338.

Rappaport, J. (1981). In praise of paradox: A social policy of empowerment over prevention. *American Journal of Community Psychology, 9*(1), 1-25.

Rappaport, J. (1986). *Terms of empowerment/exemplars of prevention: Toward a theory for community psychology.* Unpublished manuscript, University of Illinois, Champaign-Urbana.

Resnick, R. (1976). Conscientization: An indigenous approach to international social work. *International Social Work, 19*, 21-29.

Rose, S., & Black, B. (1985). *Advocacy and empowerment: Mental health care in the community.* London: Routledge & Kegan Paul.

Sarri, R., & du Rivage, V. (1985). *Strategies for self help and empowerment of working low-income women who are heads of families.* Unpublished manuscript, University of Michigan, School of Social Work.

Schaeffer, M., & Gutiérrez, L. (1980). *Parents as therapists.* Paper presented at the meeting of the New York Association for the Learning Disabled, New York.

Schechter, S. (1982). *Women and male violence: The visions and struggles of the battered women's movement.* Boston: South End.

Schechter, S., Szymanski, S., & Cahill, M. (1985). *Violence against women: A curriculum for empowerment* (Facilitator's manual). New York: Women's Education Institute.

Shapiro, J. (1984). Commitment to disenfranchised clients. In A. Rosenblatt & D. Waldfogel (Eds.), *Handbook of clinical social work* (pp. 888-903). San Francisco: Jossey-Bass.

Sherman, W., & Wenocur, S. (1983). Empowering public welfare workers through mutual support. *Social Work, 28,* 375-379.

Silver, R., & Wortman, C. (1980). Coping with undesirable life events. In J. Garber & M. Seligman (Eds.), *Human helplessness: Theory and application* (pp. 279-375). New York: Academic Press.

Simmons, C., & Parsons, R. (1983a). Developing internality and perceived competence: The empowerment of adolescent girls. *Adolescence, 18,* 917-922.

Simmons, C., & Parsons, R. (1983b). Empowerment for role alternatives in adolescence. *Adolescence, 18,* 193-200.

Solomon, B. (1976). *Black empowerment.* New York: Columbia University Press.

Solomon, B. (1982). Empowering women: A matter of values. In A. Weick & S. Vandiver (Eds.), *Women, power, and change* (pp. 206-214). Silver Spring, MD: National Association of Social Workers.

Stensrud, R., & Stensrud, K. (1982). Counseling for health empowerment. *Personnel and Guidance Journal, 60,* 377-381.

Thoits, P. (1983). Dimensions of life events that influence psychological distress: An evaluation and synthesis of the literature. In H. Kaplan (Ed.), *Psychosocial stress: Trends in theory and research.* New York: Academic Press.

Van Den Bergh, N., & Cooper, L. (Eds.). (1986). *Feminist visions for social work.* Silver Spring, MD: National Association of Social Workers.

Wilson, J. (1987). Women and poverty: A demographic overview. *Women and Health, 12,* 21-40.

Withorn, A. (1980). Helping ourselves: The limits and potentials of self help. *Social Policy, 11*(3), 20-28.

Withorn, A. (1984). *Serving the people: Social services and social change.* New York: Columbia.

Zambrana, R. (1987). A research agenda on issues affecting poor and minority women: A model for understanding their health needs. *Women and Health, 12,* 137-160.

Still I Rise

Maya Angelou

You may write me down in history
With your bitter, twisted lies,
You may trod me in the very dirt
But still, like dust, I'll rise.

Does my sassiness upset you?
Why are you beset with gloom?
'Cause I walk like I've got oil wells
Pumping in my living room.

Just like moons and like suns,
With the certainty of tides,
Just like hopes springing high,
Still I'll rise.

Did you want to see me broken?
Bowed head and lowered eyes?
Shoulders falling down like teardrops,
Weakened by my soulful cries.

Does my haughtiness offend you?
Don't you take it awful hard
'Cause I laugh like I've got gold mines
Diggin' in my own back yard.

You may shoot me with your words,
You may cut me with your eyes,
You may kill me with your hatefulness,
But still, like air, I'll rise.

Does my sexiness upset you?
Does it come as a surprise
That I dance like I've got diamonds
At the meeting of my thighs?

Out of the huts of history's shame
I rise
Up from a past that's rooted in pain
I rise
I'm a black ocean, leaping and wide,
Welling and swelling I bear in the tide.

Leaving behind nights of terror and fear
I rise
Into a daybreak that's wondrously clear
I rise
Bringing the gifts that my ancestors gave,
I am the dream and the hope of the slave.
I rise
I rise
I rise.

From *And Still I Rise* by Maya Angelou.
Copyright 1978 by Maya Angelou.
Reprinted by permission of Random House, Inc.

The Lord's Prayer from Guatemala

Julia Esquivel

Give us this day our daily bread

the bread of the freedom to associate and organize,
the bread of being able to be at home and walk the streets
without being abducted,
the bread of not having to search for a place in which to hide,
the bread of going into the streets
without seeing machine guns,
the bread of equality,
the bread of happiness.

Let the bread of your word and the bread of education
come into our huts made of cane stalks and straw,
into our cardboard shacks, and let us carry them
in our knapsacks as we travel through life.

The bread of land titles for all campesinos,
the bread of milk for all children under 2 years of age
who suffer malnutrition and hunger,
the bread of medical assistance
for those in the countryside,
the bread of land for the thousands of landless campesinos. . . .

From *Threatened with Resurrection* by Julia Esquivel. Copyright 1982
by Brethren Press. Reprinted by permission.

Chapter 10

REFUGEES AS FEMINISTS

WAWA BACZYNSKYJ

MY DEFINITION OF FEMINISM:
EQUALITY FOR ALL

As a professional of refugee background, working in a field dealing
with refugees' needs, my definition of feminism is intricately tied to the
fabric of a refugee heritage. It emerges from my roots as a refugee as
well as from my experience of working daily with refugee women. This
chapter begins with my personal experience, then moves to exploring
the interrelation between feminism and refugee status. For the Southeast Asian woman, this interconnection is embodied in the conflict of
the outer and the inner worlds. I close with a discussion of some implications for treatment with Southeast Asian refugee women.

The agency in which I practice, Metropolitan Indochinese Children
and Adolescent Services (MICAS), focuses on providing mental
health and social services to children and adolescents from Cambodia,
Laos, and Vietnam. These include information and referral, education,
advocacy, consultation, crisis intervention, and individual and family
therapy. A combination of concrete and therapeutic services is used to
assist with their daily needs, soothe the troubled turbulence of a
traumatic past, negotiate any ongoing crises, and identify the
foundations of the self upon which to build a new future. An American
social worker and a Southeast Asian social worker work together to
provide services. In working with children and adolescents, we are by
definition drawn into the network of family work, becoming involved

with adults in their roles as parents, guardians, and family members. The women with whom we work range from baby daughters to teens, young adults, mothers, aunts, grandmothers. Among these women are many who have stood witness to the definition of feminism as equality for all.

THE REFUGEE EXPERIENCE

The title of a recent book on the Ukrainian women's movement, *Feminists Despite Themselves* (Bohachevsky-Chomiak, 1988), embodies well the reality of refugee women. Why *despite* themselves? Although feminism for many refugee women is not the primary espoused goal, the actions of these women capture its essence. While men go off to fight wars of struggle out of which most refugees are born, women both fight and tend the home fires. However, it is not in comfortable living rooms, but amid the stark reality of babies crying from hunger, bombs shattering, and dangerous escape, that they must live. This is reality for all Third World women, for all survivors not privileged to partake in the discussion of equal wages and status. The women with whom I work have raised themselves well above all slogans of feminism. They are women who, seemingly unprepared for fighting a woman's cause, have embraced a human one—that of equality for all.

The image of Southeast Asian women generally held by Americans does not fit well with the characteristics typically associated with feminism. The common image is of women who are demure, quiet, sweet, feminine, and subservient to all males. Yet these are women who have walked through jungles, maneuvered their survival, and safeguarded their partners, children, and other loved ones. These women have been involved in the preservation of life. They have participated in retaining the fundamental equal right to be alive, rather than dealing with the more luxurious issues of wages, status, and work load. They were talking about the bread of life, rather than the butter. The bread comes first. In Asian terms, the rice comes first, then the sauce. What is the bread? What is the rice? The bread speaks to me, coming from a Slavic tradition. The rice is the connection that I make to those with whom I work.

MY EXPERIENCE AS A REFUGEE

I come from a family of refugees, where the need to sustain life took precedence over individual professional aspirations. The great exodus of post-World War II immigration brought us, as many others, to the shores of the United States in 1948, and into the New Land that had to be transformed into a New Life. That New Life dictated that my parents, both lawyers, struggled through mourning the loss of family, homeland, status, and material goods; they focused on preserving the life that had survived—theirs and that of their children—something labeled *family*. With limited English, my father laid aside his legal aspirations and concentrated on securing a living wage for his family as a carpenter. My parents decided that my mother would devote her energies to raising children—a not uncommon women's occupation in the early 1950s, particularly among refugee parents, whose motivation for survival and escape was often for the "children's sake." For them, having lost all else, their children were their dearest possessions. The home that they created nurtured the oft-told stories of survival, loss, reunification, and hope, strewn with an investment in retaining Ukrainian language and culture—its history, politics, literature, and current status.

Since Americans, until recently, typically did not distinguish Ukrainians as separate from Russians, our identity issues in the family and outside it often concentrated on gaining validity for being recognized as Ukrainian. This was the first definition of "equality for all" that I learned: the need to speak up for the existence of a land and a people to whom I was connected. We were carelessly and ironically labeled "Russians," when the only reason we had escaped to the United States as displaced persons was because the Ukraine had been incorporated into the Union of Soviet Socialist Republics and had lost all autonomy. If feminism engenders standing up for one's rights, then this was the first experience of self-identity that demanded a statement from me.

My primary philosophical mentor, who communicated to me the discrepancies in the meting out of equality to all, was my brother. Two years older, he ventured early beyond the ethnic enclave to participate actively in the civil rights movement, joined the Peace Corps in Thailand, worked as a journalist in Cambodia, and has to this day remained his own kind of person—a chess player, outside the established repertoire of professions. Our family circle was completed by my sister, who was born in the United States and thus became the real owner of the New Land.

While it is easier in retrospect to contemplate my parents' choices, I ask myself what I would have done. I still find it difficult to discern what my preferences would have been if I had belonged to the generation that was part of the great exodus and for whom survival was the only goal in the most creative middle years of life.

I do recognize that my roots as a refugee have clearly played a significant role in my entering the social work profession and refugee work in particular. There was something else that I always wanted to understand. There was some empathy, as well as fascination and curiosity, in hearing others' tales of separation, escape, danger, and survival. An earlier choice as a literature major and teacher eventually led me in my 30s to pursue the role of social worker. As a single woman, I have not felt discriminated against. Instead, I acknowledge the rich opportunities that I have had to pursue more than one career and to make choices and changes over the years. I realize that in doing so I am privileged by a set of educational, racial, and social factors that have shaped my life. Through my parents' nurturing a sense of freedom to develop and to become whomever we wanted, I have been given a security from which to operate. However, others have not had the opportunities that I have enjoyed, because of racism and discriminatory behavior. I received the tools with which to choose the butter for my bread. Many others have not. And many are struggling to find them.

It is within this context that I set forth my definition of feminism: a joining in and making it more possible for people to be recognized as who they are. For me, feminism is an opening of opportunities, a drawing of lines in the commonality of human interests, and a process of cooperation rather than rejection.

THE SOUTHEAST ASIAN WOMAN'S EXPERIENCE

Is there a thread of feminism in the Southeast Asian women I have met through my work? The thread is both blatant and hidden, rebelling and acquiescing. Historically, the past has been both rich and heavy for them: rich in the fabric of culture and tradition, extended family, norms and defined roles, heavy in terms of twentieth-century political strife, colonization, upheaval, war, famine, and oppression. The end result is a litany of horror, escape, separation, violence, trauma—all laced with the nostalgic sweet music of chants, graceful dance, incense, flower petals, and a descriptive indirect language with lyrical nuances punctuated by ever-enigmatic smiles.

Among the three ethnic groups—Vietnamese, Laotians, and Cambodians—there are important and essential differences in terms of political and social strife. These national and ethnic differences should not be minimized by assumptions that all refugees are the same, and that their relationship to us as Americans is the same. Vietnam fought us and at least a part of it survived as victors. Laos was used for our intelligence, for spraying Agent Orange, and then abandoned. Cambodia was supposedly never at war (except in Nixon's invisible secret compartment), and then burst out suddenly in a terror of bombs, only to be followed by the diabolical Pol Pot. Different struggles, involvements, and motives, yet one was clear and shared—each was struggling to survive. This is the unifying raison d'être for all Vietnamese, Laotians, and Cambodians who are here. They did survive. Yet there was a price to pay for survival.

Being Vietnamese often meant getting into an overcrowded, clanking fisherman's boat, being tossed by the waves of the Indochina Sea, in hopes of reaching a safe haven. Hunger, thirst, and pirate attacks were the norm. And being raped became a part of the escape ritual for many women.

Being Laotian meant abandoning the green mountaintops, since there was no longer safety for anyone who could be labeled a CIA conspirator. How does the highland and the tribe get transformed into an urban environment, where the bond with nature is broken? No more fields, no more harmony, and, for women, no more status as bearers of children.

Being Cambodian meant not only surviving a war that was officially not a war, but also living through an organized devastation of one's people by one's own people—a holocaust. Wearing eyeglasses could mean death; being educated meant annihilation. A country was transformed into killing fields, not on a movie screen but in real life. The years 1975-1979 meant that anyone over the age of 5 was in a work camp, devoid of family, urged to acknowledge Anka, and forbidden to show emotion; sudden tears or laughter at the wrong moment meant execution. One was forced into the inner world of memory and the outer world of mechanical motions. For women, for men—no difference—final equality and a national slogan, "Your death is no loss," as long as you were not Khmer Rouge.

Were these women feminists? They were feminists in the true sense of the struggle, of survival, of sharing their protection of equality for all—the equality of survival. Real events, real courage, real survival maneuvers obliterated the differences of education, class, rural, or urban upbringing. These women saw losses—real losses—executions and deaths, and continued on. Somehow, in crisis, the old traditional notions of roles and differences in strength disappeared; simply living was the main task. Whether one could survive was the only question, not one's gender or who one was. Crisis, horror, tragedy equalized all to the level of human beings struggling to escape inhumane systems. And, as seemingly unprepared as women were for that task, they embraced it.

For those of us who have not seen Southeast Asian women in that struggle for survival, it is important to remember that daily reality, particularly as we view these women from our current perspectives and environments. Their experiences of survival left no room to contemplate and reflect; the life-or-death tempo of existence postponed mourning and grief. It was only in the supposed safety of the New Land that the time would come for such reflection. Then the past experiences would unravel one more time, either to be lulled into sad memories or to be relived as intense traumatic flashbacks. These flashbacks would encompass depression, paralysis, suicide attempts, substance abuse—all enrolled in service as painkillers, although in reality they would prolong the pain.

For Southeast Asian women, both inner and outer worlds are full of conflicts and contradictions. The same woman who could outmaneuver a Khmer Rouge interrogation, who could procure food for her children in a famine-stricken land, and who witnessed torture of loved ones is the woman who stands in front of you today, smiling her enigmatic smile as you try to explain to her the rights of an abused wife. She continues to smile and stays with her abusive husband—why?

Transplanted across continents, the natural desire surfaces to create a semblance of a familiar order in the inner world. The husband, even if he is an abuser, is often the only remaining link to an old order of familiar things. Leaving him means throwing oneself, and often one's children, into the turbulent sea of the unknown and the unfamiliar. The language barrier, the lack of extended family and known supports, and problems of employability and child care further limit a woman's options within this foreign environment, still tying her to her husband.

If they do seek self-validation and protection, Southeast Asian women face a number of barriers. They rarely have support groups to which they can turn. Community agencies are mainly run by men and are oriented toward delivering basic services geared toward self-sufficiency, language, and employment; they are not concerned with women's self-actualization. The Asian preservation of face, the sense of shame and reputation, and the family as the primary orientation of identity are also barriers to seeking assistance. Access to mainstream women's shelters, for example, is barred both by language barriers and by the frightening notion of stepping outside a familiar circle.

Women's groups that do exist in the community can provide an environment within which Southeast Asian women can grapple with the traumatic past. They also allow issues to unfold slowly, as sharing overcomes shame, and the wish to survive in the here and now begins to surface. Yet even in such settings, the community often resorts to emphasizing only the age-old duties of wife and mother. A woman who leaves her husband is somewhat understood by the community only if the husband is openly acting deranged and violent. A woman who leaves her husband and children finds no sympathy in the community, even if she has left her children as a means of ensuring her own safety. She is ostracized and judged.

The past conflicts with the present in numerous ways. Marital strife expresses itself in situations where the woman earns more than her husband. The same husband who might have admired and condoned his wife's survival skills now feels not only that he has been displaced as a wage earner and provider in the outside world, but that he has lost face in the inner world. His anger then becomes focused on the achiever.

Second and third marriages, often hastily entered into during the refugee exodus, do not necessarily continue to work. Survival has been achieved; the initial goal of the union has been met. Single mothers are left alone, feeling lost and depressed as they struggle to survive on welfare. An additional conflict for many couples who stay together is that men who suffered serious head trauma during the war may have violent outbursts when they fail to take prescribed medication. During such outbursts, they may target the most vulnerable victims— their wives and children. Often, stoically, the woman, remembering the man as he was before, chooses to remain and accept the violence.

Further, the norms of male-female social interactions in the United States are highly misunderstood by Southeast Asians. Asian men will often misinterpret American men's casual manner of speech and body gestures toward Asian women. This can lead to accusations and violent encounters stemming from misplaced jealousy. Asian men's jealousy may also be intensified by American attitudes toward sex and family planning. Family planning undermines a fundamental characteristic of the woman as a bearer of children. Women, not men, are perceived to be responsible for family planning, but often only with their partners' permission. Yet to have children in America raises complex issues of financial survival. Since the Asian male's understanding of American culture may be gleaned primarily from television, misconceptions and stereotypes—such as that all sex is free and family breakup is routine—result. Any steps toward some independent self-actualization by women may be misunderstood as "women's liberation" and therefore highly negative and suspicious.

IMPLICATIONS FOR
WORKING WITH REFUGEE WOMEN

Where is feminism in all of this? How does one strengthen the rights of the refugee woman and help her move toward self-actualization? As a first step, the reality of the phases of a refugee experience has to be understood. For the Southeast Asian, this is connected with both racial identity and their relationship to an unpopular war in which many of their American neighbors suffered casualties. Women's equality becomes secondary when compared with screams of "Go home, gook," which ring louder. The kinds of choices available thus have to be seen within the context of the Southeast Asian community and its struggle for identity. Because this community is only now developing role models within the first generation, it will take several generations before Southeast Asians can partake equally of mainstream services.

One way to begin to understand the refugee's experience is through a team approach, with at least one member of the team who is Southeast Asian. While other team members may bring technical skills, the Southeast Asian member offers linguistic ability, cultural expertise, and the heart of that particular group's experience. In the best of circumstances, team members can grow to trust each other, communicate, and jointly attempt to figure out the tangled web of human existence and appropriate interventions.

The conflicts between the inner and outer worlds, and the implications of these conflicts for women's role, must also be understood. After trauma, one has to survive. Survival and safety often mean retrenching to familiar positions and roles in order to preserve a known legacy. Stepping out into a new foreign world in order to make choices does not come easily to adult women. It means the willingness, not forced by uncontrollable circumstances of war and oppression, to discard the ideals under which one has been raised and nurtured. And, although small beginnings have been made, the support systems for the new approaches are not yet constructed. For now, it may be only through identifying a goal of survival and creatively employing a familiar framework that treatment can occur.

Service delivery systems usually lack culturally and linguistically appropriate treatment environments. For example, an alcoholic Southeast Asian woman may prefer to find solace and self-esteem by "drying out" in the environment of incense, meditation, and chanting of a Buddhist temple rather than in a Western-style verbal Alcoholics Anonymous group, with its framework of admissions and confessions, even if language interpreting is available. For her, admission means confession, shame, guilt, loss of face, disgrace, and a further rupturing of self-esteem. For her, the notion of saving face is not a "therapeutic resistance maneuver"; it is actually a value.

On a personal level, both literally and symbolically, a new language has to be created, a language that can begin to synthesize the inner and outer worlds of the Southeast Asian woman. By communicating in English with bilingual people, we can mistakenly assume that our words mean the same and refer to a common framework. We forget that in the process of becoming bilingual, a person speaks for a long time with only the mind, while the heart carries on a conversation in the native language. Symbolically, the familiarity cherished in the heart may impede the necessary action perceived by the mind. And it is often only by dealing with the notion of survival that risky steps are taken by the refugee women as they grow in the recognition that a new kind of survival technique may demand their own self-assertion to deal with the enormity of a current problem. For many, self-actualization, outside of traditionally accepted boundaries, will often find its first expressions when merged with the goal of survival.

Until our interventions can create the synthesis of linguistically and culturally appropriate language, we will continue to misread one another. We will be unable to build on the strength of refugee Southeast Asian women and to move with them toward self-actualization. For the therapist, this means time and caution. Educating about choices is fine. However, only the Southeast Asian refugee woman can actually determine which choices are realistic. We cannot use our measure of what is "better," or we may manipulate a woman into making a choice that, in the long run, is foreign and alienating within her own heart and cultural framework. Although it may be described as an "acculturated" choice, it may leave her with a vacuum of more losses. If ever the task as a social worker is to listen and start where the client is, it is with these refugee women. We can assist them, within a relatively stable environment, to develop their own notion of feminism—an equality for all—on their own terms, with their own legacy.

And why should we not trust them to do it? They are the ones who have survived, in the jungles of escape, under the devastation of Pol Pot, in Vietnamese villages, and in the waters of the Mekong Delta. Having struggled for equality of survival for all, they are the ones best able to tell us how to link the refugee and the feminist.

REFERENCE

Bohachevsky-Chomiak, M. (1988). *Feminists despite themselves*. Edmonton: University of Alberta.

Untitled

Karen Cook

Our fire burns instinctively
but our minds betray us
pulling away
pushing away
and our hearts cling desperately
to the promise
of simply
being
should we ignore our minds
let the passion burn
and the hearts cling?
that
we have been taught
is what man calls
love
will we deny our individual strengths
for a common weakness?
that
we have been told
is what man calls
woman
can we dissect our souls
matching color to color
until they are identical
leaving the remains to rot
eternally mourned in an uncommon grave?
that
we have learned
is what man calls
together
or
will we let the colors remain
reflecting in the sunlight
a rainbow
of simply being alive
a celebration
of hearts and minds
and passion
our individual weakness
becoming a common strength
that
we are learning
is woman

Part III

ORGANIZATIONAL AND STRUCTURAL ISSUES

INTRODUCTION

NAOMI GOTTLIEB

Other parts of this book have addressed the issue of the impact of the setting on feminist social work practice. The two chapters in Part III deal directly with organizational and structural factors. Diane Kravetz and Linda Jones chronicle and analyze the development of grass-roots, feminist agencies; Nancy Hooyman describes feminist leadership within a traditional, large, hierarchical institution. The similarities in these two disparate organizational contexts are as remarkable as their differences.

The feminists in both kinds of organizations strive to live and work by feminist values and ideals, and to improve the lives of women. The authors of these two chapters state those values clearly, and they also describe the difference between the ideal and the pragmatic in acting on them. The analyses of these different institutional structures also attest to the constant evolutions and developments in feminist organizational practice and give us a straightforward evaluation of the forces inherent in their environments that deter feminist development. Although small feminist organizations are, by their very nature, independent of an immediate superstructure, they still need to deal with a larger, traditional community, primarily for material and other supports. Because of this, they are faced with the same kinds of dilemmas Hooyman describes in her role as a feminist leader in a hierarchical institution. Kravetz and Jones analyze the negative effects as feminist agencies grapple with those political contexts.

The major differences between these two analyses may lie in the extent to which the participants can openly proclaim their feminist convictions. The agencies Kravetz and Jones describe were purposefully established to ensure that feminist values and practices could be publicly acknowledged and implemented. Hooyman's institutional constraints not only require a more muted public stance but place serious and immediate obstacles in the path of feminist practice.

Kravetz and Jones's historical chronicle is consistent with one of the major themes of this book—our need for a sense of feminist history coupled with a new generation's need for creating its own history. Their acknowledgment of the continuing problems feminist agencies face offers an agenda for a new generation of grass-roots feminists.

As important as such alternative agencies are, Hooyman's contribution may be applicable to a wider range of practitioners. Although most social workers are not employed in academic settings, they face the same kind of heavy bureaucratic structure that Hooyman describes. Her ideas about the possibilities and strategies for incremental change within such institutions may have widespread potential.

the things that change

zana

i sit in the grass filling my hat with mushrooms
like last spring and the spring before
in this spot, and with the same hat . . .
this is for the things that do not change.

rain fell meager in this spring of '82
and the mushrooms, small and shriveled,
huddle in nests of dead grasses.
last year i filled my hat full
and had some left for drying.
this is for the things that change.

in that year since the big mushrooms
an orange cat has died
a womon and two children left the land
two children and six wimim came.

i avoid the eyes and path of someone
whose sight i loved then.
someone i hated has gone and returned;
we feel out ways to know each other's lives.

I wanted rules about numbers of dogs
and who could make noise where, when.
now those things drift over in their own flow
like clouds shifting, warmth to sorrow.
things move, and move again.

my legs are worse this year.
i no longer hunt mushrooms up near woods edge
but only these a few steps from my cabin.
it is impossible to know if I will ever be well
if my friend and i will ever laugh and sing again
if the water table will hold enough
for all the wimin on this land.

but this year salsify puffs dot the field
where there were none before
and afternoon thunder tempers out flat, hot days
so i know that it is possible to hope.

From *herb womon* by zana. Copyright 1983 by zana,
12150 W. Calle Seneca, Tuscon, AZ 85743. Reprinted
by permission.

Chapter 11

SUPPORTING PRACTICE IN FEMINIST SERVICE AGENCIES

DIANE KRAVETZ
LINDA E. JONES

While most chapters in this book discuss feminist social work practice with specific populations, this chapter discusses feminist practice within feminist service agencies. Women working in feminist service agencies have played a crucial role in analyzing, redefining, and addressing women's needs and concerns for the last 15-20 years. Therefore, it is important that these agencies be examined, as they have provided the organizational context that has helped define and has explicitly supported feminist practice in recent years.

This chapter focuses on feminist service agencies, that is, agencies that are feminist in their philosophies, goals, structures, and services, and are developed to stand in direct opposition to the ideology and structure of traditional social service agencies. Many issues have been raised about the existence and purpose of services in feminist agencies, including the inevitable tension between the provision of services, structured according to feminist principles, and political action, directed toward fundamental social change (Hyde, 1989; O'Sullivan, 1978; Schechter, 1982). This tension has led to debates among feminists who take various positions, including, for example, the stance that services cannot contribute effectively to social change, and the stance that services drain resources of time, energy, and money from social change efforts. In the feminist service agencies discussed here, services are designed to be consistent with and part of feminist social change efforts.

This chapter describes the emergence, ideology, and goals of feminist service agencies, as well as the organizational structures and characteristics that distinguish them from traditional social service agencies. The chapter also presents a variety of issues and challenges facing feminist service agencies as they evolve and mature, and as the environments in which they operate change. Finally, the current and potential influence and the mutual benefits to be derived from the interaction of feminist practice in feminist agencies and mainstream social work practice are explored, and future practice and research issues suggested. The chapter includes material from interviews that were conducted as part of our study of six feminist service agencies in Madison, Wisconsin.

Over the last 25 years, feminists have organized to influence change in every aspect of women's lives. Their goals are not only to eliminate sex bias and discrimination, but to transform cultural views of women's roles and rights. In the early stages of the new feminist movement, there was a distinct separation between the activities of the women's rights movement and the women's liberation movement. The women's rights movement consisted of large national organizations (e.g., National Organization for Women [NOW], Women's Equity Action League, and the National Women's Political Caucus) that focused on improving the status of women in education, employment, and electoral politics, and, in the case of NOW, on reproductive rights. These formal, bureaucratic organizations were concerned with achieving social change through influencing reforms in legislation and government policies.

Women's liberation groups included small, decentralized, nonhierarchical, grass-roots groups that focused on consciousness-raising, the development of feminist ideology, and social action. Their goals were to alter radically cultural and political ideology about women, to eliminate female oppression, and to transform social relationships and social institutions to reflect feminist values, goals, and processes.

Over time, the sharp distinctions between these two movements blurred, although their original philosophies, purposes, and strategies for change remain in evidence today. As the feminist movement became widespread, a multitude of diverse feminist organizations and groups emerged, focusing on a wide range of issues and addressing the needs and rights of many women. These groups represented a continuum of political ideologies, goals, and change strategies.

Within this diversity, feminist service agencies primarily evolved out of and continue to represent most closely that part of the contemporary feminist movement that has its roots in the early women's liberation movement. Their philosophical and ideological foundations and their goals, structures, and methods were shaped and continue to be influenced by the tenets of the liberation groups of the late 1960s and early 1970s. These characteristics of feminist service agencies are discussed more specifically below.

THE EMERGENCE OF FEMINIST SERVICES

In the early stages of the women's liberation movement, mid-1960s to early 1970s, its activities centered on consciousness-raising (CR) groups. These groups consisted primarily of socialist feminists and radical feminists, and their group discussions focused on political analyses and the development of feminist ideology. Also, these early CR group members educated themselves and others through projects such as writing pamphlets and newsletters, serving as a "speakers' bureau," holding demonstrations and protests, and organizing other women's CR groups. As noted by Carden (1974) and Freeman (1975), the rapid development of CR groups during this period and public awareness of feminist thought can be largely attributed to their efforts. These early groups served as mechanisms for educating and radicalizing women and for creating a broad-based social concern with women's issues.

In the 1970s, one result of these efforts was a proliferation of diverse and specialized feminist grass-roots organizations and activities. These efforts were designed to enable women to take direct control of their lives by creating alternatives to male-dominated institutions. The values and goals that women identified through consciousness-raising became articulated and reinforced through the evolution of feminist culture (e.g., woman-centered art, music, literature, and theater) and through the founding of many feminist businesses, community programs, and services.

One important example of feminist community activities was the provision of alternatives to established health, mental health, and social services. Numerous alternative feminist service agencies evolved, including women's counseling centers, abortion referral services, rape crisis centers, shelters for battered women, feminist therapy collectives, and women's health centers. In all of these activities, understanding the dynamics of female oppression in a sexist society has been the foundation for assessing needs, establishing goals, and determining the nature of alternative programs and services.

THE IDEOLOGICAL BASE
OF FEMINIST SERVICE AGENCIES

Feminist service agencies emerged from and remain highly identified with the philosophies and strategies of the women's liberation movement. In general, these include feminist principles of equality and sisterhood, the legitimacy of personal experience, the merging of the personal and the political, and female empowerment (Carden, 1974). More specifically, the underlying feminist principles guiding these agencies, which are consistent with and support the assumptions of feminist practice theory, principles, and methods, include the following:

(1) *The conviction that personal and sociopolitical transformation are inextricably linked; that is, the personal is political.* It is understood that institutionalized systems, especially patriarchy, foster social inequality, powerlessness, and dependency, which are determining factors of women's individual problems and victimization. Thus the elimination of gender inequality and female subordination is essential for meaningful change to occur for women.

(2) *The importance of empowering women to take control over their everyday lives and their bodies.* Both women workers within feminist service agencies and their clients are empowered by the creation of an agency environment that models feminist ideology through its philosophy, goals, and operation. This agency environment supports the feminist direct practice methods and techniques employed (e.g., self-help groups, consciousness-raising methods, supporting clients in determining and making choices, encouraging collective action).

(3) *The importance of nonhierarchical, nonelitist interpersonal relationships and consensus-based, collective decision making, as well as the equal sharing of resources, responsibility, and power among women and between women and men.* This cooperative model is seen as a goal in relationships both among workers and between workers and

clients. In these groups, the process and the product must both adhere to basic feminist principles.

These tenets continue to shape the goals, processes, and structures of feminist service agencies. However, their translation into specific policies, programs, and practices differs across agencies. These differences depend on the political orientations and involvements of agency members; on organizational factors, including size, range of services, diversity of the staff, extent of staff turnover, and requirements of funders; and on environmental factors, such as location (urban, suburban, or rural), geographic region of the country, and the existence of and relationship with other organizations working with the same population.

THE GOALS OF
FEMINIST SERVICE AGENCIES

Feminist service agencies were organized to meet the unmet needs of women, to provide alternatives to existing services that were viewed as oppressive and unresponsive to women's problems, and to alter women's sociopolitical circumstances. They also provided feminists an opportunity to work with others who shared their visions and values in a manner that was empowering to all involved. Referring to herself and the other original workers in a battered women's shelter, one woman we interviewed expressed this by saying, "We had a tremendous belief in the rightness of what we were doing and the wrongness of what we saw going on in society and how that had to be changed, and we had a really strong commitment to seeing that that was done."

Like other alternative service agencies emerging outside the established social service system at various points in time, such as services for youth and people of color in the 1960s, feminist alternative agencies arose in response to changing social conditions and the increasing visibility of new client groups. They provided new approaches to service delivery as well as innovative theories and techniques of intervention (Miller & Philipp, 1983). Unlike other alternative agencies, the ideological and philosophical base of feminist agencies lay in the emerging feminist analyses of male privilege and female subordination. The provision of alternative services for women was one part of the larger goal of transforming the nature of women's social and economic circumstances so that they could function with economic, social, and psychological autonomy.

Feminist critiques of traditional social, mental health, and health services include the following:

(1) Traditional services are based on gender-biased, androcentric theories and research.

(2) Traditional approaches to service delivery for women are adjustment oriented, designed to help women to understand, accept, and adjust to traditional gender roles and norms.

(3) Traditional services are controlled and administered by men.

(4) Traditional services are delivered by practitioners who do not recognize or value the unique aspects of female experience, who are uncritical of the social circumstances of women and of traditional gender roles and inequality, and who are negative in their attitudes about and behaviors toward women.

(5) Traditional services reinforce female subordination by placing women in another powerless situation.

(6) Traditional services exacerbate women's powerlessness and victimization by failing to protect women from predominantly male violence and by blaming women for their own victimization.

(7) Traditional services often are racist, classist, and heterosexist. These services do not take into account or address the multiple oppression and special needs of lesbian women, women of color, poor women, older women, and women who are differently abled.

Rape crisis centers, women's health programs, and women's centers that provided a range of services addressing women's needs are examples of some of the earliest feminist services and programs. By 1971, the lack of adequate laws, policies, and services related to rape had led to the grass-roots development of the first rape crisis centers. Their goal was to help victims move through a system that defined rape as a crime of passion, labeled the victim as the provocateur, and assumed that the victim was guilty until proven innocent. Women were being victimized by their attackers and then again by the law enforcement system. In an interview, a founder of a rape crisis center described her motivations to develop the program in 1972:

> One was the really brutal treatment that women get in the courts if they decide to prosecute. There was some feeling that it was a really inhuman

kind of process and that there was no advocate there for the woman to support her, and often she was attacked—her character assaulted by the attorneys. The other was in the reporting of the actual rape in a crisis situation. There was some feeling that at times the police did not handle that in a real sensitive way and the emergency rooms didn't know what to do. And again, often the woman was alone and without support.

Typical services of rape crisis centers initially included 24-hour hot lines, accompanying victims to hospitals and police stations, and providing victim advocates for women throughout court proceedings (O'Sullivan, 1978). Rape prevention efforts, including community education, women's self-defense courses, and escort services, were also part of their services. Over the next decade, feminists broadened their analysis and understanding of violence against women, especially domestic violence. Responses to the lack of services for victims of rape, incest, and partner abuse led to the emergence of the antirape movement and later to the battered women's movement (Schechter, 1982).

Another example of feminist services that developed in the early 1970s is the women's health movement, which combined the grassroots efforts of the community health movement and the women's liberation movement. Feminist activists in this movement worked to change health care delivery based on their analysis of the ways in which physicians, administrators, and legislators, who were generally male, controlled women's health and health care: "The medical care system is seen as supporting, under the guise of science, societal sexism through its depiction of women's physical and mental capabilities and its emphasis on women's reproductive organs" (Marieskind, 1980, p. 289).

Working for the provision of adequate, quality abortion services for women has been a central focus of feminist health care efforts. Also, grass-roots self-help clinics and women's health centers provide health education for women, including breast and vaginal self-examination, pregnancy screening and counseling, birth control education, and, in some centers, abortion services. In addition, many health activists are involved in rape crisis centers. Understanding and controlling their bodies were seen as core aspects of empowering women to control their own lives and destinies (Marieskind, 1980; Withorn, 1980; Zimmerman, 1987).

Since the early 1970s, small women's centers have developed as multiservice agencies, providing a wide variety of services and addressing unmet needs in many diverse arenas. They assist women in dealing with issues around employment, general health care, abortion, child care, aging, sexual identity, separation and divorce, widowhood, rape and self-defense, family violence, sexual harassment, legal problems, substance abuse, and difficulties in personal relationships. Typical services provided by these centers include advocacy for women (on legal issues, education, employment, housing, social services), community education, support groups, counseling, 24-hour hot lines, referral services, feminist literature, and information about women's community activities (see Galper & Washburne, 1976; Gottlieb, 1980; Masi, 1981; Women and Mental Health Project, 1976).

ORGANIZATIONAL STRUCTURE AND OPERATION

Although the organizational structures and day-to-day operations of feminist service agencies vary, several characteristics are typical. In collective feminist agencies, authority belongs to the collectivity, although it may be temporarily delegated. Every member is responsible to the group, and all decisions are made by the group. There is minimal division of labor, with staff responsibilities being shared or rotated. The structure is egalitarian, with limited differences in rewards and shared decision making by staff and consumers. Specialized training and degrees are viewed as much less important than shared values, network contacts, and personality (Ferree & Hess, 1985).

Some agencies have maintained this "ideal" structure, often limiting their range of services in order to continue as collectives. Over time, however, many other feminist agencies moved toward more formal decision-making structures (e.g., steering committees and other standing committees, task forces, and written policies), with more internal task differentiation and specialization. These modifications were generally tailored to maintain the egalitarian norms of these agencies and, at the same time, respond to problems created by increased size and the high level of demand for a range of services, the time-consuming nature of consensus building, and the requirements of external funders and conventional service agencies.

Nonetheless, the organizational approaches of feminist service agencies continue to be well within the broad spectrum of goals, values, and methods that define the feminist movement. These small, community-based agencies remain "alternative" agencies, and their organizational structures and methods of operation can be differentiated from conventional agencies in the following ways (Grossman & Morgenbesser, 1980; Hooyman & Cunningham, 1986; McShane & Oliver, 1978; O'Sullivan, 1978; Schwartz, Gottesman, & Perlmutter, 1988; Women and Mental Health Project, 1976):

(1) Their authority structure is a flattened hierarchy or nonhierarchical; decisions are made on a cooperative or collective basis.

(2) Relationships with the women who use the services are conducted in a personal, humanistic fashion. There is a conscious avoidance of the "objectivity" and "value-free" orientation that reputedly characterizes professionalism.

(3) Terms such as *patient* and *client* are avoided to eliminate the elitist assumptions they imply.

(4) Agency staff include volunteers, paraprofessionals, and/or professionals, and may include women who formerly used the services of the agency.

(5) Staff members see themselves as accountable to the women who use the services and to the other staff, not to taxpayers or agency administrators.

(6) Initial funding is often outside of traditional agency, community, or government sources; services are either free or fees are much lower than those of conventional service agencies.

(7) The agencies are controlled by women. They may exclude men from staff, board, and volunteer positions and from using the services of the agency.

(8) In addition to direct services, the roles of staff include public education, educating professionals in and changing policies of established institutions, and working for changes in law enforcement, the courts, and legislation.

ISSUES FACING
FEMINIST SERVICE AGENCIES

A central problem for small, local feminist agencies is that of balancing priorities and multiple objectives. For example, consciousness-raising and political analysis are time-consuming and, in the short run, detract from the provision of direct services. In tracing the development of rape crisis centers, O'Sullivan (1978) notes that there were often different priorities, including altering the social forces that support and promote rape, changing professionals, obtaining legislative and administrative reforms, and assisting victims. Highlighting the difficulties in choosing among these priorities, O'Sullivan points out:

> These priorities were not static. Women intending to aid victims found themselves questioning the capabilities of public institutions. Others, who rejected "working within the system," found themselves making accommodations to meet victims' needs. . . . The hardest decisions have been made by small feminist collectives. Often overwhelmed by their obligations to victims, they have questioned whether they were effectively contributing to ending rape and its effects. (pp. 46-47)

There is an ongoing debate regarding service provision versus political activism (Hyde, 1989; O'Sullivan, 1978; Schechter, 1982). Related to this, one woman we interviewed who worked at a battered women's shelter said:

> We had a real strong ideological base, I think. . . . There was a tension that got built up real early on between how are we going to make these changes in society that would prevent this battering from occurring versus providing services to people. It was like opening a Pandora's box to start that crisis line. We felt really overwhelmed with the need for immediate care that women had, and then discovered all the ways the system was not cooperating with them. And, at the same time, we were trying to hold onto this vision of ourselves as this kind of social change, advocacy agency.

As noted by Schechter (1982), some have argued that feminist agencies must focus solely on service delivery, not on their role as part of the feminist movement. This position asserts that feminist activism and ideology should be pursued through actions and organizations other than the service agency. However, feminist critiques of society and analyses of needed social change were the foundation for the development of feminist services; their contributions and significance for women will continue only if these agencies maintain their dual mission of structural change and service delivery (Ferguson, 1984; Sullivan, 1982; Withorn, 1980). This position is articulated well by Schechter (1982), who points out: "Self-help creates the environment in which women demonstrate that society can be changed and that women no longer have to endure abuse, inequality, and powerlessness" (p. 253). Further: "As women experience egalitarian service models, they themselves will start to question hierarchical and authoritarian relations. As more and more women are offered a new vision of how people should treat one another, new political possibilities emerge" (p. 318).

Only through linking services with a political analysis will the relationships between women's personal problems and their socioeconomic circumstances be evident in agency goals, structure, and processes and become part of the consciousness of women. The goal of feminist service agencies is to empower women, not only to meet their immediate needs. This can be accomplished only when feminist service provision is understood to be an integral part of the larger feminist social change agenda.

The involvement of professionals has presented a complex set of issues for feminist service agencies. Many of the early founders of these agencies were professionals, including many social workers, although their involvement often was based primarily on their identity as movement activists. Working in feminist agencies, they could escape the conflicts, lack of support, contempt, and ostracism frequently experienced by feminists in the early 1970s when they tried to work for change from within traditional social service agencies. Most important, in feminist agencies feminists can actively incorporate their political values into their work and truly integrate their personal, professional, and political goals; they can also work closely with other women who share their values and goals (Freeman & McMillan, 1976-1977a, 1976-1977b; Galper & Washburne, 1976; Withorn, 1984).

However, as the feminist movement became more diversified, so did the women who were attracted to working in feminist agencies. Professionals in these agencies, who served as paid staff, as volunteers, and/or as members of boards of directors, represented a range of different feminist political orientations. Also, some professionals who chose to work in feminist agencies did not have a feminist perspective and were not identified with the feminist movement (O'Sullivan, 1978; Schechter, 1982; Women and Mental Health Project, 1976).

Feminists with professional training brought information, contacts, and expertise to these alternative agencies, including skills in writing, lobbying, fund-raising, group facilitation, counseling, and public speaking. However, in many instances, they also promoted status hierarchies, professional "objectivity," emphasis on professional services instead of self-help, and concern with higher wages and paths for advancement that characterize conventional services. It is often difficult for professionals to share their knowledge and experience in ways that empower other staff and consumers and are consistent with feminist goals and methods. Further, since professionals tend to be white and middle-class, expanding professional participation tends to replicate forms of racism and classism found in traditional services (Sullivan, 1982).

Particular problems were created by those women who were motivated by professional goals and career interests and had no prior involvement with the feminist movement. For some, their participation in these agencies has led to their developing a feminist perspective and commitment. In other instances, the participation of nonfeminists has led to painful divisions and conflicts within agencies and ultimately to feminists leaving as the agencies became indistinguishable from other small conventional service agencies (Ahrens, 1980; Withorn, 1980).

A final core problem for these agencies is that of maintaining alternative status and emphasis on self-help in the face of the requirements of external funders. As discussed earlier, in their purest form, feminist self-help agencies stress collective decision making. In contrast, public and private funding sources demand accountability, evidence of professional expertise, a designated division of labor and lines of authority, a board of directors, and a less explicitly politicized mission (Ferree & Hess, 1985; Morgenbesser, Natkin, McCall, Grossman, & Nachreiner-Cory, 1981).

In order to obtain external funding and the cooperation of conventional social services, feminist agencies often must shift their goals to conform to changing funding priorities, spend considerable time on data collection for funders and researchers, and participate in contract billing systems that ignore the work of volunteers and the value of peer assistance and emphasize one-to-one counseling instead of women's self-help and peer support groups (Sullivan, 1982).

Women we interviewed offered some examples of issues created by external funding requirements. One said, "If there were only one funding source, it would be one thing, but because there are five major ones, we have to reproduce the same information into their language first, and it becomes an incredibly cumbersome task." Another said, "Funding influences the way I write a proposal. . . . It's no different from sales in so many ways, because somebody doesn't want to hear what you're saying, you figure out what he does want to hear . . . tell him the same thing from a different approach. . . . funding has certainly influenced the way we present goals." A third woman said, "We've known there's certain pockets of money available, and this is what they're willing to fund, and we may design a program that's going to fit into that, so yes, it has affected our programs. Not to a great extent, but it has."

The dilemma for feminist agencies is clear. Attracting outside funding and coordinating agency efforts with conventional agencies stabilizes feminist agencies, legitimates their efforts, increases their influence and impact in the community, and may provide the resources and support necessary for their survival. However, working in close association with established systems may also lead to their co-optation, including a diminished commitment to feminist goals and weakened ties to the feminist community, and ultimately to conversion into a conventional community service.

FEMINIST SERVICE AGENCIES AND SOCIAL WORK PRACTICE

In many ways, the clear split between women as professionals and women as feminist activists has diminished. In social work, feminist scholars, educators, and practitioners have developed new knowledge about social work policies and practice with women, have influenced the incorporation of feminist theory and research into all parts of the social work curriculum, and have integrated feminist approaches into every field of social work practice with women. As evidenced by this book and others (e.g., Bricker-Jenkins & Hooyman, 1986; Hanmer & Statham, 1989; Norman & Mancuso, 1980; Van Den Bergh & Cooper, 1986), feminist social work practice is no longer confined to alternative agencies. However, there remains a unique and essential role for feminist agencies.

Feminist agencies provide inspiring evidence of the psychological and social benefits of self-help for women, encouraging conventional agencies to find ways to incorporate aspects of self-help into their services (e.g., support groups for women). Also, the relative flexibility and autonomy of these agencies, compared with traditional agencies, allow them to be more responsive to changing needs and issues. As these agencies develop new understandings of women's issues and establish new services for women, they provide information and innovative models and methods that can be incorporated into established agencies.

Feminist service agencies give feminist social workers unique opportunities: (a) to work in the field of human services in an environment that explicitly values and promotes solidarity among women as workers and between women workers and the women who use the services, and (b) to provide services that are deliberately designed to make a contribution to social change. As Withorn (1984) notes, "Feminist services have given a model to many feminists and socialists that shows how services can be something valuable in themselves, not merely as organizing tools or as palliatives to an unfair society" (p. 45).

Involvement of feminist professionals can increase the credibility and contacts of the feminist agency, enhancing community support and the stability of its funding. Feminist social workers possess specialized skills and knowledge that benefit the development and continued viability of these agencies (Perlmutter, 1988; Valentich & Gripton, 1984).

In addition, feminist service agencies provide excellent settings for the recruitment of feminists into the profession of social work. As volunteers and staff, women learn new skills, gain a sense of accomplishment and confidence, and often become interested in and motivated to seek professional training. Their understanding of the ties between the personal and the political, their concern with individual and social change, and their substantial experience as "generalist practitioners" all suggest that the field of social work would greatly benefit by their presence.

Differences are likely to exist between feminists in alternative agencies and those in conventional agencies, especially with respect to attitudes toward professionalism, willingness to work within bureaucratic structures, salaries, and status among traditional professionals. However, their shared political beliefs, their mutual interests in improving services for women, and their shared commitment to feminist practice provide the bases for collaboration, mutual support, and collective action.

Democratically structured feminist service agencies provide opportunities for women to develop new skills and abilities, to raise their social consciousness and develop a more detailed understanding of the nature of female oppression, and to work actively to change the political, economic, and social conditions of women. They continue as impressive models of the vitality and potential of feminist self-help and activism.

PRACTICE AND RESEARCH ISSUES

As feminist service agencies continue to develop, numerous practice and research issues will emerge and evolve. Researchers and practitioners, working together in feminist service agencies, need to develop an understanding of and take into account the multiple and interacting forms of oppression affecting women's lives, including sexism, racism, classism, and heterosexism. Feminist service agencies must work to ensure that no women are excluded. Analyses of problems, as well as policies and practices, must be sensitive to differences among women related to race, class, sexual orientation, and other factors. For example, African-American, Native American, or lesbian women may find domestic violence programs and services primarily developed from the experience of white, heterosexual women to be unhelpful and insensitive to their needs and circumstances. An essential aspect of feminist service agencies is understanding what types of practices and services are most needed by and effective with different groups of women. Moreover, feminist service agencies must be diligent in including women from diverse backgrounds and communities, especially women of color, among their workers.

Another crucial question for feminist practitioners and researchers to consider is how feminist service agencies can maintain their core feminist principles while operating within traditional, nonfeminist environments. An additional challenge for researchers, in alliance with practitioners, is to examine the ways in which the programs and services of feminist service agencies, in both urban and rural settings, can inform each other as they work to address the issues faced by women who live in these different environments.

No doubt, feminist service agencies will be challenged to continue to provide models for addressing new problems and issues, such as services for women and children who are HIV positive or who have AIDS. Current threats to women's reproductive rights, as well as rapidly developing reproductive technologies and the emergence of numerous alternative family forms, will also necessitate that feminist service agencies, as well as other feminist organizations, be vigilant in their advocacy for women in a time of fast-paced social change and intensified efforts to control women's bodies and lives.

As feminism, feminist service agencies, and the social climate for women continually change, both new and ongoing practice and research issues will become evident. Both feminist practitioners and researchers committed to feminist service agencies must analyze and communicate the continuing importance, influence, and roles of these organizations in addressing the oppression of all women.

REFERENCES

Ahrens, L. (1980). Battered women's refuges: Feminist cooperatives vs. social service institutions. *Radical America, 14*(3), 41-47.

Bricker-Jenkins, M., & Hooyman, N. R. (Eds.). (1986). *Not for women only: Social work practice for a feminist future.* Silver Spring, MD: National Association of Social Workers.

Carden, M. L. (1974). *The new feminist movement.* New York: Russell Sage.

Ferguson, K. E. (1984). *The feminist case against bureaucracy.* Philadelphia: Temple University Press.

Ferree, M. M., & Hess, B. B. (1985). *Controversy and coalition: The new feminist movement.* Boston: Twayne.

Freeman, A., & McMillan, J. (1976-1977a). Building feminist organizations. *Quest, 3*(3), 73-80.

Freeman, A., & McMillan, J. (1976-1977b). The feminist workplace: Interview with Nancy MacDonald. *Quest, 3*(3), 65-73.

Freeman, J. (1975). *The politics of women's liberation.* New York: David McKay.

Galper, M., & Washburne, C. K. (1976). A women's self-help program in action. *Social Policy, 6*(5), 46-52.

Gottlieb, N. (Ed.). (1980). *Alternative social services for women.* New York: Columbia University Press.

Grossman, B., & Morgenbesser, M. (1980). Alternative social service settings: Opportunities for social work education. *Journal of Humanics, 8,* 59-76.

Hanmer, J., & Statham, D. (1989). *Women and social work: Towards a woman-centered practice.* Chicago: Lyceum.

Hooyman, N. R., & Cunningham, R. (1986). An alternative administrative style. In N. Van Den Bergh & L. B. Cooper (Eds.), *Feminist visions for social work* (pp. 163-186). Silver Spring, MD: National Association of Social Workers.

Hyde, C. (1989). A feminist model for macro-practice: Promises and problems. *Administration in Social Work, 13*(3/4), 145-181.

Marieskind, H. I. (1980). *Women in the health system.* St. Louis: C. V. Mosby.

Masi, D. A. (Ed.). (1981). *Organizing for women: Issues, strategies, and services.* Lexington, MA: Lexington.

McShane, C., & Oliver, J. (1978). Women's groups as alternative human service agencies. *Journal of Sociology and Social Welfare, 5,* 615-626.

Miller, H., & Philipp, C. (1983). The alternative service agency. In A. Rosenblatt & D. Waldfogel (Eds.), *Handbook of clinical social work* (pp. 779-791). San Francisco: Jossey-Bass.

Morgenbesser, M., Natkin, S., McCall, N., Grossman, B., & Nachreiner-Cory, E. (1981). The evolution of three alternative social service agencies. *Catalyst, 11*, 71-83.

Norman, E., & Mancuso, A. (Eds.). (1980). *Women's issues and social work practice.* Itasca, IL: F. E. Peacock.

O'Sullivan, E. (1978). What has happened to rape crisis centers? A look at their structures, members, and funding. *Victimology, 3*, 45-62.

Perlmutter, F. D. (1988). Administering alternative social programs. In P. R. Keys & L. H. Ginsberg (Eds.), *New management in human services* (pp. 167-183). Silver Spring, MD: National Association of Social Workers.

Schechter, S. (1982). *Women and male violence: The visions and struggles of the battered women's movement.* Boston: South End.

Schwartz, A. Y., Gottesman, E. W., & Perlmutter, F. D. (1988). Blackwell: A case study in feminist administration. *Administration in Social Work, 12*(2), 5-16.

Sullivan, G. (1982). Cooptation of alternative services: The battered women's movement as a case study. *Catalyst, 14*, 39-56.

Valentich, M., & Gripton, J. (1984, September). Ideological perspectives on the sexual assault of women. *Social Service Review*, pp. 448-461.

Van Den Bergh, N., & Cooper, L. B. (Eds.). (1986). *Feminist visions for social work.* Silver Spring, MD: National Association of Social Workers.

Withorn, A. (1980). Helping ourselves: The limits and potential of self help. *Radical America, 14*(3), 25-39.

Withorn, A. (1984). For better and for worse: Social relations among women in the welfare state. *Radical America, 18*(4), 37-47.

Women and Mental Health Project. (1976, September). Women-to-women services. *Social Policy*, pp. 21-27.

Zimmerman, M. K. (1987). The women's health movement: A critique of medical enterprise and the position of women. In B. B. Hess & M. M. Ferree (Eds.), *Analyzing gender: A handbook of social science research* (pp. 442-472). Newbury Park, CA: Sage.

The Tax Assessment

Carie Winslow

Chipawayyayayaya
The pen cuts tight into my hand
I try and squeeze the letters of your name   into the little squares
                             on the form.
               you are de/formed
               never formed
I say your name with my heavy English tongue
I can taste   the dried blood of the women in the moon hut.
Your child cries
I hear the flesh drum sounds that came with him from your womb.

You circle my government regulation desk
You shuffle my papers.
You laugh at me.
     White woman.

I measure your furs and your fish.
I enter 0 in the dollar column and I hear my Mother's voice . . .
     "another useless Indian, those people would still be in teepees
     if it weren't for us"
My heritage rattles in my head
     blood and ink on my hands.
You would still be in teepees if it weren't for us,
               my haunted voice echoes.

Except
It's me who is uneasy
and you who casually shifts your full woman's body on my
polyurethane chair.

I remember that you know how to sit in a circle on the earth.
You know how to use her medicines in a sacred way.
I look at the dirt under your fingernails,
              the weather grain on your skin,
          it's evidence that I can trust.
My White daughter's heart rests
          glad
        the land is still in your hands.

Chapter 12

SUPPORTING PRACTICE IN LARGE-SCALE BUREAUCRACIES

NANCY R. HOOYMAN

Previous chapters have demonstrated the richness of feminist practice in diverse practice settings. This chapter focuses on the macro level of administration or leadership as a primary variable that sets the context for feminist practice within organizations. In the particular instance described, the setting is a large public school of social work, in which, as dean, I am attempting to implement feminist principles and values in my work with faculty, students, staff, and community constituencies. Despite the unique collegial governance structure of academic settings, many of the principles described are applicable to implementing a feminist approach within human service agencies, including other large public bureaucracies (Weil, 1988).

Throughout this chapter, the terms *feminist leadership* and *feminist administration* are used interchangeably. This recognizes that leadership qualities are not tied to a particular management position or associated with a position's visibility. Rather, all of us exert power and influence at different levels within an organization, without necessarily holding a specific administrative position. In fact, many of the direct service practitioners who have contributed to this book are leaders, although they may not be managers formally. Such an assumption reflects the feminist perspective that the personal is political: that there is nothing we do—no matter how individual and personal it seems—that does not reflect our part in a system of power.

This chapter begins with a presentation of my perspective on feminist administration; briefly reviews the literature on women in social work administration, including the question of whether or not differences exist between male and female administrators; and concludes with a description of my efforts to implement feminist values within a large public hierarchical organization. I will share some of my own process of development as an administrator, a process in which I am continuously learning, changing, and struggling with my own contradictions as a woman socialized to traditional bureaucratic norms who is now attempting to infuse feminist values into those norms. This ongoing process reflects the feminist principle that the changer and the changed are one: As we strive to implement changes within our own organizational work settings, we also are changed (Bricker-Jenkins & Hooyman, 1986).

Disagreement exists in the literature and among practitioners about whether it is even possible to implement feminist values in an organizational environment that does not incorporate feminist structure and decision-making processes, because of the dissonance between values and form (Weil, 1988). My perspective is that feminist leadership within hierarchical organizations can be conceptualized as a way to bring about organizational change, to create environments that support and empower individuals by maximizing their potential. An underlying assumption of such organizational change is that both male and female participants within the organization will ultimately benefit from these changes.

DEFINITIONS

In my work setting, I find Harstock's (1979) definition of feminism useful: as a mode of analysis, a method of approaching life and politics, a way of asking questions and searching for answers. As a mode of analysis, feminism does not present a clear-cut, right/wrong way that works for all women—or men. In fact, to assume so is counter to feminist values. But feminism does have clear implications for action, for permitting choices, and for acting to change existing institutions.

My own development as a feminist began while I was in graduate school in the early 1970s. Then, and later as a new faculty member, I was disturbed by the lack of women in social work administration and worked to create opportunities for women to advance within the profession. At that stage of my development, however, I operated primarily from a women's issues framework, preoccupied with achieving equal opportunities within current structures. Given my own relatively privileged situation, I was fortunate to be able to take advantage of such opportunities, moving relatively quickly up the academic ranks. I became increasingly aware, however, that such an individualistic, incremental approach left the lives of many women unchanged. I recognized the need for fundamental changes in how work and family roles are determined and how rewards are allocated in our society. I saw that the feminist principle of the interconnection between personal and structural change was one way to address the gaps inherent in a women's issues or nonsexist approach.

My perspective on feminist administration is also shaped by my own experience of being in a leadership position in a predominantly female profession in which the majority of students, staff, clients served, and people serving them are women, often underpaid and undervalued. Social work is a profession that tends to be devalued by our society, in part because it is characterized by female values of care and concern that are viewed as secondary in status compared with marketplace values of competition and gain. Recognition of these interconnections between gender and societal values fuels my determination to work for larger changes within the social work profession.

My perspective is also influenced by my operating within an academic setting. Despite the norm of faculty governance and participation, universities are hierarchical and patriarchal organizations that can be oppressive to women and that discourage the questioning of authority. As women, most of us have been socialized to hierarchy as the predominant organizational form and to male models of leadership as the primary model. As Chernesky (1980) has documented, for models of organization we have hierarchies, for power we have models of oppression, and for expressing conflict we have examples of violence and sanctions. In my effort to make changes within the university hierarchy, I have had to acknowledge that my apparent success in advancing within it is partially due to my possessing behavior and skills traditionally valued by the predominantly white male culture. Therefore, along with my growing awareness as a feminist, I continually experience conflicts over my own successes within the bureaucratic system that I seek to change.

In contrast to hierarchical approaches and male models of power, feminist leadership aims to reaffirm and build upon women's unique processes and experiences as strengths, not characteristics to be negated (Schwartz, Gottesman, & Perlmutter, 1988). It seeks to institute, as legitimate, the feminine values of caring, service, and concern with relationships. A feminist perspective begins by recognizing that women's place in the social structure is fundamentally different from men's, because of women's daily experiences with oppression. Given this, women bring to organizational positions distinctive experiences, values, relationships, cognitive and emotional perspectives, ideas, and needs that differ from those of men (Lyons, 1983; Miller, 1976, 1984; Schaef, 1981). Accordingly, a feminist approach stresses the absolute necessity of taking action to improve women's lives. In fact, efforts to build upon and reaffirm women's strengths, processes, and experiences in human service agencies may be even more critical now under conditions of fiscal austerity and program cutbacks, which affect women most negatively. It is precisely at such times, when both women staff and clients may be particularly anxious and experiencing low morale, that efforts to create supportive environments are most needed.

A major theme of this chapter, however, is that a feminist perspective on leadership is not for women only; instead, it aims to cross-cut concerns shared by both men and women by developing work environments that empower all individuals by facilitating the development of their full potential. As identified by Bricker-Jenkins and Hooyman (1986), a feminist approach recognizes that self-actualization is the inherent purpose and goal of human existence. A feminist administrator thus tries to identify and mobilize inherent capacities for individual and collective self-actualization for all members of the organization.

STUDIES ON WOMEN IN ADMINISTRATION

Although women predominate in lower-status and lower-paid positions within social work, the majority of deans, agency administrators, and individuals in key leadership positions are men—an inequity that has motivated much of my own work to support women's preparation for and movement into administrative positions (Faver, Fox, & Shannon, 1983; Rubenstein, 1981; York, Henley, & Gamble, 1985). Given this gender imbalance in the social work profession, there has been considerable interest in and a growing number of studies about whether women's leadership style is different from men's and whether, in fact, it may be more effective (Larwood & Lockheed, 1979; Lyons, 1983).

This question about gender differences in effectiveness parallels the growing concern with a crisis of leadership generally in our society, with resultant interest in the need for fundamental changes in major organizations. This interest is reflected by the recent organizational and leadership literature on peer group supervision, participatory and democratic management, matrix organization designs, and quality-control circles (Kanter, 1983; McCormack, 1989; Ouchi, 1981; Peters & Waterman, 1982). Some of the themes of this literature are the destruction of hierarchy, replaced by boundaryless, ambiguous networks of organizations; empowerment, ownership, and information sharing; team-centered organizations; partnerships with clients and vendors; lifelong learning and development for every employee; and constant change and fluidity as the norm.

Similarly, organizational and management literature is replete with advice for effective leadership, and a new formula for leadership that is more person centered, consensual, creative, and caring is gradually emerging (Lenz & Meyerhoff, 1982; Loden, 1985; Maccoby, 1981; Pearson, 1981). For example, Kanter (1983) maintains that organizations must be altered to be more flexible in order to adapt to evolving technology and changing competitive environments. Discussing the necessary "change master" skills, Kanter identifies kaleidoscope thinking, persistence, the ability to articulate and communicate visions, the capacity to build coalitions as well as a working team to carry out ideas, and the sharing of credit to reward everyone who works. Similarly, Rosener and Schwartz (1980) call for a leadership style based on synthesizing, creativity, intuition, and qualitative thinking.

At the same time, as noted earlier, most of the models of leadership in this society have been based on male norms for career success within bureaucratic structures (Dexter, 1985; Riger & Galligan, 1980; Shakeshaft, 1987). Women who have moved into administrative positions have generally been expected to adapt to positions as defined by men rather than have the opportunity to change the position's requirements and characteristics to reflect a female-centered approach (Chernesky & Bombyk, 1988; Dexter, 1985; Hooyman & Cunningham, 1986). In fact, most of the early social work research on gender differences in management focused on personality traits and their relationship to the leadership qualities of men and women—in other words, whether women possessed those traits and qualities that were held by men and considered necessary for effective leadership. It was frequently assumed that successful managers possessed characteristics that are more frequently and stereotypically associated with men than with women, such as aggression, self-confidence, rationality, and emotional control (Dexter, 1985; Putnam & Heinen, 1985).

Women have been presumed to be at a disadvantage for administrative positions because they are primarily socialized to family roles and feminine norms. In fact, this assumption was perpetuated recently by the "Mommy Track" concept, whereby women presumably "choose" whether to place a higher value on family than on career and thus to advance more slowly within organizations. One explanation of the scarcity of women in administrative positions is the discrepancies in fit between ascribed and achieved role prescriptions that preclude women from developing attitudes and skills appropriate for managerial roles in bureaucratic organizations, and that result in male decision makers' perceiving women as unqualified for managerial positions. As a result, it is presumed that women have to undergo a two-stage process, from socialization to their ascribed roles to resocialization to the norms appropriate for being a manager (Hanson & Tyach, 1981). These person-centered explanations, essentially psychological in nature, maintain that female socialization practices encourage the development of personality traits and/or behavior patterns that are contrary to demands of the managerial role. Therefore, it is agreed that women must discard the attitudes and behaviors learned in childhood that are inappropriate to managerial roles. In fact, some authors suggest that women who have succeeded as managers are those who have never been traditionally socialized and who have learned two different types of expected behavior (Symons, 1984).

Consistent with such person-centered explanations, many management and leadership training programs for women have tended to convey the message that in order to succeed, a woman must "think like a man, dress like a doll, and work like a horse" (Hooyman, 1978). A review of books for women managers identifies the theme that managerial success requires such male qualities as assertiveness; competitive drive; cooperative team spirit; strategic, logical, and analytical skills; and compulsion to assume leadership and achieve authority and power (Chernesky, 1979). Chapter headings such as "Whatever You Do, Don't Cry," "Packaging Yourself," and "Creating and Controlling Your Territory—Strategies to Create an Executive Image" all convey that women have to learn the management game and its rules, are personally responsible if they do not get ahead, and must make the individual effort if they are to succeed. A "slice-of-the-pie" model of occupational mobility has held women responsible for their own successes and failures within organizations. In fact, I was trained in such a male-based model, which I initially perpetuated through my own training in individualistic skills strategies for women in the 1970s.

The person-centered model encourages personal growth strategies, such as assertiveness training, to help women take charge of their lives and to overcome the presumed "fear of success," as well as enhancement of specific management-related or technical skills (Riger & Galligan, 1980). In other words, women have frequently received the message that in order to be effective leaders, they must become more like men in terms of personality traits such as assertiveness and rationality, and adopt a model of organizational behavior that is essentially male. In turn, so-called feminine characteristics, such as concern and compassion for others, empathy and nurturance, interpersonal skills, and intuitive and creative problem solving, have been viewed as weaknesses to be negated or minimized. Since what women valued or how they behaved was considered inappropriate for effective management, the focus of much of the research on administration has been to demonstrate that women managers were equal to or as good as male managers. Even recent surveys of workers across types of organizations have found persistent support for the belief that better managers are masculine (Bailey & Neilsen, 1987; Camden & Witt, 1983).

These individualistic strategies have a number of fundamental limitations. First, person-centered strategies do not acknowledge the existence of a gender hierarchy in which males are at the top and females are at the bottom. Second, the efficacy of the traditional male model of optimal organizational functioning is questionable, given growing concern with problems of worker morale and productivity under hierarchical models. There is increasing recognition that characteristics associated with traditional female gender-based roles might actually produce better outcomes (Ferguson, 1984; Loden, 1985; Rosener & Schwartz, 1980). What is of even greater concern is that viewing women's characteristic ways of behavior and thought as secondary, inferior, and ineffective, and therefore locking women into positions of less power and visibility, has resulted in losses to social work organizations, programs, and the profession. By defining women within a male framework, person-centered strategies fail to acknowledge that the activities that women undertake and their motivations for doing so are in addition to and different from those that men perform and thereby can enrich and strengthen organizations.

Even more important, these individualistic approaches fail to address fundamental questions about the impact of work and organizational settings on people. Simply filling slots in organizational charts with "masculine" women ignores both the negative consequences of typically masculine work styles and the unique contributions that can be obtained from more traditionally feminine orientations. As Kanter (1977) noted more than a decade ago, organizational reform is not enough. There is a need to move beyond the issues of whether or not individuals receive their share of organizational rewards to questions of how shares are determined in the first place—how labor is divided between men and women and between the marketplace and the family, and how power is concentrated.

A second wave of research produced mixed findings about the extent of similarity between male and female leaders. For example, Broverman's (1970) work on gender stereotypes found that men were seen as more competent than women, but as less warm and expressive. Subsequent research suggested that when male/female differences in leadership styles and behaviors exist, they are consistent with sex-role stereotypes (Camden & Witt, 1983; Greenhaigh & Gilkey, 1986; Lenz & Myerhoff, 1982; Lyons, 1983, 1985). Women have knowledge of a female culture and socialization that they bring to the job, a female world that researchers have often failed to investigate when they have studied male/female differences (Bernard, 1987; Ferguson, 1984; Schaef, 1981). This perspective on a female culture and world has been most clearly articulated by Gilligan (1982), who asserts that women view the world differently from men in terms of interpersonal relationships and a morality of responsibility and care; women speak with "a different voice." Yet in organizations that promote objective, rational methods of knowing, women are disadvantaged in gaining access to their own voices (Belenky, Clinchy, Goldberger, & Tarule, 1987). Women have been socialized to make and sustain human relationships in a world that devalues sustenance and care and therefore limits the potential of women and men.

A more recent research focus demonstrates that the leadership behaviors of women are not only different from men's, but may, in fact, be more effective (Chusmir, 1985; Greenhaigh & Gilkey, 1986). So-called feminine characteristics—the capacity to sustain and affirm others through empathy and mutuality, an emphasis on cooperation and creativity—are viewed as strengths, not liabilities. Therefore, utilizing the gender-linked strengths of women can alter the standard of effective leadership for both men and women (Bailey & Neilsen, 1987; Lyons, 1983; Miller, 1984). For example, an empirical study of women executives in human service organizations in New York City found a leadership style characterized by a nonhierarchical approach, cooperation, participation, and sensitivity and empathy to others (Chernesky & Bombyk, 1988). Similarly, Loden (1985) distinguishes women's leadership style by its emphasis on empathy, collaboration, and cooperation. A review of the literature on women and management over the last 20 years concludes that where women once rejected stereotypically female behaviors, many such characteristics are now considered appropriate management behavior, particularly for a style that is more democratic than autocratic (Rosener & Schwartz, 1980). Such an approach has been conceptualized as combining the strengths of masculine and feminine styles—cooperative and competent, yielding and dominating, nurturing and collaborative (Sargent, 1981).

As a next stage, and one oriented to the future, there is increasing interest in a feminist approach to leadership that reaffirms and builds upon women's unique strengths, processes, and experiences in their own right (Ferguson, 1984; Schwartz et al., 1988; Weil, 1988). The major assumptions and principles that underlie a feminist leadership style are as follows:

- affirming the value and dignity of each individual as central to a clearly explicated value framework
- valuing multidimensional thought processes
- reconceptualizing power
- creating open problem-solving structures
- valuing of process

The next section reviews each of these principles and describes briefly my own efforts to implement them in my position as dean of a school of social work in a public university. In doing so, I acknowledge the dilemmas inherent in such efforts and that I am not always as effective as I would like to be.

PRINCIPLES OF FEMINIST LEADERSHIP

Affirming the Value
and Dignity of Each Individual

Affirming the value and dignity of each individual is fundamental to a feminist approach in working with people within all levels of an organization. This value underlies all social work practice, but it takes shape explicitly in feminist practice by affirming women's perspectives and experiences, recognizing and building upon women's strengths, and anticipating, interpreting, and responding to the needs of others within the organization (Ferguson, 1984; Weil, 1988). It means utilizing one's position and skill to make a difference in the options available to women, and continually identifying ways in which one can have a positive impact upon the conditions faced by women students, faculty, and clients. In facilitating new opportunities for women, it is assumed that all organizational members—men and women—will benefit in the long run from the greater integration of women's values and processes into the organization's structure.

In terms of my administrative practice, this translates into facilitating others' development, believing that all individuals can change, and identifying their areas of strength as a basis for changes. As I meet with faculty, staff, or students, I am constantly looking for ways to build upon their strengths, facilitate choices for them, and support their choices. In doing so, I try to balance the value I place on being equitable with enhancing both individual and organizational competence and productivity. Although these values are at times conflicting, keeping both of them at the forefront of my decision-making processes and of my interactions with others permits me to try to balance them deliberately over time. Maintaining a long-range, developmental orientation about decisions that affect individual faculty, students, and staff prevents me from making hasty, idiosyncratic decisions about individuals' well-being.

To affirm each individual's value is also to seek deliberately to increase and encourage diversity as a source of strength, not as something to be merely tolerated. Diversity includes not only differences by gender, but also by race, sexual orientation, culture, religion, degree of physical ability, and socioeconomic status. To create an environment that celebrates diversity requires listening carefully to others' ideas and viewpoints; hearing the unspoken as well as the spoken, the emotional and personal issues as well as the facts; creating a climate where people feel free to disagree; and then encouraging dialogue and coalitions among diverse groups in order to arrive at agreement on overall direction. Differences are thus not a basis for separation, but a means toward unity, commonality, and synthesis. Noncompetitive working principles, techniques of noncoercive conflict resolution, and language that shows consideration, concern, and appreciation, and that stresses the inclusive "we," are strategies that help attain this unity (Kahn, 1984; Schwartz et al., 1988).

One example of my working to ensure diversity has been how I have responded to student and faculty concerns about racist, sexist, anti-Semitic, and homophobic graffiti in the school of social work. My initial reaction—common to most administrators—was one of disbelief and denial: that in a school of social work, with a mission statement espousing diversity, such acts could not occur and, in fact, must be caused by someone from "the outside." However, by opening myself up to the possibility that such intolerant behavior could occur within our school, and by *really* listening to students' and faculty's concerns and suggestions, I have been able to work productively with them (through a new group involving students, faculty, and the three deans) to create a safe, supportive environment for all members of our diverse school community. Through my being open to students' input regarding orientation and classroom structure, the students and I have made clear that we will not tolerate any form of discriminatory behavior within the school. By creating an environment in which all members of our school community have viable choices, we are conveying to students, faculty, and staff the institutional value placed on diversity.

A dilemma that accompanies such developmental approaches and openness to others' viewpoints is that one may be labeled a "weak administrator," or not "tough" enough. From other more traditional perspectives, a feminist approach, by encompassing diverse perspectives, can be equated with softness or lack of strength. This reflects the societal tendency to view *soft* and *hard* as polarities rather than recognizing that the two kinds of behaviors can coexist and can have value among both men and women, depending upon the particular situation.

Valuing Multidimensional Thought Processes

Closely related to the value placed on diversity is that of multidimensional thought processes rather than traditional linear explanations. A feminist administrator recognizes the richness that can emerge from varied explanations being brought to bear on decisions. This means seeking to avoid defining issues in black or white polarities, by recognizing and acknowledging the complexities and contradictions inherent in organizational issues, the shades of gray, and the interconnections of differences among organizational members.

As a feminist administrator, I have tried to create a safe environment in which people can take risks, exercise options, and present different ways of defining and solving problems. In decision-making processes, such as during faculty meetings, the emotional aspects of decision making are valued as well as the rational and cognitive ones. I try to listen carefully to the feelings that lie behind the words, and to what is *not* being said as well as what is stated. Such an approach clearly conflicts with traditional patterns of decision making and may be viewed as irrational, nonadaptive behavior that slows down the decision-making process.

It also means being completely open to new ideas, many of which may conflict with traditional approaches or with my own way of doing things. In many ways, the principle is comparable to "believing the client" in a practice setting. As an example, when faculty, staff, or students approach me excitedly about an idea or project, I try to listen carefully to the enthusiasm beneath the proposal and to reinforce them for their creativity. Rather than respond with "It can't be done that way, because . . . " and enumerate the barriers to change, I encourage joint problem solving for a solution that has both individual and organizational benefits. In many instances, individuals who have felt empowered by a supportive reaction have gone on to achieve something that previously seemed impossible. Even if an idea cannot be implemented, the presenter generally feels affirmed and is more likely to engage in creative initiatives in the future that benefit the organization.

I have also tried to acknowledge my own limits, by recognizing the complexity of issues, qualifying my assertions, and admitting my doubts when I do not know the answer or when I have made a mistake. An approach of modeling tentativeness, self-exploration, and disclosure is intended to encourage others to take risks, to admit their

own fallibilities, to reduce their need for defensiveness, and to minimize defining new ideas as threatening. I also seek to acknowledge
the impact that others have upon me, that their thinking has power
and meaning for me, and thus that reciprocity and mutuality exist in
our interactions.

Reconceptualizing Power

The reconceptualization of power is fundamental to changing organizations in a feminist direction. Under such a reconceptualization,
power is defined as influence and responsibility that everyone within
an organization can possess in terms of who can perform particular
functions and tasks rather than as a limited, zero-sum commodity.
Shared power expands. Expertise is not correlated with hierarchical positions, but varies with the tasks to be performed (Hooyman &
Cunningham, 1986; Schwartz et al., 1988; Weil, 1988).

Feminist administrators, similar to the other practitioners in this
book, are therefore concerned with ways to empower others through
developing their potential fully. Feminist leadership is determined by
the functions the leader performs and her ability to move others to action, not by her public visibility. As noted by Van Wagner and Swanson (1979), power can be expressed by building on others' internal
strengths and expressing concern for others rather than through competitive, aggressive models. A feminist administrator places a high
value on the long-term relationships of the people involved and seeks
to avoid tactics that might jeopardize those relationships. Rather than
striving to win, the feminist administrator is willing to compromise.

One way in which I have attempted to empower others is to try to
move power out of the dean's office by actively delegating to faculty
and administrative staff. In order to do so, I must be able and willing
to trust others to carry out their responsibilities and functions. Rather
than directing others, I seek to involve them in mutual planning, problem solving, and decision making. I struggle with my own need to
control and to achieve perfection, recognizing that I need to set overall directions and standards, and then be willing to let go, since the
autonomy of other administrative staff is essential both to their job
satisfaction and to their overall effectiveness. It also means that I
must be able and willing to accept that others may not perform a task
exactly as I would. I seek to convey support and appreciation for their
decisions, expressing disagreement only when I feel I absolutely

cannot live with their choices—whi h happens rarely because of the relationship of mutual trust developed over time.

Letting go of my need for control and perfection has not been easy, because of my high standards and my uneasiness with asking others for help. As dean and as a woman, I frequently hold myself to the unrealistic expectations that I should be able to manage on my own and "do it all myself." Given our socialization as women to be responsible and responsive and to take care of others, it is easy to fall into the trap of trying to do it all.

Yet to empower others can also be freeing to the administrator. In a more traditional hierarchical model, the administrator conveys, "I'll take care of you, trust me, I'll make the decisions for you," which produces dependence. The need to be in control creates the burden of carrying dependent people and of trying to do it all—to sit on every committee, to attend every meeting, to be involved in every detail of the organization, and to be the one who feels responsible for its overall success. However, when power and the presumed responsibility for organizational success do not rest with one person, the risk of burnout is reduced.

When I was unable to "let go," even to ask my immediate administrative staff person to assume certain tasks, I faced exhaustion. Such control was unhealthy not only for me, but also for some staff who felt that I did not trust them to perform adequately. As I have struggled to delegate tasks in a way empowering to others, it has been necessary to clarify our different functional levels of responsibility and the areas where consensual decision making is possible versus those where I make the final decision. This process of clarification of the focus and differentiation of decision making has benefited both my administrative staff and me.

Another difficulty that I initially encountered in my efforts to diffuse power was that delegation was perceived as abandonment and lack of caring by some staff and faculty accustomed to traditional hierarchical models of decision making. For some staff and faculty, there is a certain comfort and security when one person makes most of the decisions—and carries most of the burden of the organization. As noted above, over time, staff welcome the opportunities created by the sharing of power; but the immediate experience can be disquieting for those who have worked only in hierarchies and must "unlearn" attitudes of powerlessness inherent in most traditional workplaces (Schwartz et al., 1988). When collaborative efforts are to occur within an overall hierarchical framework that has traditionally stressed competitive individualism, autonomy, and personal achievement at the expense of community goals, the administrator needs to invest time in preparing staff for her different approach that values cooperation, collaboration, and the diffusion of power.

Part of this preparation includes involving staff in the decision to delegate and decentralize, rather than announcing such changes as a fait accompli. This also means deliberately thinking through who is affected by major administrative decisions and how to involve them effectively in the decision-making process. For example, in order to decentralize and move toward a more consensual decision-making model within the university hierarchy, I recently instituted an administrative team involving the directors of all the key units within the school of social work. Although such a team approach is typically used in the private sector, it is less common in academia. This approach recognizes the diversity of viewpoints reflected by the different administrative units and seeks to prevent their working at cross-purposes. Discussion and consensual decision making regarding complex administrative issues appear to lead to greater understanding and ownership of decisions and commitment to their effective implementation.

At the same time, despite my efforts to diffuse power, the reality within the university hierarchy is that the formal position of dean carries a weight that cannot be denied. The chief administrator who is struggling to implement feminist values must therefore come to terms with the power and authority of her position accorded it by others and inherent within the organizational structure. To attempt to deny the existence of such power is to be dishonest. It is a myth that we all are or can be equally powerful. Within hierarchical organizations, there needs to be a differentiation of the functional areas in which others can participate and decisions can be made consensually versus those for which one individual has the final responsibility and accountability. The challenge then becomes how to utilize that power of formal position in ways consistent with underlying feminist values in order to act on issues that will benefit the people within and served by the organization.

Reconceptualizing power within a traditional hierarchy also involves modifying the existing reward structure to recognize members' differential contributions. I have sought to utilize my access to rewards to create a sense of community, where there are no insiders or outsiders, but rather everyone feels that he or she is "in." This has meant developing a broader definition of the types of behaviors that are rewarded, and expanding the number and types of rewards given at different times. For example, in faculty salary allocations based on merit, I have also rewarded behaviors required for organizational well-being, such as chairing major school committees, rather than only the individualistic behaviors (e.g., number of publications) traditionally rewarded within hierarchies.

Creating Open Problem-Solving Structures

Redefining power also means developing more open structures for two-way communication and mutual problem solving to create access to issues and information. Meetings should include both content time and process time—open space that allows for considering new possibilities, for being receptive to others' ideas, and for developing mechanisms for people to work together on problems rather than one person giving orders to another. Greater involvement in the decision-making process, such as through the administrative team, will over time create greater investment and commitment to decisions among different units in the organization.

Within hierarchies, the administrator as the central figure is traditionally expected to be the problem solver. When staff have complaints or conflicts with each other, they usually turn to the administrator to resolve those issues for them. In an effort to develop horizontal methods for sharing information and solving problems, I have tried to create the norm that individuals deal directly with each other, rather than turning to me. In effect, I have tried to "flatten" the hierarchy. When an individual comes to me with a complaint or concern, I consistently refer him or her back to the individual of concern rather than become involved initially in trying to solve the problem. As individuals identify common goals through such interactions, coalition building among diverse groups and individuals can occur.

At the same time, as noted earlier, I have had to differentiate between situations in which there can be open participation in the decision-making process and those in which I, as the person who is ultimately accountable within the hierarchical university structure, must make the tough decisions about personnel, budget, space, and administrative arrangements. This has meant coming to terms with the inherent tension between my own value of openness in problem solving and the reality of the hierarchical structure. This tension, which creates a degree of isolation, must be acknowledged; I must be careful not to encourage participation in situations where it cannot be honored.

Valuing of Process

Underlying all of these efforts is a valuing of process and of relationships—a developmental orientation concerned with long-run effectiveness, not only short-run efficiency, and with the long-range institutional impact of decisions, not isolated individual cases. This does not mean endless meetings and "process" time. Rather, it means attending to both content and process in time-delimited meetings, determining the extent of agreement, and involving the group in resolving conflicts and disagreement. Since majority decisions are more feasible than consensus within a large and diverse faculty, the goal is generally to achieve as much agreement as possible. Focusing on the ends in the means translates into developing mechanisms for feedback upward as well as horizontally and downward, for expressing support and appreciation as well as criticism, and for dealing directly with conflict and differences. As an example, faculty are provided with opportunities to give me feedback on all major issues. Because I place a high value on accessibility and responsiveness, I convey a message that I will listen to their ideas and concerns. A guiding principle has been that when faculty, staff, or students express a concern or make a request to me, they should receive an immediate response. Even if the response is no, or "I need more time and/or information, but will get back to you in a week," they know that they have been heard.

Valuing of process also means recognizing the interaction between personal/familial and professional concerns within the work setting—trying to create a fit between individual and organizational needs in order to build a positive work environment. A feminist administrator can play a central role in developing work environments that are supportive of individuals' personal/familial concerns as well as encouraging the formation of social networks that support personal development. On a pragmatic level, this means adjusting work schedules, tenure clocks, and other expectations to take into account child-care and elder-care demands. For feminist administrators, the line separating the public world from the private is generally blurred.

SUMMARY

I have been able to present in this chapter only a few of what I perceive to be differentiating characteristics of a feminist approach to leadership. In doing so, I recognize that writing about these principles is easier than implementing them, and that I am not always successful in my attempts. To be successful requires openness and flexibility, valuing of diversity and conflict, setting aside time for reflection and feedback, and accepting that there is no right and perfect way. As a feminist dean within the university hierarchy, my leadership approach is constantly evolving, creating both the excitement and the challenge of the position. The bottom line is that we as women must exert our leadership on behalf of women's interests so that we can make a substantial impact on the increasingly desperate needs of women at the bottom. In my setting, this means structuring the work and learning environment to encompass this larger goal.

In social service agencies, the work setting can also be modified to develop alternative demonstration programs built on feminist values, regardless of the particular organizational context. Feminism is not about individual mobility up the corporate ladder, so that women with proper credentials will succeed while others will not. Rather, it is about changing institutional norms and practices that deny women access to essential resources. Our incremental efforts within large, traditional hierarchies, whether within academia or in social service agencies, may seem minuscule at first glance. But they are ultimately oriented to how feminist values can become the basis for fundamentally changing organizations and institutions so that women and men are able to act according to their potential and abilities rather than according to traditional gender-based modes of thought and behavior.

REFERENCES

Bailey, D., & Neilsen, E. (1987). Life scripts as sources of reward for women executive directors. *Affilia: Journal of Women and Social Work, 2*(4), 46-56.

Belenky, M., Clinchy, B., Goldberger, N., & Tarule, J. (1987). *Women's ways of knowing: The development of self, voice and mind.* New York: Basic Books.

Bernard, J. (1987). *The female world.* New York: Basic Books.

Bricker-Jenkins, M., & Hooyman, N. R. (Eds.). (1986). *Not for women only: Social work practice for a feminist future.* Silver Spring, MD: National Association of Social Workers.

Broverman, M. (1970). Sex role stereotypes and clinical judgments of mental health. *Journal of Consulting and Clinical Psychology, 34*(1), 1-7.

Camden, C., & Witt, J. (1983, May-June). Manager's communication style and productivity: A study of female and male managers. *International Women's Studies*, pp. 258-269.

Chernesky, R. (1979). A guide for women managers: A review of the literature. *Administration in Social Work, 3*, 91-97.

Chernesky, R. (1980). Women administrators in social work. In E. Norman & A. Marcuso (Eds.), *Women's issues: Social work practice* (pp. 241-262). Itasca, IL: F. E. Peacock.

Chernesky, R., & Bombyk, M. (1988). Women's ways and effective management. *Affilia: Journal of Women and Social Work, 3*(1), 48-61.

Chusmir, L. H. (1985). Motivation of managers: Is gender a factor? *Psychology of Women Quarterly, 9*, 153-159.

Dexter, C. (1985). Women and the exercise of power in organizations: From ascribed to achieved status. In L. Larwood, A. Stromberg, & B. Getek (Eds.), *Women and work: An annual review* (Vol. 1, pp. 239-259). Beverly Hills, CA: Sage.

Faver, C., Fox, M., & Shannon, C. (1983). The educational process and job equity for sexes in social work. *Journal of Education for Social Work, 19*(3), 78-87.

Ferguson, K. E. (1984). *The feminist case against bureaucracy.* Philadelphia: Temple University Press.

Gilligan, C. (1982). *In a different voice.* Cambridge, MA: Harvard University Press.

Greenhaigh, L., & Gilkey, R. W. (1986). Our game, your rules: Developing effective negotiating approaches. In L. L. Moore (Ed.), *Not as far as you think: The realities of working women,* (pp. 135-148). Lexington, MA: Lexington.

Hanson, E., & Tyach, D. (1981). *The dream deferred: A golden age for women school administrators* (Policy Paper No. 81-C2). Stanford, CA: Stanford University, School of Education, Institute for Research on Educational Finance and Governance.

Harstock, N. (1979). Feminist theory and revolutionary strategy. In Z. Eisenstein (Ed.), *Capitalist patriarchy and the case for socialist feminism* (pp. 71-73). New York: Monthly Review Press.

Hooyman, N. (1978). Redefining models of power and administrative style. *Social Development Issues, 2*, 46-54.

Hooyman, N., & Cunningham, R. (1986). An alternative administrative style. In N. Van Den Bergh & L. B. Cooper (Eds.), *Feminist visions for social work* (pp. 163-186). Silver Spring, MD: National Association of Social Workers.

Kahn, C. S. (1984). Group process and sex differences. *Psychology of Women Quarterly, 8*, 261-281.

Kanter, R. M. (1977). *Men and women of the corporation.* New York: Basic Books.

Kanter, R. M. (1983). *The change masters.* New York: Simon & Schuster.

Larwood, L., & Lockheed, M. (1979). Women as managers: Toward second generation research. *Sex Roles, 5*, 659-669.

Lenz, E., & Myerhoff, B. (1982). *The feminization of America: How women's values are changing our public and private lives.* New York: St. Martin's.

Loden, M. (1985). *Feminine leadership or how to succeed without being one of the boys.* New York: Times Books.

Lyons, N. (1983). Two perspectives: On self, relationships and morality. *Harvard Education Review, 53*, 136-147.

Lyons, N. (1985, October). *Overview: Perspectives on what makes something a moral problem.* Paper presented at the annual meeting of the American Educational Research Association, Boston.

Maccoby, M. (1981). *The leader: A new face for American management.* New York: Simon & Schuster.

McCormack, M. H. (1989). *What they don't teach you at Harvard Business School.* New York: Bantam.

Miller, J. B. (1976). *Toward a new psychology of women.* Boston: Beacon.

Miller, J. B. (1984). *The development of women's sense of self* (Working Paper No. 12). Wellesley, MA: Wellesley College, Stone Center.

Ouchi, W. G. (1981). *Theory A: How American business can meet the Japanese challenge.* Reading, MA: Addison-Wesley.

Pearson, S. S. (1981). Rhetoric and organizational change: New applications of feminine style. In B. L. Forisha & B. H. Goldamon (Eds.), *Outsiders on the inside* (pp. 54-76). Englewood Cliffs, NJ: Prentice-Hall.

Peters, T. J., & Waterman, R. H. (1982). *In search of excellence: Lessons from America's best-run companies.* New York: Harper & Row.

Putnam, L., & Heinen, S. (1985). Women in management: The fallacy of the trait approach. In B. A. Stead (Ed.), *Women in management* (pp. 322-332). Englewood Cliffs, NJ: Prentice-Hall.

Riger, S., & Galligan, P. (1980). Women in management: An exploration of competing paradigms. *American Psychologist, 35,* 902-910.

Rosener, B., & Schwartz, A. (1980). Women and leadership in the 1980s: What kind of leaders do we need? In *New leadership in the public interest* (pp. 25-36). New York: NOW Legal Defense & Education Press.

Rubenstein, H. (1981). Women on organizations: A review and some implications for teaching social work practice. *Journal of Education for Social Work, 17*(3), 20-27.

Sargent, A. G. (1981). *The androgynous manager.* New York: AMACON.

Schaef, A. W. (1981). *Women's reality: An emerging female system in the white male society.* Minneapolis, MN: Winston.

Schwartz, A. Y., Gottesman, E. W., & Perlmutter, F. D. (1988). Blackwell: A case study in feminist administration. *Administration in Social Work, 12,* 5-15.

Shakeshaft, C. (1987). *Women in educational administration.* Newbury Park, CA: Sage.

Symons, G. L. (1984). Career lives of women in Canada: The case of managerial women. *Work & Occupations, 11,* 331-352.

Van Wagner, K., & Swanson, C. (1979, January-February). From Machiavelli to Ms.: Differences in male-female styles. *Public Administration Review,* pp. 66-72.

Weil, M. (1988). Creating an alternative work culture in a public service setting. *Administration in Social Work, 12,* 69-82.

York, R., Henley, H. C., & Gamble, D. (1985). Barriers to the advancement of women in social work administration. *Journal of Social Service Research, 9,* 1-15.

CONCLUSION

THE PROPOSITIONS AND ASSUMPTIONS OF FEMINIST SOCIAL WORK PRACTICE

MARY BRICKER-JENKINS

Attention to women's issues in social work has resulted in many dramatic changes in the language of practice, riveted attention on many previously unattended dimensions of women's experiences, and generally given greater voice to the perspectives and aspirations of the community of women in the profession. However much one may applaud (or bemoan) these indicators of movement toward balance, equity, and inclusiveness, such challenges to sexism are a necessary but insufficient expression of feminist visions and commitments. As the work described in the foregoing chapters reveals, underneath the visible and sometimes dramatic waves of woman-centered energy and events we have experienced in the last two decades lies a deep reservoir of consciousness and commitment that will likely have even more far-reaching consequences: the feminist practice movement. While the aim of the women's issues movement is equity and inclusiveness for women, the work of the feminist practice movement is the creation of a method of practice designed to engage all persons in the process of personal and political transformation. This concluding essay will examine the recent history of that movement and the underlying principles of its practice as they are expressed in the daily work of the contributors to this volume.

THE EMERGENCE OF
FEMINIST SOCIAL WORK PRACTICE

Feminist practice began as an attempt by social workers to integrate feminist theory, commitments, and culture with conventional approaches to practice (Bricker-Jenkins & Hooyman, 1986; Valentich, 1986; Weick, 1983b). These efforts have resulted in the emergence of a distinguishable approach to practice that goes beyond a "nonsexist" or "women's issues" orientation, and beyond a grafting of feminist perspectives onto a humanistic core. Lying well within the tradition and mission that distinguishes social work from other "helping" professions, it is an attempt to link the personal and political dimensions of human experience and action both theoretically and methodologically. While certainly not the first or only mode of social work practice to attempt this integration, feminist practice contributes uniquely to the endeavor by virtue of its roots in a liberation movement. As such, it is grounded in a worldview that is fundamentally different from that which informs much of the practice of the profession and the structures that support it. As such, it aspires to be a practice of personal/political transformation.

The work of personal/political transformation may be motivated and nurtured by visions and commitments, but it is accomplished by action. We may think of a model of practice as a patterned set of prescribed and proscribed actions. The prescription and proscription derive from a value and theory base; the pattern is the structure of its method. These elements stand in dynamic interaction with one another. By definition, a model of practice that has personal/political transformation as its purpose will be incomplete, evolving, dialectical, diverse, and replete with the contradictions that both contain it and compel it to methodological maturation. Today it is both possible and necessary to examine the work of feminist practitioners as an emerging model of practice—to search for patterns in the daily activities of feminist practitioners, and to articulate the theoretical and value propositions that appear to underpin those patterned actions.

This examination was, in fact, the work of the Feminist Practice Project sponsored by the Committee on Women's Issues of the National Association of Social Workers in the mid-1980s. That project resulted in the articulation of a set of propositions and assumptions that appear to inform the activities of feminist practitioners working in a variety of settings and using the full range of modalities typically used by social workers (Bricker-Jenkins, 1989; in press). In the remainder of this chapter, those propositions and assumptions are presented and illustrated by reference to the feminist practice in clinical settings described in foregoing chapters.

ASSUMPTIONS ABOUT HUMAN BEINGS AND THEIR ENVIRONMENTS

All social work action is informed by a set of assumptions about human beings and the environments we create to meet human need. Those that appear to be most significant in shaping feminist practice are discussed in this section. They can be summarized as follows:

- The inherent purpose and goal of human existence is self-actualization; self-actualization is a *collective* endeavor involving the creation of material and ideological conditions that facilitate it.
- We have created and institutionalized systems and ideologies of domination/subordination, exploitation, and oppression that are inimical to individual and collective self-actualization; patriarchy is only one of these, but it has resulted in specific and profound injuries to women.
- Since people strive for self-actualization, it is possible to identify and mobilize inherent individual and collective capacities for healing, growth, and personal/political transformation.
- The worldview informing all practice posits (a) that all things are connected; (b) that individual and collective pain and problems of living always have a cultural and/or political dimension; (c) that "reality" is a multidimensional process; (d) that diversity creates choices for all and is thus a source of strength, growth, and health; and (e) that women have unique and relatively unknown histories, conditions, developmental patterns, and strengths that must be discovered and engaged by social work practitioners.

Self-Actualization as Human Purpose

Implicit in feminist practice is a belief that the inherent purpose and goal of human existence is self-actualization. As one of the participants in the Feminist Practice Project stated, "Feminism originates in a belief in the worthiness of all to have an opportunity to develop to their fullest" (quoted in Bricker-Jenkins, 1989, p. 2). For feminist practitioners, this fundamental tenet is both a value position and a hypothesis of human behavior.

Self-actualization—or the achievement of potential—is viewed by most social workers as a basic human imperative, as suggested by Maslow (1968, 1970, 1971/1976; see also Gil, 1981, 1987). Feminist practitioners emphasize two dimensions of this concept: collectivity and conditions. Self-actualization is viewed as a collective endeavor involving the creation of conditions that facilitate it. It proceeds necessarily from social interactions and within a sociopolitical matrix. Because all things are seen as connected, self-actualization of one individual or group at the expense of another is presumed to be not only morally wrong, but existentially impossible.

As a corollary, feminist practitioners assume that it is possible to discover and create ways in which human beings can achieve self-actualization without inhibiting that of others. Such common contemporary phenomena as maldistribution of resources and power, interpersonal violence and aggression, exploitation, and denial of rights and liberties are presumed to be functions of confusion and distortion about human needs, nature, and potential—ineffective solutions to the human problematic—and not expressions of inherent nature. Specifically, men do not exploit, dominate, and abuse women because they are inherently aggressive, but because they have learned these behavior patterns through a "curriculum" based on a set of false assumptions about human nature and potential, and particularly those of women. Even those feminist practitioners who believe that social behaviors of men and women are inherently different and may be biologically determined suggest that these differences result from centuries of social behavior patterns that have become genetically encoded; they posit that this biological condition can and will change as we create new ideological and cultural conditions that stimulate different patterns of human development (Bricker-Jenkins, 1989, p. 184).

The concept of self-actualization as a collective endeavor pervades the practice described in this book. In the Caregiver Support Program described by Rathbone-McCuan, Tebb, and Harbert (Chapter 2), an attempt is made to operationalize the concept of self-actualization. The worker uses the instrument developed from this attempt to explore with the caregiver her unique personal meaning of self-actualization and the conditions they will enhance to support the process. Among those conditions are the creation of choices and connections with others who are experiencing similar challenges in their lives. The work to establish those connections has led inexorably to a recognition by workers and clients of "the larger context of ageist sexism that traps older women in the isolation of caregiving" and the need to change that context.

Similarly, a feminist perspective on empowerment "views individual problems as arising not from personal deficits, but from the failure of the society to meet the needs of all people" (Gutiérrez, Chapter 9). Whereas personal and interpersonal power may be enhanced through cognitive and skill development, a feminist practice of empowerment reaches for political power through collaboration and collective action to change oppressive structures. Wedenoja (Chapter 8) describes her own process of empowerment as "a process of identifying, examining, and asserting our individual needs and wants within the context of our commitment to a valued collective of feminists, [a] challenge [that] ran parallel to that of our clients."

The creation of conditions that make individual/collective self-actualization possible is also a central theme of feminist practice. Many would agree with the Feminist Practice Project participant who said:

> I have a philosophy that I espouse to a lot of clients, and to any other person who would listen. As clinician/therapist/counselor, I would suggest that if I could guarantee every woman and working class and minority person in this country an annual income of ten thousand dollars, ninety-nine percent of all mental health problems would go away. (quoted in Bricker-Jenkins, 1989, p. 202)

Similarly, in her discussion of feminist administration, Hooyman (Chapter 12) asserts that "feminism is not about individual mobility up the corporate ladder, so that women with proper credentials will succeed while others will not. Rather, it is about changing institutional norms and practices that deny women access to essential resources." Thus the goal of the practice of feminist leadership is "to create environments that support and empower individuals by maximizing their potential."

The "conditions" that feminist practitioners attempt to create are both material and ideological. The notion that "the personal is political" underscores the presumed dialectical relationship of material and ideological conditions by proposing that the values and beliefs expressed through our social, political, and economic structures are identical to those belief systems and values that shape our self-concepts and intimate relationships. Thus much of feminist practice begins with an examination of those values and beliefs that impede individual/collective self-actualization and then seeks ways to create material conditions that embody a different configuration—one that makes it possible for all persons to grow to full potential.

Patriarchy Is Only Part of the Problem

Feminist practitioners concern themselves with *all* institutionalized systems and ideologies of domination/subordination, exploitation, and oppression that are inimical to individual and collective self-actualization. Whether one believes that patriarchy is the wellspring of racism, for example, or a categorically different phenomenon, they both embody supremacist beliefs and attendant behaviors.

Wherever one enters the realm of private pain with this perspective, the intersections of the "isms" are soon encountered. Smith (Chapter 4) describes how his own efforts to shed sexist behaviors in his community of men were confounded by heterosexism and homophobia; Baczynskyj (Chapter 10), Gutiérrez, and Liddie (Chapter 6) describe the ways in which the struggles of the women with whom they work are confounded at the intersection of sexism, racism, and an economic deprivation that is an inevitable by-product of capitalist competition; Rathbone-McCuan, Tebb, and Harbert's efforts are confounded by the economic exploitation of women's labor in the capitalized health care system and by ageism even within the feminist movement.

Increasingly, as feminist practitioners work to untangle the web of beliefs and behaviors that contain women's potential, it becomes clear that feminism is not for women only, but provides a mode of analysis and action that can and must contend with all the "isms" that threaten human well-being. Palmer (Chapter 3) illustrates, for example, how a feminist analysis can help us see not only the common experiences of all victims of incest, but also the ways in which these experiences are differently processed by people of color, people with disabilities, and old persons. Smith describes the way he uses his feminist analysis of the dynamics of oppression in his work with an African-American adolescent father.

Inevitably, most feminist practitioners will concern themselves primarily with the specific and profound injuries to women that devolve from patriarchy. As Wedenoja and Rathbone-McCuan et al. reveal, a woman's caregiving is not seen as necessarily limiting in and of itself, but it becomes so in a system that regulates and enforces it in order to sustain a system of privilege and profit. Palmer describes the ways in which women's processes of growth and self-definition through relationships—whether these be natural or learned patterns—are distorted and converted from splendid strengths to agonizing vulnerabilities through the exercise of patriarchal hegemony. In a world where domination/subordination and coercive dynamics prevail, women "de-self" in order to survive physically and psychically.

In order to work effectively with women, it is necessary to view them through a lens that produces a double exposure—one that simultaneously locates them in the context of patriarchy and defines them as unique and whole by removing them from the tangle of gender roles defined by that context. Only then can we begin to construct a practice system that does not replicate and exacerbate women's victimization and silencing.

People Are Inherently Healthy

The construction of that practice system is rooted in the conviction that it is possible to identify and mobilize inherent individual and collective capacities for healing, growth, and personal/political transformation. The feminist practitioner approaches work in search of alliances with people's innate health-seeking aspirations and efforts. Thus Mermelstein (Chapter 7) scans the landscape of devastated rural communities for signs of renewal and reclamation; she goes prepared to teach specific skills that will reinforce these efforts. Baczynskyj approaches her work with Southeast Asian refugee women, many of whom are experiencing anxiety and depression, cognizant of the cultural imperative to "save face" and culturally generated healing processes: meditation, incense, flowers, solitude. She views the women's returning to battering husbands as "retrenching to familiar positions and roles in order to preserve a known legacy." Similarly, Palmer views the "pathology" of survivors of incest as their health-seeking attempts to secure psychic safety; she trusts that "persons will work to grow, to take on their sufferings when they are ready." In his work with African-American adolescent fathers, Smith acknowledges their fears and threats to survival and masculine identity as reality based in a racist and heterosexist environment; such acknowledgment is a necessary first step in helping "young fathers realize that the power of domination over the women in their lives is not real power."

The assumption of health and the possibility of mobilizing strengths pertains to groups and communities as well as to individuals. In all of the situations described above and elsewhere in this book, there is a tremendous trust in the power of natural, self-help, and support groups. While acknowledging the silencing and competitiveness that will inevitably emerge in such groups, the practitioner locates the roots of these dynamics not in the group itself but in a social context in which people have learned to distrust themselves and each other. As one of the participants in the Feminist Practice Project affirmed:

> I think people profoundly really do want to help each other. I think people function best in groups, in concert with each other. I think there is a certain amount of skill to helping people have good group experiences, and I think some of those skills can be taught. . . . There is no end to the human potential. There are cultural differences, there are gender differences, but in the grand scheme of things those are really very minor compared to the similarities. Most people really want the same things for themselves and for the rest of the world. (quoted in Bricker-Jenkins, 1989, p. 201)

A Different Worldview

As Kravetz and Jones (Chapter 11) point out in their discussion of feminist agencies, feminist approaches to practice are like other "alternative" models in their origins in "changing social conditions and the increasing visibility of new client groups." They differ, however, in that the "ideological and philosophical base . . . [lies] in the emerging feminist analyses of male privilege and female subordination." In describing the influence of the ideological and philosophical base on the structures and processes of organizations, Kravetz and Jones help us understand that the way we view reality determines the way we try to change it. Moreover, although feminists may have begun with a narrow analysis of women's position in society, the process and content of that analysis has led inexorably to a much more fundamental and comprehensive analysis—to a worldview that differs from the dominant worldview either in content or in emphasis (Bricker-Jenkins & Hooyman, 1986; Bricker-Jenkins & Joseph, 1980; Morell, 1987; Van Den Bergh & Cooper, 1986; Wetzel, 1986).

One of the elements of that worldview that most influences practice is the *connectedness of all things.* As Palmer suggests, "Practice within a feminist perspective is . . . the experience of our interconnectedness,

the mutual relationship, the oneness with all living things that is crucial to our fragile existence. When we desecrate, subordinate, alienate, and oppress, we are doing the same to ourselves." The prevailing
worldview leads us to view the social worker as the changer and the
client (person/environment) as the changed; for the feminist practitioner, the changer and the changed are one.

This perspective forms the basis for such characteristics of feminist
practice as mutuality and reciprocity in relationships, consensual decision making, the valuing of process—"preserving the ends in the
means"—and attention in practice to dimensions of human experience, such as the physical and spiritual, often neglected in conventional practice. As we have seen throughout this book, much of feminist practice involves analyses of the precise ways in which things are
connected, efforts to create or strengthen connections that work for
people, and confrontation and transformation of those that do not.

A feminist perspective on interconnections and interdependencies
expands and strengthens an ecological systems approach to social
work (Germain & Gitterman, 1980) in the way it focuses on the relationship between the personal and the political. Feminist practitioners
lead with the assumption that *individual and collective pain and problems of living always have a political and/or cultural dimension.* That
is, they reflect and express ideologies, relations, structures of power
and privilege, or other salient features of the cultural milieu. Con-
versely, through our actions—or inactions—people participate in shaping
those realities. We are culture bound, and we are culture builders. Feminist social work practice is a culture-building practice that proceeds
from an analysis of the binding features of the cultural terrain.

One of the ways in which we are culture bound has enormous consequences and implications for practice: We are often unaware of the
ideological context that simultaneously reflects and sustains the overt
political/cultural realities that we experience. "Effectance"—the ability to influence one's environments and thus participate fully and effectively in the collective culture-building process—is supported by
bringing to full consciousness the ideological themes embedded in
cultural realities as we experience them. Becoming conscious of the
ideological content of the cultural terrain, of the interdependence of
ideology and culture, and of the ways we participate individually and
collectively in sustaining or revising them constitute the essence of
"consciousness-raising" and the foundation of personal/sociopolitical

transformation (Kirk, 1983; Longres & Bailey, 1979; Longres & McLeod, 1980; Wesley, 1975).

Closely related to the concepts of interconnectedness and personal/political interactions is the view that *all reality is a multidimensional, unfolding process.* This ontological perspective stands in marked contrast to the positivist philosophical tradition that has prevailed in the world for several centuries, "a philosophical 'ordering of the world' such that the building blocks of social reality are assumed to be dichotomous, polarized categories arranged in hierarchical order" (Collins, 1986, pp. 214-215). Feminist theorist Elizabeth Janeway (1980) summarizes the alternative perspective in very simple terms: "There is always more reality around than we allow for; and there are always more ways to structure it than we use" (p. 34).

Palmer reflects this view of reality in stating her belief that "being and practice are one and the same" and links it to the concepts of self-actualization and inherent health: "Practice becomes an evolving process; that is, there is no specific outcome that finishes work. This means that there is no grand 'cure,' no final 'fix.' Persons will work to grow, to take on their sufferings when they are ready."

In addition to the many implications for practice methods and techniques that will be discussed below, feminist assumptions about the nature of reality influence the content of the knowledge base used for practice and the methods used to create it. Because feminist practitioners tend to view life as process and in multidimensional terms, they tend to use with caution knowledge derived from positivist research. In addition to the issues that feminists have raised about the invisibility and distortions of women's experience in such research, the use of the paradigm itself is being subjected to scrutiny as potentially inadequate to the social and behavioral dynamics it attempts to elucidate (Gottlieb & Bombyk, 1987; Heineman, 1981; Imre, 1982, 1984; Weick, 1983a, 1986, 1987). In particular, feminist practitioners will be wary of linear, unicausal models of behavior constructed from such research efforts. The study of a multidimensional world of ever-changing processes with methods that perforce focus on only a few of the potentially relevant variables has limited utility in a world of practice as complex as that of social work.

Gary (Chapter 1) and others who work with battered women, for example, have little research that accommodates in its design such variables as the ideology and personal beliefs of family members, and the many ways that power and control can be used and abused in the family. Much research has focused on discrete acts of aggression in a decontextualized way. Practice informed by such research may be useful in teaching people how to manage a particular act of physical aggression, but the contextual dynamic and the belief system that support the abuse of power remain unaddressed. Soon perpetrators devise new ways to exercise control by using their power in less direct but equally abusive ways.

Examples like this illustrate the difficulties of using the existing depoliticized, positivist-based fund of knowledge for practice. Aware that epistemologies are themselves politically shaped, feminist researchers are attempting to find and create research paradigms and methods that can accommodate the multidimensional processes of social life (Gottlieb & Bombyk, 1987). Methods that begin with a fluid examination of women's experiences, rather than existing conceptualizations and abstract variables, provide a necessary corrective. Ethnography and grounded theory provide useful existing approaches. Others conduct action-oriented research in which their "subjects" become participants and set the agenda, pose the questions, and function as coinvestigators. The protocols and purposes of such research advance the participants' political interests. The knowledge generated is primarily for their use; the researcher's interests must be subordinated to theirs.

In contrast to the positivist assumptions that research can be value free and "controlled" in relation to a presumably static "truth," feminists assume that all knowledge is infused with values, and that we are constantly creating reality. Like any other form of feminist practice, feminist research is political in purpose and method. In fact, research itself becomes a method of practice.

In sum, viewing reality in multidimensional/process terms has enormous implications for the way knowledge of it is understood, developed, and used in practice. It is always contextualized and always tentative. Moreover, there is an ethical responsibility implied in the related notions that there are many truths and that people create their own truths, their own realities. The perspective compels an active posture in the world, but also a profoundly humble one. As one of the Feminist Practice Project participants said:

> So we really get to the point of identifying and defining people on their own terms and not with reference to other things that are somehow presumed to be normal or superior. . . . The neatest thing about being a feminist is that I

don't have to sit in judgment of other people. And I'm free to grow and learn and incorporate new ideas. This is the wonderful "weaving of feminism." There's always room to add more stuff; [truth] just grows! It's so great. (quoted in Bricker-Jenkins, 1989, p. 226)

The belief that there are many truths of equal validity reflects and reinforces another element central to the feminist worldview: that of *valuing diversity.* The notion that diversity is not only a fact of life, but a source of strength, growth, and health, is a fundamental principle of the physical world—where genetic diversity enhances opportunities for survival, growth, and adaptation—and has an underrecognized and underdeveloped analogue in the social world. Feminist practitioners not only accept diversity, but actively seek to promote it and incorporate it into practice. Just as we see in the physical world, promoting diversity and diverse solutions to the problems of living supports the practice goal of creating choices. In other words, promoting diversity is not merely a value orientation; it becomes a technique of practice. Specific examples of the use of individual and cultural diversity in practice pervade the chapters in this book and will be discussed further in the section on practice methods and techniques.

That discussion invariably will highlight the diversity among feminist practitioners themselves. As indicated in the introduction to this book, the editors and contributors expressed concern about the tendency within feminism to define "the" feminist approach. Feminism must remain an open, evolving ideology and diverse practice in order to be true to itself and viable as a system. This requires the intentional construction of a diverse feminist community and ongoing dialogue. A participant in the Feminist Practice Project described the way she does this through her peer clinical consultation group, in which each member defined herself as having a feminist orientation, but each had a different training and interest area. There were psychoanalytically trained clinicians like herself, community organizers, "alternative practitioners," and many others. "My personal preference in terms of clinical support is not to have clones of myself. . . . I haven't found the discussions in depth to be as interesting as looking at a particular case through a different prism" (quoted in Bricker-Jenkins, 1989, p. 215). Such groups are essential to the evolution of a system of practice that not only values diversity, but uses it as a source of strength, growth, and health.

The tendency of the dominant patriarchal culture to suppress diversity and silence difference has resulted in a view of women that either grossly distorts their image or obliterates it altogether. Feminists regard as incomplete and oppressive any worldview that does not include in its field of vision the woman defining herself. Like members of other groups rendered invisible in patriarchal systems, *women have unique and relatively unknown histories, conditions, developmental patterns, and strengths that must be discovered and engaged by practitioners.*

As Smith points out, male social workers who choose to work from a feminist perspective must put aside their formal training and socialization to ask themselves, "What was it like for women?" He notes, however, that he learned to do this from a feminist author, Adrienne Rich, who had to develop this technique in order to do her own writing. So penetrating is the patriarchal worldview that being a woman—even a woman-loving woman—is not enough to ensure that women's realities and interests will be held in one's consciousness.

In her discussion of the evolution of the Stone Center's "self-in-relation" theory, Turner (Chapter 5) says that "the premise undergirding the evolving theory was the belief that a closer examination of women and their development can lead to a new understanding of both women and men." If social work theory and assumptions about people and their social environments are to inform a practice of empowerment, this premise must pervade all of them.

THE PURPOSE OF PRACTICE

In the tradition of the social work profession, feminist social workers view their mission as facilitating human purpose in social contexts. The assumptions and propositions regarding people and their environments calibrate the sense of purpose, however. As stated in the report of the Feminist Practice Project, *the purpose of social work practice is to enable self-actualization.* Given structural and ideological barriers to self-actualization, practice must address itself explicitly to them. All practice is inherently political in consequence; feminist practice is explicitly political in intent (Bricker-Jenkins, 1989). In accordance with the view that human purpose is self-actualization—and the corollary that this purpose requires re-creation of symbols, structures, and social relationships that support it—feminist practitioners view their role as that of allies and agents of this process. Given the political nature of symbols, structures, and relationships, all practice is necessarily political.

In speaking of their purposes, practitioners will variously accentuate the several components of their worldview. In their chapter on practice with caregivers, Rathbone-McCuan, Tebb, and Harbert emphasize health, choices, action, and collectivity: "Our feminist practice base attempts to help the caregivers find their strengths, frame their choices, take steps to empower themselves, and support others to do the same." A social work practitioner and educator who participated in the Feminist Practice Project articulated the proposition well, punctuating the political dimension:

> Well, in *my* definition, since what you are talking about is helping everybody realize their potential and then fighting the barriers that keep that potential from happening, the only way that people can do that is to do that themselves. Your role, then, as worker or teacher is first to help people *understand* the barriers, and then help them find the power to fight the barriers. (quoted in Bricker-Jenkins, 1989)

The very language of feminist practice as it relates to purposes is political language: advocacy, empowerment, liberation, transformation. In fact, there is a tendency to critique and avoid the language of conventional definitions of purpose. *Provision of social services*, for example, suggests a disempowering, active-to-passive process; *mediation* between people and between people and environments may lead to an obfuscation and denial of power imbalances believed to be at the core of human pain and containment; *treatment* and *therapy* presume pathology; *intervention* is an invasive term that also suggests and directs a conflictual rather than a collaborative process.

Even the standard "dual-purpose" definitions of social work are called into question, as they have led to a bifurcation of professional activity (cause or function, micro or macro, case or cause, direct or indirect, clinical or everything else); more fundamentally, such dualistic definitions obscure the potential for developing methods for integrating personal and social transformation. A primary effort of feminist social work practice is to achieve and articulate that methodological integration as it presumes that personal and social transformation are, in fact, a single, integrated process to which practice is directed (see, for example, Collins, 1986; Morell, 1987).

Although all practice embodies ideologies, conventional practitioners do not generally make their ideologies explicit and consciously examine their performance against them. For feminist practitioners, ideology is at the core of practice—the measure of all choices to be made—and is consciously used to motivate and evaluate action. As the chapters by Hooyman and Kravetz and Jones document, feminist practitioners purposefully seek and highly value the congruence of practice goals, process, structure, and program with feminist ideology.

In sum, as a countervailing ideology (and as a social movement), feminist practice insists on a critical evaluation of the individual and collective choices that shape women's lives. Those choices, in turn, are measured against the imperatives of human need and social justice; feminism insists on removing any sanction from choices that are judged to be inimical to human development, freedom, and health. Feminists may argue the details of analysis and program, but an underlying consensus exists that barriers to the realization of the full and unique potential of women and other oppressed groups can and must be challenged and changed (Bricker-Jenkins & Joseph, 1980).

PRACTICE PROCESSES

Goals

As we have seen throughout this book, feminist practitioners can work in conventional settings and with the same needs, issues, and problems as conventional practitioners. To the goal-setting process, however, they bring a set of assumptions and analyses that result in a politicized agenda that includes attention to the power dynamics operating in the situation of concern.

Wedenoja illustrates this well in her comparison of conventional, collaborative, and feminist approaches to practice with caregivers of persons with mental illness: Goals include such items as "increased awareness of the sexist nature of societal expectations of and dependence on women as primary caregivers," a goal sought simultaneously at individual, family, and societal levels. Moving from and reinforcing that awareness, the goal of restructuring the assignment of responsibilities for providing care is added to the agenda. The practitioner works with other family and community members to relieve women of tasks and, involving the family in the effort, pursues changes in public policy to shift responsibility for support services from the individual and family level to the societal level.

Goals will be expanded as persons move through stages of recovery from the injuries of oppression. Gutiérrez identifies the developmental psychological stages of empowerment, each of which can become a goal of collaborative work: increasing self-efficacy, developing a group consciousness, reducing self-blame, and, finally, assuming personal responsibility for restructuring oppressive conditions. Similarly, Palmer describes the process of her work with a victim of incest as moving "from victim to survivor to the potential of thriving" through a process in which the woman was supported in her growing strength and capacity for collaborative structuring of the therapeutic relationship and process. In her approach to her work, Palmer attempts to provide opportunities for people to experience in the therapeutic environment the possibilities of self-definition that they can experience in the rest of their lives.

In sum, what the feminist practitioner will bring to the collaborative goal-setting process is an intent *to help women and other persons recover from the specific injuries of oppression, exploitation, and domination, and to facilitate their use of individual and collective power to redefine and restructure their realities.* Through the structure and methods of their work on this agenda, they pursue an overarching goal of personal/political transformation.

Assessment

Consonant with these goals, assessment is viewed as a *dialogical process* in which client and worker share their perspectives, meanings, and analyses. Mermelstein, Liddie, and Smith all identify the critical factor that catalyzed the merger of their conventional and feminist practice perspectives in terms of an experience of partnership with their clients: each was serendipitously confronted with a need to begin revealing his or her own struggles, frustrations, and personal visions. The kind of dialogical process that emerges from such sharing is characteristic of feminist practice and has specific application in assessment.

Rathbone-McCuan, Tebb, and Harbert describe the use of an openended assessment form and the Well-Being Scale as instruments their workers use to refocus attention from the needs of the dependent person to those of the caregiver. Completing the form jointly becomes a shared learning experience. They assert that the worker's self-disclosure and expression of her own emotions is essential to the search for mutual understanding of the meanings that the caregiver ascribes to her situation. During this process, the worker's caring for the caregiver—expressed through concrete and emotional support—creates the conditions for transforming a position of self-neglect to one of self-care. For many caregivers, this reciprocal process of exploration and definition may be the first experience of hearing their own voices without the distortions imposed by others' demands to define their truths for them. Similarly, to begin the dialogue and shaping of common understanding, Palmer uses literature on incest and the victim's own reflective writings on its application in her own experience.

Mermelstein provides an illustration at the community level of assessment as a dialogical process of building a common analysis through use of action research. This method—in which the "subjects" define the research agenda, collaborate through all stages of the research process, and "own" the data—fosters mutual discovery, interpretation, and use of the findings to influence change. Through its use in her project, Mermelstein reports, "we were able to give voice to rural Missourians at national levels of policy-making."

Content introduced by the worker is designed to *depathologize and politicize*—that is, to uncover the links between the personal and the political in the condition of concern under assessment. Gary describes the AWAKE program as a response to enlarging the focus of assessment from the role of the mother in a child abuse situation to encompass her culturally prescribed position in the family. This expanded focus enabled the AWAKE workers to see the mother's victimization; even if she was not herself being abused by her partner (which was often the case), she had less power than her partner to provide safety for her child. Similarly, the conditions of women care- givers must be assessed in terms of the politics of caregiving in our culture. As Mermelstein states, women are "savaged by the very societal institutions and processes that purport to protect, value, and enhance their well-being." The savagery is exercised not by virtue of the caregiver's desire to attend to the needs of her family, but by the societal appropriation of her labor and the cultural mandate to provide limitless care.

Characteristically, feminist practitioners' attention is not only on the dynamics of sexism, but more broadly attentive to the dynamics of oppression.

All of the authors working with people of color, for example, provide examples of ways in which their adaptational and survival patterns become "pathologized" in conventional assessments. Turner, for example, describes the ways in which an African-American woman's connectedness to family and ethnic identity—essential for survival, health, and growth in an environment that is hostile to biculturalism and racial pride—is defined as "deviant" and "dependent" in conventional assessments. By validating in assessment the rage and frustration of women of color derived from their experience with race, class, and gender oppression, Gutiérrez sets the stage for movement through the stages of empowerment from enhanced personal power to group-based exercise of political power. Most often, feminist practitioners accomplish this validation by gradually introducing their own analysis of the societal roots of personal pain through discussion and literature, examining both the objective conditions of oppression and the ways in which people internalize belief systems that contribute to their maintenance.

Exploring the belief system—both its roots and its consequences—related to the condition of concern is an essential part of an assessment that will lead to collective action. As Liddie's and Gutiérrez's experiences with groups illustrate, women—and especially women of color—have learned to distrust themselves. They know too that they may pay a price for speaking up and stepping out of line. In order to participate effectively in group action, they must first identify and shed the belief that they are not entitled to self-care and self-definition. Liddie, working with women who feared their own rage and the possibility of reinforcing "Black bitch" stereotypes, began by teaching them to confront each other and by modeling confrontation behaviors with her colleagues. Before using group methods, Palmer works individually with women whose victimization has silenced them until they are able to voice their own needs in some small way. Rathbone-McCuan and her colleagues relate how a student in the DVA program identified her caregiver's need to give herself permission to feel anger about her exploitation and work through the guilt she felt about seeking her own safety before she could enter a process of transformation.

Counterbalancing this attention to disempowering dynamics, assessment will also focus on preferred and available *patterns of strength* in intellectual, emotional, social, cultural, physical, and spiritual domains. Given the feminist perspective on multidimensionality, each of these areas demands attention as each is presumed to be a locus of existing personal/political strength and potential power. As Rathbone-McCuan, Tebb, and Harbert illustrate, people are presumed to be the experts on their own strengths; they train their workers to encourage the caregiver "to examine her inner knowledge of the best ways to care for herself," trusting that "opportunities for self-actualization [will] come from drawing on her knowledge and applying it to choices and actions." It will be the responsibility of the worker to help create the choices and opportunities for action. As Baczynskyj, Turner, and Gutiérrez point out, the strengths that women of color have developed in their struggles with racism can be analyzed to fashion a template for struggles with other forms of oppression.

Moreover, each culture and spiritual system has provided healing and helping mechanisms that can be assessed and incorporated into action plans. Baczynskyj's Southeast Asian women are more likely to withdraw from alcohol addiction in a Buddhist temple than in Alcoholics Anonymous meetings. In defiance of stereotypes of passive and homebound rural women, Mermelstein's survey of rural communities during a farm crisis revealed the women as more willing than the men to value and work on community revitalization. Merging this finding with knowledge of such rural strengths as community loyalty and mutual aid networks, Mermelstein and her colleagues constructed a platform for collaborative action with rural women.

Moving outward from an exploration of belief systems and strengths, assessment will attend to the *power dynamics* operating in the situation of concern. Gutiérrez describes the use of vignettes— drawn either from the women in her group or from the worker describing similar situations—to engage the members in analysis of disempowering dynamics and sources of potential power "such as forgotten skills, personal qualities that could increase social influence, members of past social support networks, and organizations in the community." Smith explores the fantasies and dreams of his teenage parents to assess their perceptions of personal power.

Palmer and Gary reframed their conventional assessments of abuse by using a power analysis to pierce the wall of legal and medical definitions that contained both worker and client. Smith, believing that the pregnant adolescent with whom he was working could not leave the boyfriend who was beating her, engaged both of them in an analysis of the ways each was contributing to their oppressor/ oppressed relationship. Like Liddie, he reminds us that work can and must be done on both sides of the equation, however asymmetrical it may be, to achieve a balance of power in relationships.

Like Gutiérrez, Wedenoja points out that workers must themselves be clear about the ways that sociopolitical structures and ideologies disempower both workers and the people with whom they work; through their own studies and participation in consciousness-raising and peer supervision groups, they can expand their analyses and receive support and guidance as they restructure their practices. Since, as Hooyman and Smith point out, feminist practice demands a yielding of the power derived from hierarchical positions, it can exact major penalties in the form of professional self-doubt and marginalization. Clients and coworkers socialized in conventional relationships can be confused and angered by nonconventional approaches. Feminist practitioners themselves need support, validation, and a long-term perspective to sustain their vision and build their skills for pacing the changes they seek.

In sum, feminist assessment will include a mutual examination of constraints and opportunities in personal, interpersonal, and political power dynamics. Both concrete and ideological dimensions of power are explored through a dialogue about who benefits, how, and why in the existing arrangements. Finally, the practitioner takes responsibility for restructuring the working relationship as people gradually claim their rights to define the conditions of work.

Throughout the process of assessment—indeed, in all phases of work—special attention is given to *basic, concrete needs and to physical and psychological safety.* Liddie could have conducted self-esteem and assertiveness classes for her child day-care mothers, but knew that they were more likely to grow in these areas as they engaged in creating a food-buying cooperative that enabled them to meet a basic family need. Practitioners working with victims of violence know well the risks of moving too precipitously without a safety plan. Palmer highlights the significance of securing a sense of psychic safety as she respects the pace set by the incest survivor. Resistances are viewed as structures of safety that will ripen away as they are respected and validated as such.

Finally, knowledge of *women's unique history, conditions, developmental patterns, and strengths* is used in assessment. This knowledge helps both partners frame the condition of concern and the possibilities that it contains. Practitioners report using popular and professional literature, poetry, music, art, theater, storytelling, journal writing, and myriad other techniques to convey information about and pride in women's culture, to build a sense of community, and to document the political roots of private pain. Against this backdrop, some practitioners encourage people to write their own social histories. This experience both validates the individual and supports the development of analytical skills. This practice also provides a concrete experience of collaboration for those who may be more eager to please than ready to see themselves as partners in a healing and helping process.

Whatever the source or the medium of communication used, the preponderance of material shared in assessment is based on strengths. As the chapters in this book document well, the feminist practitioner is ever mindful that one cannot build a therapeutic alliance with pathology. The "pathological lens" of much conventional social work is replaced by a "political lens" in feminist assessments. Then, as one of the participants in the Feminist Practice Project said, assessment becomes an educational and agitational process that leads to a search for solutions in women's individual and collective histories.

Methods and Techniques for
Personal/Political Transformation

Feminist practitioners use a range of conventional and nonconventional approaches in their practice but appear to select and organize them around a proposition that is "strong enough to permit us to break through our commitments to various methodologies" (Walters, Carter, Papp, & Silverstein, 1988, p. 16). The proposition is stated in the findings of the Feminist Practice Project (Bricker-Jenkins, 1989) as follows:

> Healing, health, and growth are functions of validation, consciousness, and transformative action; these in turn are supported and sustained through resources to meet basic needs, relationships that preserve and nurture uniqueness and wholeness, and the creation of validating environments.

As stated at the outset of this book, feminist practitioners tend to view all their practice essentially as a practice of social change—or, more precisely, as the transformation of culture (Bricker-Jenkins & Hooyman, 1986). Implicit in this proposition is one theory about how "macro" change can happen: through the integration of personal and sociocultural transformational processes. As we heal ourselves from the injuries we have collectively inflicted on ourselves and each other, we heal our social relations and structures; as we take action to heal those, we heal ourselves. As we turn to a discussion of each element of the proposition, it is important to bear in mind that they are interrelated.

Validation refers primarily to the actions taken to affirm that the person's subjective experience of reality is believed in, important, and valuable. It is achieved through such techniques as encouraging the "telling of one's story" in journals, pictures, or drama; "active listening"; reflecting back the person's reality in her or his own words; sharing information from the worker's own direct and indirect experience that conforms to a person's experience; creating and working with groups of people whose concrete realities, issues, and experiences of them are similar; and encouraging the client to "set the agenda," whether in a clinical setting, research, or the community.

An essential first step in validation is "believing the client"—working from within her definition of realities, concerns, and issues. Gutiérrez points out that by accepting the client's definition, the worker not only communicates belief in her ability to understand her situation, but also takes a first step in building a relationship of shared power. Gary's case example demonstrates how "beginning where the client is" creates the safety needed to enlarge the agenda for work: Even though the AWAKE staff did not believe that "Ms. Z" would be able to protect her child as long as she remained with the man who battered her, working from her agenda helped her feel safe enough to acknowledge and end the battering. This is analogous to the process described by Palmer, who reminds us that what is often called "denial" in conventional practice represents behaviors adopted by survivors "to gain a perception of control. These survival behaviors must be respected and gently worked with in order not to strip persons of their only means of coping."

Working with people of color requires recognition and validation of a reality central to their lives: the need imposed by biculturalism to conform simultaneously to two often conflicting sets of values and norms. As Turner suggests, "a major task of the clinician is to learn to understand the client's functioning within her own cultural environment and value system (as well as how she functions within the majority culture) as a 'norm.' By doing so, the clinician is in a better position to determine mutually with the client the extent of conformity and deviation."

Indeed, it may be appropriate to view all women as facing an analogous task as they attempt to live in a patriarchal culture. In a sense, to live in a man's world that marginalizes women's realities and denies them the right to speak their truths demands a form of bicultural adaptation. Baczynskyj reminds us that "in the process of becoming bilingual, a person speaks for a long time only with the mind, while the heart carries on a conversation in the native language." If we regard all women as being in exile, validation will involve reaching for the silent language of their hearts. The Well-Being Scale described by Rathbone-McCuan, Tebb, and Harbert provides one mechanism to do this; Palmer uses working with clay, and Smith explores fantasies and dreams. All of these and other techniques, mostly nonverbal, provide a means of giving voice to the silenced native language of the heart.

Validating and working with the client's realities does not mean that the worker's own reality or interpretations of it are withheld; on the contrary, the open sharing of the worker's perceptions and assessments is part of the validation process. In sharing their own material, practitioners convey the notion of partnership in discovery of solutions that draw on the worker's knowledge but conform to and build on the client's own expertise derived from a lifetime of successful problem solving. The effort is to depathologize, to establish that the client and her community have competence, and to reinforce the client's need, ability, and right to "name the world" for herself.

Validation is the first step in a consciousness-raising process that can lead to healing and empowerment. It also lays the foundation for working with all dimensions of people's experience—intellectual, emotional, social, ethnic and/or cultural, physical, and spiritual—as appropriate to their preferences, interests, and patterns of self-healing and action. Whether practitioners work in these domains directly or through alliances with other healers and helpers in a person's environment, their bedrock assumption is that each domain must be validated as a source of strength and solutions.

Consciousness-raising is "the process by which [people], not as recipients, but as knowing subjects, achieve a deepening awareness both of the socio-cultural reality which changes their lives and of their capacity to transform that reality by acting upon it" (Freire, 1970, p. 205). It begins with an examination and affirmation of one's reality (validation) and then moves to an exploration of the forces and factors that contribute to that reality as well as to one's experience of it. It is a search for meanings, and of how those meanings were derived. One of the participants in the Feminist Practice Project described her own experience of consciousness-raising in the ecclesiastical "base communities," or culture circles, of Brazil, where the method was first developed:

> They really had what Freire called the "conscientization process"—his word was "conscientizaçao." That means to make oneself conscious, not just within a rational-linear perspective, but as an overview of the person in the world—the center and the circle at the same time. And within the culture circles, there were dialogs happening. As you know, it was the beginning of the group process in our [feminist] style, and each contribution was felt as significant, and even the ones that had a conservative or unrealistic basis were felt as significant because it opened the windows for more questioning, for deeper questioning. So there was nothing there to be lost. (quoted in Bricker-Jenkins, 1989, p. 244)

As this account suggests, the basic technique for consciousness-raising is problem-posing dialogue. As other participants describe it in their practice, the problem-posing dialogue involves an exploration of a series of questions that can be summarized as follows:

- *Who am I?* What are my needs, my desires, my visions of a life that is safe, healthy, and fulfilling?
- *Who says?* What is the source of my self-definition and that of my reality? Does it conform to my experience of self and the world?
- *Who benefits from this definition?* Does it conform to my needs, my "truths"? Is it possible for me to live by these definitions? If not . . .
- *What must change, and how?*

The last question in this dialogical process is the bridge to transformative action. It is the point at which one begins to formulate a vision of the possible in concrete terms and to experience oneself as active in the world. "To even imagine that one has the capacity to create a new definition for oneself is a radical act" (Weick, 1987, p. 226). The worker infuses her or his analysis, however tentatively, to challenge the authority of those in the person's life that have imposed definitions and recipes for living that are not working for the person or, indeed, for anybody but those who have imposed their definitions.

Consciousness-raising is not simply providing information and analysis, although these can help. Rather, it evolves from a process in which the practitioner creates the conditions for others to develop their own analyses. Like all other components of empowerment, as described by Gutiérrez in her chapter, it is not something that can be done for another person (Simon, 1990).

It is, however, most fully accomplished in groups. It is in a group, as several of the authors suggest, that it is most possible to experience directly a sense of belonging and the potential for social power, and to develop the supportive bonds and skills needed to claim that power. As Palmer suggests, many people will need to experience their personal power in individual work until they feel safe and confident enough to take on the agendas of enhancing interpersonal and political power. Meanwhile, the development of an identity as a member of a class of disenfranchised people—and the concomitant reduction in self-blame—can be fostered through readings, attendance at meetings and cultural events that provide analysis, doing oral histories with family members and friends, and the like.

Liddie, in attempting the process with members of her group of child day-care mothers, discovered that the movement from consciousness-raising to action is not necessarily linear. So deeply ingrained were the women's feelings of powerlessness that they had first to experience themselves as able to do something for themselves as a group before they could formulate a notion of themselves as worthy of self-definition. Liddie describes the combined use of task-oriented work, for which the women were prepared by role-playing new skills, and cognitive work, in which they learned positive self-talk and the avoidance of persons and situations that would reflect negative images to them. Like Palmer and Smith, who use these techniques with individuals as well, Liddie worked simultaneously to reduce status differentials between herself and the group members, thereby helping to socialize them to a culture of collective, participatory action.

Transformative action can be as simple as asking that furniture be moved—as Palmer's client did—or as complex as organizing a campaign to change national policy, as Mermelstein and Wedenoja's clients have done. What makes the action transformative is that it is rooted in an analysis of the network of social, historical, and material realities that both prevent and compel action; it evolves from a vision of oneself as co-creator of those realities and therefore responsible for

them; and it contributes, however minutely, to the restructuring of relationships and processes to augment self-definition and choices for
self and others. As a participant in the Feminist Practice Project said,
"Transformative action is self-healing that becomes actualized in the
world" (quoted in Bricker-Jenkins, 1989, p. 247).

Another Feminist Practice Project participant described transformative action as "a rolling process of having a vision, and revising it"
(quoted in Bricker-Jenkins, 1989, p. 248). The worker's role is to assist in the articulation of the vision; to identify and/or create the opportunities for the person to actualize it in the social, historical, and
material context of her life; to teach the skills and mobilize the resources needed to do so; and to put forth and reinforce the notion that
each of us is, in community, capable of and responsible for the creation of reality. Having posed the question "What must change?" the
necessary next questions are "What can I do to effect the change?"
and "What are the sources of power for effecting change?" The
practitioner's knowledge of action and life-style alternatives and her
skill in teaching people how to take action in complex and entrenched
environments are called upon in this process, during which consultation and partnership become the prevailing means of work.

Perhaps the biggest challenges faced by practitioners at this stage
of work are resisting "doing for" and supporting the choices made by
the people with whom they are working. Refraining from "doing for"
is a challenge to one's ego and—as Smith and Hooyman relate from
very different settings—involves yielding some conventional practice
techniques and much of the formal power derived from one's status in
hierarchically structured professional relationships. Getting out of the
way of other people's growth means both creating opportunities for
choice and supporting those that people make. Having a process orientation and a vision of people as striving for self-actualization provides
ballast in the churning oceans of oppression and unrelenting assaults
on people's physical and psychic safety. Perhaps it is the combination of
their assumptions about human purpose and their expanding knowledge
of techniques of transformative action that account for the tenacious but
gentle optimism of feminist practitioners.

Although beliefs and visions may provide the energy for personal/
political transformation, the core feminist practice principle also contains concepts relating to the *contexts* of validation, consciousness,
and action. As stated earlier, these processes must be supported and
sustained by resources to meet basic human needs, nonexploitive rela-

tionships, and environments that reinforce new realities. We turn now to a consideration of these concepts as they are expressed in feminist practice.

Mobilizing resources to meet basic human needs, providing for safety, and building skills—all traditionally concerns of social work—have a special significance in feminist work. Once again, human need is viewed in terms of material, social, cultural, and spiritual dimensions. As I have indicated throughout, particular attention is paid to the cultural and spiritual dimensions of human experience. Contributors have reported a variety of techniques and methods already described for engaging and addressing these either directly or indirectly. At the very least, practitioners will establish recognition of the importance of cultural and spiritual dimensions in their dialogues with people.

As we have seen throughout this book, attention to people's basic, concrete, material needs—food, clothing, shelter, health care, physical safety—was the necessary beginning place in the practice system. The reality and psychic experience of safety is of particular concern in working with women whose concrete realities often render them quite unsafe. Whatever techniques that will secure these basic needs—whether provision of shelters, case advocacy and management, or teaching self-defense or stress- and aggression-containment techniques—are seen as a sine qua non of an effective practice system and worthy of a social worker's full attention and skill. The creation and exercise of choices—which may be seen as a common purpose in all practice—cannot happen unless this foundation is established.

Methods and techniques for mobilizing social resources include such common social work approaches as teaching skills for problem solving; skills in assertiveness (or, more precisely, self-confidence); "life skills" for such tasks as parenting, employment, and self-defense; group communication skills—especially learning to hear and reflect others' meanings, as modeled by the worker in the dialogical process; and how to identify and engage resources in one's formal and informal networks.

Once again, these skills are taught within a context of analysis of the possible reasons that women have been denied opportunities to learn them and how they may be used for political action to redefine their collective place in the world. The value of collective social experiences—particularly for validation, support, and demonstration of the strengths and wisdom available among "nonexperts"—is established through the use of groups, both mutual aid groups and those facilitated by professionals, used for mobilizing social resources and building skills to access them.

Creation of relationships that nurture and sustain uniqueness and wholeness as well as connectedness is of critical importance in feminist practice. In effect, the creation and development of the worker-client relationship is an opportunity to establish experientially with the client that it is possible to have nonexploitive relationships in which she is valued and affirmed as a responsible and capable actor in the world. The worker-client relationship becomes a template for the kinds of relationships that can prevail throughout the environment— in political and economic systems as well as among friends, in families, and between lovers. By participating in the creation of relationships that are open, egalitarian, mutual, and reciprocal, people can begin to formulate a vision of these becoming the norm in their families, workplaces, and communities. "Macro" systems can then be experienced as resulting from people's choices of how to structure social, political, and economic relations, and not as inevitable and immutable "facts of life."

Much of the practice described in this book—in some cases, most of it—extends beyond the practice setting and into the life space of the client, and is focused on searching out and building a network of affirming and nonexploitive relationships. The workers will also teach the process of evaluating the dynamics and structures of new relationships. They not only affirm that such relationships are possible and—as Palmer indicates—imperative for human development, but advocate vigorously for the elimination of exploitation and domination from all human relationships, whether intimate or formal. As several of the contributors affirm, empowerment and transformation come down to the creation of relationships in which "power over" as a dynamic is replaced by a balanced blending of "power from within" and the "social power" of people connected with each other in common cause.

The creation of validating environments is an integral component of a practice of transformation. If alternative values and visions are to be sustained, they must be validated in the environment. Contributors to this book describe two aspects of this culture-building method: validating the strengths of groups of people that are ignored or trivialized in the dominant culture, and infusing alternative values into the structures and processes of their organizations.

Whether working with women-as-women, lesbians, men attempting to learn nonsexist behaviors, people of color, or any other "common identity" around which a practice is organized, practitioners attempt to incorporate in their work symbols that reflect the strengths of that cultural heritage. Feminist and culture-specific music, poetry, graphic arts, and novels can all be used to convey images of realities created not by those whose values and definitions are in ascendancy in the dominant culture, but by those whose visions and strengths are different and valued by the practitioners.

The implicit message in the use of cultural symbols is that there are indeed many realities, many truths, and that these have found concrete expression in people's collective experiences. It reinforces the notion that choices can be and are created by people who value their own experience and commit to actualizing it in the world. By experiencing images of cultural diversity, the notion that choices exist is conveyed. In this sense, the use of culture becomes a metaphor for the pathways available for healing, health, and growth.

The metaphor becomes concrete through action to expand the repertoire of cultural choices available to clients in their own environments. Thus, as Turner describes, people are encouraged to immerse themselves in their own cultural histories and networks, viewing them not as deviant and "alternative" but as primary and complete in themselves. Palmer describes the formation of incest survivor groups in which people can experience their "maladaptive" behaviors as having been adaptational to real threats to their safety; their experience of their strength and creativity in the face of danger becomes the foundation for learning new behaviors. Liddie provides an example of cultural action at the most fundamental level in her account of the creation of an alternative economic system: a food-buying cooperative that enhanced the group's ability to meet their families' basic needs. And Mermelstein demonstrates the potential of organizing rural women around a common identity as a disenfranchised population who refuse to accept that status.

The second application of the concept of creating validating environments entails the restructuring of organizational structures and processes. Feminist practitioners tend to view the organizational context of practice as a component of the practice system. While most feminist practitioners would agree that their unique approach to practice can best be developed in explicitly feminist organizations like those described by Kravetz and Jones, most of the authors in this book work in conventional, hierarchically organized agencies. Believing that striving for consonance of value and form is integral to feminist practice, the contributors have struggled with ways to incorporate feminist structure and decision-making processes in their workplaces. The chapter by Rathbone-McCuan and her associates and that of Hooyman demonstrate the possibilities by describing successful attempts to infuse a feminist worldview into relatively unyielding patriarchal structures—a veteran's hospital and a state university.

What makes these efforts necessary is a conviction that the organizational context of practice is not merely context, but an integral component of a practice system. What makes the efforts possible is a creativity that is stimulated by a worldview in which each of us is responsible for and capable of creating his or her own reality. Practitioners undertake in their own environments the same challenges faced by the people with whom they work. In so doing, they reinforce the definition of their work not as "providing services" to clients but as uniting with other people in the common cause of collective empowerment.

Feminist practitioners use a range of other conventional and nonconventional methods and techniques in their work, but appear to use a set of criteria for selecting and using them that relate to the notion of creating practice processes and environments that reflect and validate their clients' subjective realities. These criteria include *process orientation* (that is, does the approach "preserve the ends in the means"?); *congruence with the values* of both practitioner and client; *potential for self-empowerment* in the sense of helping people to act out of their own inner knowledge and repertoire of skills; and *potential for transformation* of the realities a person is experiencing as injurious, whether a bad marriage, an unfulfilling job, a chemical dependency, or a negative evaluation of self and the person's group based on an internalization of somebody else's definition of their worth, capabilities, or health.

CONCLUSION

The purpose of feminist practice is consonant with the traditional social work practice framework; however, as a practice it has emerged from social workers' efforts to deal with the forces and consequences of sexism in peoples' lives. This practice has as its primary purposes healing the injuries of sexism and facilitating liberation from this particular form of oppression, as well as all others. In order to achieve this purpose, feminist practitioners are building knowledge of its effects on the development and lives of all people, and on women in particular. They are attempting to create, select, and organize into a system of practice those skills, techniques, methods, and relationships that foster simultaneously individual and sociocultural transformation. In other words, rather than seeing the mission of social work as a dual mission, feminist practitioners attempt to integrate the personal and political dimensions of practice into a single practice system.

Feminist practitioners operate from shared experience with the people called clients. Together, practitioners and clients engage in relationships that affirm the differential but equally important expertise of each. They introduce an analysis of the many dimensions of power operating in people's lives that result either in containing or creating choices—opportunities to "live one's stance in the world." Living one's stance with consciousness of oneself as capable of creating new realities and taking responsibility for them is, in itself, a transformational act in a world that has been viewed as defined primarily by others. The process is an unfolding one: We change the world as we change ourselves as we change the world.

Because the approach is holistic and process oriented, contradictions and diversity become sources of strength, opportunities for unfolding new ways of being and doing. Unafraid to attempt shared power and uncertainty, feminist practitioners create new choices and realities with their clients, fully expecting and hoping that their perceptions and lives too will change in the process. One Feminist Practice Project participant encapsulated this concept well by saying that the most important quality to encourage in feminist social workers is humility. As he explained:

> The feminist process is different from classic or traditional social work process because it's far more engaging, dialogic, admitting to uncertainty. There's no such thing as overidentification with the client. There is such a thing as skill, and I think we have to own that, but that's different from being "the social worker helping others." And I think that's a real difference. Not that we don't work to help others, but as we work to help others, we admit that we're helping ourselves. (quoted in Bricker-Jenkins, 1989, p. 256)

Although there appears to be a common set of principles and assumptions held by feminist social workers—including a set of assumptions about the nature, process, and potential for fundamental social transformation—there is no one single approach to feminist practice. It must be viewed as an evolving and collective endeavor of and by people who share a culture and worldview quite different from that in ascendancy today, but who see themselves as able and willing to work through the contradictions imposed by those differences. Because they choose to root themselves collectively in a common ground—a community of women and profeminist men—they derive information, analyses, and energy for transforming the destructive experience of centuries of oppression into material to nurture and sustain a different set of social relations and symbolic expressions of those relations. They are about creating a new culture.

Like the ancient communities of female healers and helpers who were both revered and despised, honored and feared for their differences, their knowledge, and their skills, feminist social work practitioners are blending seemingly disparate and contradictory elements in their work. To a core of knowledge, values, and skills shared with other social workers they add politics and spirituality, art and new scholarship, ritual and psychic energy, new alliances, and an insistence that their values, concerns, and reverence for life become the currency of both public policy and private exchange.

REFERENCES

Bricker-Jenkins, M. (1989). *Foundations of feminist social work practice: The changer and the changed are one* (Doctoral dissertation, Fordham University, 1988; Publication No. 9015943). Ann Arbor, MI: University Microfilms International. (UMI Dissertation Abstract No. 5104 A)

Bricker-Jenkins, M. (in press). *The changer and the changed are one: An introduction to feminist social workers and their practice.* New York: Columbia University Press.

Bricker-Jenkins, M., & Hooyman, N. (Eds.). (1986). *Not for women only: Social work practice for a feminist future.* Silver Spring, MD: National Association of Social Workers.

Bricker-Jenkins, M., & Joseph, B. (1980, September). *Social control and social change: Toward a feminist model of social work practice.* Paper presented at the National Association of Social Workers Conference on Social Work Practice in a Sexist Society, Washington, DC.

Collins, B. G. (1986). Defining feminist social work. *Social Work, 31,* 214-219.

Freire, P. (1970). The adult literacy process as cultural action for freedom. *Harvard Educational Review, 40,* 205-225.

Germain, C. B., & Gitterman, A. (1980). *The life model of social work practice.* New York: Columbia University Press.

Gil, D. G. (1981). *Unravelling social policy* (3rd ed.). Cambridge, MA: Schenkman.

Gil, D. G. (1987). Human services and human liberation: Notes on practice and education. *Journal of Teaching in Social Work, 1*(2), 155-165.

Gottlieb, N., & Bombyk, M. (1987). Strategies for strengthening feminist research. *Affilia: Journal of Women and Social Work, 2*(2), 23-35.

Heineman, M. B. (1981). The obsolete scientific imperative in social work research. *Social Service Review, 55*, 371-397.

Imre, R. W. (1982). *Knowing and caring: Philosophical issues in social work.* Washington, DC: University Press of America.

Imre, R. W. (1984). The nature of knowledge in social work. *Social Work, 29*, 41-45.

Janeway, E. (1980). *Powers of the weak.* New York: Knopf.

Kirk, S. (1983). The role of politics in feminist counseling. *Women & Therapy, 2*, 179-189.

Longres, J. F., & Bailey, R. H. (1979). Men's issues and sexism: A journal review. *Social Work, 24*, 26-32.

Longres, J. F., & McLeod, E. (1980). Consciousness-raising and social work practice. *Social Casework, 61*, 267-276.

Maslow, A. H. (1968). *Toward a psychology of being* (2nd ed.). New York: Van Nostrand Reinhold.

Maslow, A. H. (Ed.). (1970). *Motivation and personality* (2nd ed.). New York: Harper & Row.

Maslow, A. H. (1976). *The farther reaches of human nature.* New York: Penguin. (Original work published 1971)

Morell, C. (1987). Cause *is* function: Toward a feminist model of integration for social work. *Social Service Review, 61*, 144-155.

Simon, B. L. (1990). Rethinking empowerment. *Journal of Progressive Human Services, 1*, 27-39.

Valentich, M. (1986). Feminism and social work practice. In F. Turner (Ed.), *Social work treatment: Interlocking theoretical frameworks* (3rd ed.; pp. 564-589). New York: Free Press.

Van Den Bergh, N., & Cooper, L. B. (Eds.). (1986). *Feminist visions for social work.* Silver Spring, MD: National Association of Social Workers.

Walters, M., Carter, B., Papp, P., & Silverstein, O. (1988). Toward a feminist perspective in family therapy. In M. Walters, B. Carter, P. Papp, & O. Silverstein (Eds.), *The invisible web: Gender patterns in family relationships.* New York: Guilford.

Weick, A. (1983a). Issues in overturning a medical model of social work practice. *Social Work, 28*, 467-471.

Weick, A. (1983b). Women's issues. In *1983-84 supplement to the encyclopedia of social work, 17th edition* (pp. 177-182). Silver Spring, MD: National Association of Social Workers.

Weick, A. (1986). The philosophical context of a health model of social work. *Social Casework, 67*, 551-559.

Weick, A. (1987). Reconceptualizing the philosophical perspective of social work. *Social Service Review, 61*, 218-230.

Wesley, C. (1975). The women's movement and psychotherapy. *Social Work, 20*, 120-124.

Wetzel, J. W. (1986). A feminist world view conceptual framework. *Social Casework, 67*, 166-173.

A Membership Claimed

Carie Winslow

One out of two girl children will be raped by the time we are 13.
We were 15 in my all girl, 9th grade class.

I want to know . . .
Which one of you waited until the gym room was empty
      for fear that we would see the fingerprints and the bruises,
                              long since faded?
Which one of you rushed home after volleyball or choir
           frantic and more afraid of what happened
                        while you were away?
Which one of you didn't bother to say "no,"
                    your first time with a boy?
Which one of you starved or stuffed your body
              in hopes of making yourself invisible?
Which one of you held the blade too close to your wrist
              while shaving your legs?
Which one of you lied compulsively so if you did blurt the "truth" out
              no one would believe you?
Which one of you lay in bed
      so still

              watching the bedroom door every night
           only to wake up naked, pillow over your face
                       again?

I want to say me too!
I want to tell you I'm sorry we wasted so much time alone
      or laughing behind each other's backs.
I want you to know that I lived to tell the truth.
Did you?

ABOUT THE AUTHORS

WAWA BACZYNSKYJ, M.S.W., is Clinical Services Coordinator at Metropolitan Indochinese Children and Adolescent Services in Chelsea, Massachusetts. For the last 10 years she has coordinated services for refugee populations and has taught about issues for immigrants and persons of color.

MARY BRICKER-JENKINS, M.S.W., D.S.W., is a mother, farmer, and social worker who prefers to practice in the public sector. She was born and bred in New England and educated on the streets of New York. She now lives in the hills of Tennessee at WIT's End Farm—"a place for women to go when they're already there"—and teaches social work and women's studies at Western Kentucky State University. She is currently working on a book based on her dissertation, *Foundations of Feminist Social Work Practice: The Changer and the Changed Are One.*

LISA TIESZEN GARY, M.S.S.A., is the Project Director of Advocacy for Women and Kids in Emergencies (AWAKE) at Children's Hospital, Boston. Since 1980, she has worked with abused and neglected children and their families in Chicago and Boston. Out of that work has grown her deep concern and commitment to battered women and their children.

NAOMI GOTTLIEB, M.S.W., Ph.D., is Professor, School of Social Work, at the University of Washington. She originated the specialization on women at that school 15 years ago, and was one of the cofounders of the Association for Women in Social Work and of *Affilia: The Journal of Women and Social Work*, where she is currently Book Review Editor. Her interests include older women, feminist research, and women in the workplace.

LORRAINE GUTIÉRREZ, M.S.W., Ph.D., is Assistant Professor at the School of Social Work at the University of Washington. She teaches courses on generalist practice and life-span development, and in the specialization on minorities. She has extensive social work experience with women of color and an expertise in creating and providing programs for victims of domestic violence. She has written in the area of empowerment of persons of color, which is one of her main areas of interest.

TERRY LEE HARBERT, M.S.W., is Chief of Social Work Service at the Colmery-O'Neil V.A. Medical Center in Topeka, Kansas. Her areas of interest are aging and psychiatric social work and program evaluation.

NANCY R. HOOYMAN, M.S.W., Ph.D., is Professor and Dean at the School of Social Work at the University of Washington. She has served as Chair of the Commission on the Role and Status of Women in Social Work Education of the Council on Social Work Education, as well as on a number of other national committees related to social work education, gerontology, and women's issues. She has written extensively on gerontology, caregiving, and feminist social work practice, including administration and community organization.

LINDA E. JONES, M.S.S.W., Ph.D., is Assistant Professor at the School of Social Work, University of Minneapolis, where she is also affiliated with the Center for Advanced Feminist Studies, the Women's Studies Department, and the Hubert H. Humphrey Institute of Public Affairs. Her research and publications are in the areas of women and poverty, feminist service agencies, and teenage dating violence.

DIANE KRAVETZ, M.S.W., Ph.D., is Professor, School of Social Work, University of Wisconsin–Madison, and a member of the Women's Studies Program there. Her research and teaching focus on women and social work practice. Her publications include articles on women and mental health, women in social service administration, women's conscious-raising groups, and feminist service agencies.

BERNICE W. LIDDIE, M.S.W., R.N., is a doctoral candidate at Fordham University Graduate School of Social Service and an Assistant Professor of

Social Work at Marymount College, Tarrytown, New York. She has been in private practice as a psychotherapist for the last 10 years and is a longtime advocate for the rights of families and children.

JOANNE MERMELSTEIN, M.S.W., Ph.D., is on the faculty of the University of Missouri–Columbia and carries a joint appointment with the University Extension Service. She has been a theoretician, writer, and practitioner of rural generalist social work for three decades. She is a founding member of the rural social work movement in the United States and holds national office in the Association for Rural Mental Health.

NANCIE PALMER, M.S.W., has practiced social work in Kansas for the last 20 years. She also teaches practice courses at the University of Kansas School of Social Welfare. She is currently a doctoral candidate, researching the aspect of resilience in adult children of alcoholics. She has worked extensively with the Kansas State Department of Social Welfare, in direct practice and serving as supervisor and administrator for child protective services. Her interests include working with alternative paradigms to the medical model, issues of human diversity, adult survivors, and women's issues.

ELOISE RATHBONE-McCUAN, M.S.W., Ph.D., is Associate Chief of Social Work Service at the Colmery-O'Neil V.A. Medical Center in Topeka, Kansas, and Adjunct Professor, School of Social Welfare, University of Kansas. Her areas of interest are geriatric mental health, older women, and adult public services.

ARMANDO SMITH, M.S.W., is currently employed as Information and Referral Coordinator for the AIDS Foundation of Chicago. His other professional affiliations include Horizons Community Services and the State of Illinois AIDS Hotline/Gay and Lesbians Helpline, where he is a Supervisor and Trainer of Resource Counselors. He also maintains a small private practice and consulting service.

SUSAN TEBB, M.S.W., is Research Social Worker at the Colmery-O'Neil V.A. Medical Center in Topeka, Kansas. Her areas of interest include veteran caregivers and older families.

CLEVONNE TURNER, M.S.W., until her recent move to Knoxville, Tennessee, maintained a private practice in Lexington, Massachusetts. She has also been a Clinical Instructor at Boston College, Boston University, Indiana University, and Simmons College Graduate Schools of Social Work. She was formerly Clinical Director of the Stone Center for Developmental Services and Studies at Wellesley College. Since moving to Knoxville, she has become heavily involved in civic and community services. She has published in the areas of high-risk underachievers, career development, and self-in-relation theory.

MARILYN WEDENOJA, M.S.W., is a doctoral student in social work and psychology at the University of Michigan. She is the Family Education Coordinator, Department of Psychiatry, Chelsea Community Hospital, Chelsea, Michigan. She has taught courses on women's issues, social work practice with families and groups, and clinical research at the University of Michigan's Women's Studies Program and School of Social Work. Her research interests include stress and coping in families with seriously mentally ill members.